BAREFACED CHEEK:
RUPERT MURDOCH

On November 22nd, 1979, Rupert Murdoch
declared: "To buy *The Times* would be a highly
irresponsible thing to do for your shareholders."
Nobody could quarrel with that judgment, since
the paper, plagued by industrial disputes, was
losing millions of pounds a year. Yet ten months
later Murdoch had a chance meeting with its
Canadian owner, the second Lord Thomson, in
the Concorde lounge at New York's Kennedy
airport. And six months after that, at his fiftieth
birthday party at his ranch near Canberra, the
Australian media tycoon cut a cake iced to
resemble the front page of *The Times*, celebrating
his acquisition of the world's most famous
newspaper . . .

BAREFACED CHEEK:
RUPERT MURDOCH

'Neither distortingly biased nor unfair . . .
a reasonably balanced account of a very
remarkable career'
Sunday Telegraph

'A fascinating vignette of a modern
entrepreneurial personality'
The Listener

'Michael Leapman . . . has done us all a
great service. His book makes fascinating
reading . . . an engrossing portrait'
The Scotsman

'An entertaining and important essay on the
mechanics of international capitalism'
New Society

'Packed with critical, disparaging and sometimes
hilarious anecdotes'
Sunday Express

Michael Leapman, born in London in 1938, has been a journalist since he was twenty. He left *The Sun* shortly before its acquisition by Rupert Murdoch in 1969 and joined *The Times*, where he was New York correspondent (twice) and editor of the popular Diary column. In 1981, after Murdoch bought *The Times*, Leapman left to begin writing this book and became a columnist for the *Daily Express*, where he stayed until 1983. His first book was ONE MAN AND HIS PLOT (1976), about his allotment in London. In 1982 some of his New York columns for *The Times* were collected into a volume called YANKEE DOODLES, and in 1983 his COMPANION GUIDE TO NEW YORK won the Thomas Cook award as the guide book of the year. His latest book is TREACHERY? THE POWER STRUGGLE AT TV-AM. He lives in London with his wife and teenage son.

BAREFACED CHEEK:
RUPERT MURDOCH

'Full of fascinating gossip and anecdote'
Yorkshire Evening Post

'Michael Leapman might have titled his book:
One of the most intriguing men of our
Times . . . It is one of the most interesting books
of our times'
Guernsey Evening Press

'An engrossing study of media obsession'
Irish Independent

'Mr Leapman's research has been deep and
disciplined . . . A remarkable picture emerges'
Eastern Daily Press

'Pictures of editors and executives . . . brilliantly
etched in acid'
Daily Telegraph

'Readable and enjoyable'

Glasgow Herald

Barefaced Cheek:
Rupert Murdoch

Michael Leapman

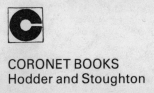

CORONET BOOKS
Hodder and Stoughton

Copyright © 1983 by Michael Leapman

First published in Great Britain 1983 by
Hodder and Stoughton Ltd under the title
BAREFACED CHEEK: THE APOTHEOSIS OF
RUPERT MURDOCH

Coronet edition, revised and updated, 1984

British Library C.I.P.

Leapman, Michael
  Barefaced cheek.
  1. Murdoch, Rupert   2. Newspaper owners—
  Australia—Biography
  I. Title
  070.4'092'4   PN5516.M8

  ISBN 0-340-35907-2

Printed and bound in Great Britain for
Hodder and Stoughton Paperbacks, a
division of Hodder and Stoughton Ltd,
Mill Road, Dunton Green, Sevenoaks,
Kent (Editorial Office: 47 Bedford
Square, London, WC1 3DP) by
Richard Clay (The Chaucer Press) Ltd,
Bungay, Suffolk. Photoset by
Rowland Phototypesetting Ltd,
Bury St Edmunds, Suffolk.

To Times past,
present and future

Preface

Since the hardback edition of this book was published in 1983, Rupert Murdoch has amply fulfilled the predictions I made in it. I wrote that he had scarcely begun to exploit the scope for expansion in the United States and that I expected him to "continue to live dangerously" through an aggressive and ambitious programme of acquisitions.

As if to prove my point, a few months later he bought two satellite television companies with a view to establishing networks in the United States and Europe, beaming programmes to individual homes. The investment was substantial and so was the risk. That became evident not long afterwards, when he announced a delay in the introduction of the system, due to unforeseen snags.

Dangerous living, certainly. But undeterred, Murdoch continued to deploy his cheque book. In November 1983 he paid ninety million dollars for the *Chicago Sun-Times*, the most he has ever paid for a newspaper. That gave him daily press outlets in three of America's most important cities – New York, Boston and Chicago.

A few weeks later came another dramatic announcement. Murdoch had become the single largest shareholder in Warner Communications, with a stake of nearly seven per cent that cost him ninety-eight million dollars. It fuelled speculation that he might eventually seek control of the giant conglomerate, which would give him an abundant supply of film material for his satellite venture. The Warner management thwarted him, but he withdrew with a profit of $41.5 m.

I have greatly expanded the last chapter of this book to take these and other recent developments into account. For the original edition I interviewed more than 120 people in Britain, the United States and Australia. Since then I have made a return visit to America to catch up with the latest moves there.

Because many of those I interviewed would agree to talk only in the strictest confidence, I feel it best to name none of them. But I offer my renewed thanks to all, and to the many others who have helped in the production of both editions.

Neither Rupert Murdoch nor Charles Douglas-Home would agree to see me, although I again invited both to do so while this new edition was in preparation. Therefore descriptions of conversations and incidents in which they took part rely on the evidence of others present or, in a handful of cases, on previously published material included in the bibliography.

Mr Douglas-Home did write to me about unspecified "inaccuracies" in the book, but said he was too busy improving *The Times* to list them for me. Colin Webb, managing editor of *The Times*, also mentioned inaccuracies in his review of the book in that paper, but he was too busy even to reply to my letter asking him to be more precise. I suspect that both men were referring to what they saw as wrong or mischievous interpretations of events in which they took part, rather than errors in salient facts, of whose accuracy I am entirely confident.

Harold Evans was unhappy at my description of his brief but dazzling year as editor of *The Times* and, at his request, I have omitted from this edition one sentence he found especially offensive. His own book *Good Times, Bad Times*, published in October 1983, confirms my account of events, in particular of his crucial failure to understand or respect *The Times* as an institution. I have incorporated some new information gleaned from his book where it seems useful to strengthen my narrative.

Michael Leapman

Contents

Prologue

THE SHARK SCENTS BLOOD

I desire that my said son Keith Rupert Murdoch should have the great opportunity of spending a youthful, altruistic and full life in newspaper and broadcasting activities and of ultimately occupying a position of high responsibilities in that field.
— *Sir Keith Murdoch's will.*

The Concorde lounge in the British Airways terminal at Kennedy Airport in New York differs decidedly from a conventional departure lounge. It has comfortable settees and armchairs, trays of canapés with caviare and a running champagne bar. On a more workmanlike level, there are desks with typewriters for executives who need to take executive acts moments before they board the plane for their three-and-a-half-hour dash across the Atlantic. The two newspaper owners who met there by chance on a September morning in 1980 were not much interested in the champagne and led sufficiently ordered lives not to need the typewriters. But Rupert Murdoch and Kenneth Thomson were inordinately interested in each other. Like lovers in a bad movie, they came directly and inexorably together. They sat on one of the deeply cushioned settees and, in the few minutes before take-off, spoke earnestly.

Superficially, the two men shared a bond: both had inherited a newspaper empire – in Murdoch's case the skeleton of one – from notable fathers. Yet, beyond that, they were in most respects precise opposites. Murdoch, an Australian, was twenty-one when his father Keith died, leaving him, after death duties had been accounted for, only the Adelaide *News* as the remnant of his small newspaper group. Both his father and mother had doubted that he had the capacity to run even this successfully. But in twenty-eight years, by perfecting the aggressive business methods that came naturally to an ambitious man in his twenties, he had expanded it into one of the world's largest media companies, with newspapers on three continents, as well as television stations, a publishing company, and now even half ownership of an airline.

Thomson had to wait until 1976, when he was fifty-three, before he inherited the world-wide conglomerate that his father Roy, the son of a Toronto barber, had created quite late in his life. The most prized of all Roy Thomson's achievements – he called it "the summit of a lifetime's work" – was his acquisition of *The Times* in 1966. He had owned the more successful *Sunday Times* since he bought Kemsley Newspapers in 1959, but *The Times*, the paper of the ruling class, had a much greater cachet. He had even been prepared to agree to the humiliating conditions that the British establishment exacted as the price for allowing their house organ to go to an outsider. He was made to pledge that he would not himself serve on the newspaper's board and would not interfere editorially.

Kenneth had been inordinately fond of his father but did not completely share his excitement at being the owner of *The Times*. He was in truth more comfortable at home in Toronto, surrounded by his fine paintings, than on the international press circuit where such as Roy Thomson and Rupert Murdoch thrived. He felt himself a Canadian essentially; although he had inherited his father's peerage, he preferred not to use the title.

On that September morning he was hurrying to London in response to a call from Gordon Brunton, the head of the Thomson companies there. *The Times* and the *Sunday Times* had been in dire trouble since their closure from November 1978 to November 1979 in a failed gamble by the management to force the printing unions to take a more docile attitude to the introduction of new printing methods and to stop disrupting production. When the papers spluttered back to life, scarcely any of the issues at stake had been resolved and things had deteriorated since. Now Brunton had told Thomson that, after considering all the options, he and his board thought he would be well advised, as soon as was decently possible, to rid himself of the papers his father had been so proud to acquire.

Murdoch, whose intelligence service is the best in Fleet Street, was aware of the bleak mood of the Thomson management and wondered routinely whether there might not be some opening here for him. This was almost a reflex action to any news concerning an impending change in newspaper ownership. It was not that he needed to increase his holdings in Britain – indeed, as the publisher of the country's largest-circulation daily and Sunday papers it might be that the Monopolies Commission would not let him acquire any more. Still, his undoubted business success had been based largely on doing the unexpected, on seeing opportunities in situations from which others would shy away. That was how he had built on the meagre inheritance from his father, and created an international empire.

In Britain, though he owned the *Sun* and the *News of the World*, it was his delight to bid for almost anything that was going. In 1976 he had almost got his hands on the *Observer*, a prestige Sunday newspaper, but because its journalists had thought him too controversial a figure it had been sold instead to an American oil company. And when the Express newspapers had been up for sale he tried to do a private deal for them with Lord Beaverbrook's son, Max Aitken. No wonder one press executive likened him to a shark cruising in the waters, ever alert for the slightest whiff of blood.

He loves being in the know and trying to steal a march on his competitors. The process of wheeling and dealing intrigues him as much as the result of the deal. The bigger his empire the greater his delight in running it. He uses the jet plane and the international telephone system like most people use the bus to work and the office chat. His element is a desk piled with newspapers, all published by him. As he makes phone calls to all parts of his empire, he flicks through the papers, taking a second or two over each page, only occasionally pausing longer when he finds something of unusual interest.

If anything bothered Murdoch about his papers, it was that for the most part they attracted readers at the bottom end of the social scale. There was nothing wrong, surely, in providing people with what they wanted to read and doing it in the slickest, most professional fashion. But he felt that the style of his papers caused those connected with more serious publications to look down on him. They were not the kind of reading that people of his – and his mother's – social standing would normally have in the house. That was why he had been so pleased years earlier to be invited to join the board of Reuters, the international news agency owned by the major papers in consortium. At their periodic board meetings he had struck up a friendship with Sir Denis Hamilton, the stiff, officer-like editor-in-chief of *The Times* and the *Sunday Times* – and the man who, ironically, had once been one of his fiercest critics. Moreover, in the Newspaper Publishers' Association, he had won the respect of, among others, Gordon Brunton.

Murdoch had known for a while that the future of Times Newspapers hung in the balance, and when he caught a glimpse of Thomson in the Concorde lounge in New York, in September 1980, he moved alongside him.

"So how are things going?" he asked the Canadian, with his casual familiarity.

"Not too well," Thomson replied, never diffident about sharing his burdens with a fellow. "In fact, it's a mess."

Later, Thomson and Brunton were anxious to play down the significance of the encounter and those remarks. "It's always a mess," Thomson would explain. "It's what I would say to anyone who asked." But to Murdoch, at least, it was more than a routine bout of venting steam against a hostile world.

"The conversation was pretty general," he told the *Sunday Times* the following February, after his purchase of the papers had been finalised. "All about what a mess England was in and how dreadful the unions were. But I sensed he was getting sick of it and wanted out."

The two men boarded the plane and sat apart. Enough had been said to set Murdoch's mind racing. The shark had scented blood. *The Times* – the most famous newspaper in the world: wouldn't it be grand if it were part of his empire? Wouldn't it vindicate him once and for all in his mother's eyes? Certainly it would, but at a price. Thomson's, in most respects a competent enough outfit, had failed to make it pay in fourteen years and the losses were mounting. Why should he be able to effect a miracle? Ah yes, but hadn't they said the same about his *Daily Mirror* in Sydney and the *Sun* in London? Hmmm . . . surely the problems of *The Times* were of a different order.

But the *Sunday Times* – what sweet revenge for being spurned by its closest rival, the *Observer*. And itself a much more viable proposition. Would Thomson be willing to sell the one without the other? If he couldn't find a buyer for both, he might be forced to. Maybe Murdoch should set his sights on that. Its editor, Harold Evans, had a higher reputation than almost any other journalist in the world. How marvellous to buy him into his stable!

Yes; on reflection, the *Sunday Times* looked a decidedly worthwhile proposition. No need to make a move yet, though: wait to see what Thomson decided finally and how he was going to dispose of it. There might be a possibility of getting something for very little – quite Murdoch's favourite way of doing business. Yes, the *Sunday Times* was the one to go for. No earthly point in taking aboard *The Times*, with its hopeless losses and the encumbrances that went with being a national institution. Even for him, that would be imprudent, well nigh unthinkable.

Wouldn't it?

Chapter 1

PUFF THE MAGIC FOUNDER

You don't realise that there's a great deal of iron behind the boyish exterior.

– *Maxwell Newton.*

Sir Keith Murdoch spent the last few years of his life worrying about two matters: money and his son Rupert. His wife Elisabeth, nearly twenty-five years his junior, would certainly outlive him, and he was not sure that he had provided sufficiently for her and their four children. As for Rupert, Sir Keith was never convinced that his son had the tenacity and application to assume his mantle as probably the most influential newspaperman in Australia.

In the event, only the first of these fears was justified. After death duties, the only business venture Rupert and his mother inherited was a paltry evening and Sunday paper in Adelaide, capital of South Australia. Though chairman of the giant Herald and Weekly Times group in Melbourne, Sir Keith owned only a few shares in it. Yet, paradoxically, the greatest favour Sir Keith did for his heir was to die in 1952 at the fairly early age of sixty-six, when Rupert was twenty-one and still at Oxford. The young man soon returned to become the "boy publisher" of the Adelaide *News* and was never anything but boss of his own show. If he felt that he had somehow been manoeuvred by his elders out of a larger inheritance, he had a working lifetime ahead to prove his worth and expand the empire. Sir Keith's legacy of time, and a lingering sense in Rupert that he had been cheated of part of his patrimony, proved a more potent spur to achievement than anything tangible he could have bequeathed.

Sir Keith had been a distinguished correspondent in the First World War and was, in an Australian context, something of an old-world aristocrat. The son of a Presbyterian minister from Scotland, he had forged a successful career in journalism entirely on the strength of his determination and ability. He had served five years as a district reporter for the *Age* in Melbourne, despite being hampered by a serious stammer. In 1908, aged twenty-three, Keith Murdoch took himself to London and spent a frustrating eighteen months trying to break into Fleet Street: his Melbourne references secured him many interviews but his stammer deterred editors from hiring him.

Returning to Australia in 1910, he had five years to wait for his breakthrough. Then he was appointed manager and editor of the United Cable Service, an Australian news agency in London. World War One was a year old and thousands of Australian volunteers were fighting in the Dardanelles. Murdoch was asked by the Australian government to investigate their mail facilities, but when he got to Gallipoli he found that not only the mail was a subject of concern. He was appalled at the conduct of the war and was encouraged in his dismay by Ellis Ashmead-Bartlett of the London *Daily Telegraph*, who persuaded him that things were much worse than anyone had admitted in London or Melbourne, and that the situation was deteriorating. Working under strict military censorship, the British reporter had been unable to hint at any of this in his despatches. Murdoch agreed to smuggle out a report by Ashmead-Bartlett, although he had, as a condition of being allowed to visit the front, signed a specific undertaking not to try to skirt the censor.

Another British correspondent "sneaked" and the despatch was taken from Murdoch at Marseilles, before he reached London. Yet he remembered much of it and wrote it in a letter to the Australian Prime Minister, recommending the dismissal of Sir Ian Hamilton, commander of the Allied forces at Gallipoli. "The conceit and complacency of the red feather men are equalled only by their incapacity," he wrote. The letter reached prominent British politicians and Sir Ian was dismissed. Through that incident Murdoch became intimate with the powerful in Britain and Aus-

tralia. In 1916, when the new Australian Prime Minister
Billy Hughes visited Britain, Murdoch arranged private
meetings with members of the establishment. Thus, when
the fast-maturing journalist returned to Australia in 1921,
as editor of Melbourne's afternoon paper the *Herald*, he
was already an influential figure. In London he had forged a
close friendship with Lord Northcliffe, founder of the
Daily Mail and the father of British popular journalism.
Murdoch took many of Northcliffe's ideas with him to the
Herald.

He soon established himself as a tough and competent
editor of strict conservative views. Within a few years he
had become editor-in-chief of the group, now including a
morning paper, the *Sun News-Pictorial*. In 1928, at the age
of forty-two, when he seemed to be settling into confirmed
bachelorhood, he met and married a young debutante,
Elisabeth Greene, at nineteen less than half his age. The
Greenes were a highly respectable Melbourne family – her
father Sir Rupert was a steward at the races. Murdoch
doted on his young wife and as a wedding present he bought
her a charming farm near Langwarrin, some thirty miles
south of Melbourne. They called it Cruden Farm, after the
town in Scotland where his father came from.

Helen, their first child, was born in 1929 and Rupert,
their only son, two years later. Two more daughters, Anne
and Janet, came in 1935 and 1939. In his book *In Search of
Keith Murdoch*, Desmond Zwar paints an idyllic picture of
family life at Cruden, with the children playing under their
father's feet as he genially and single-mindedly dealt with
work he had brought home from the office. That is also how
Dame Elisabeth remembers it at a distance of over forty
years, but it is not the entire story. Sir Keith was born in the
Victorian era and ran his household in the patriarchal
tradition. He was specially strict with his heir Rupert.
Against the boy's will, he was sent to Geelong Grammar,
the most exclusive boarding school in Australia. In the
holidays when he returned to Cruden he was not allowed to
live in the house but made to camp out in a hut in the
garden – "Rupert's sleep-over" – not equipped with heat
or running water or electricity, in the belief that this would
strengthen his character and self-reliance; though he was

allowed indoors for a shower. This strict regime lasted for eight years, until he was sixteen.

Sir Keith often worried about Rupert's capacities, and he would discuss his fears with masters at Geelong. The boy was an introverted student with few friends. Sir Keith, who had become managing director of the Herald and Weekly Times group a year after his marriage and was knighted in 1933, hoped to bequeath to his son a lucrative newspaper empire but was unsure whether he would prove worthy of it.

It might have been hard for Sir Keith to accept that he was himself a large part of Rupert's problem. For the conservative nature of the newspapers he ran made him the butt of satire and scorn from fashionable young radicals, including many of Rupert's schoolmates. He was nick-named "Lord Southcliffe" and his name was inserted into pastiche music-hall songs. The boy's cocksureness, later to develop into ruthlessness, probably originated as a defence mechanism against such barbs. Ironically, the ruthless streak that so worried Sir Keith was one of the qualities to which he owed his own success. For, as a newspaper executive, Sir Keith had a short way with incipient competition. In 1933 the *Argus*, a successful Melbourne morning paper, decided to launch an evening paper, the *Star*, to rival the *Herald*. Many senior people on the *Herald* were lured to the new paper, including Crayton Burns, a reporter whose son Creighton was many years later to edit the *Age*. When Burns gave his notice at the *Herald*, Sir Keith called him in and said: "I hear you're leaving us. Are you dis-satisfied?" Burns replied that he was being offered more money and a better job at the other newspaper. "But what are you going to do when I run it off the streets within twelve months?" Sir Keith asked. Burns joked that his son would by then be fifteen and could sell copies of the *Herald* on street corners. Sir Keith's boast was not quite justified; the *Star* survived two years and five months before folding. Burns had jumped back to the *Herald* a few months earlier.

An intriguing insight into Sir Keith's desire for power came with World War Two, when he was made Director-General of Information and introduced rules that gave him the right effectively to control the press. After an outcry he was forced to withdraw them.

His worries about his son persisted even after he was awarded a place at Worcester College, Oxford, to study politics, philosophy and economics. The London correspondents of the *Herald* – first Rohan Rivett and then Douglas Brass – were deputed to keep an eye on the lad, and Sir Keith exchanged voluminous correspondence with him. He regarded Rupert's letters as tests of his ability as a journalist. When one would arrive sketchy and ill thought out, he would be cast into gloom, but a well-turned letter would delight him. His widow, Dame Elisabeth (she was made a Dame of the British Empire in 1963) recalls that, shortly before his death, Sir Keith looked up from a letter in which Rupert was describing a meeting of the Labour Club, where he was active. "He's got it," declared the proud father, rather in the manner of Professor Higgins in *My Fair Lady*.

Thus pressure on Rupert to succeed was powerful, and when his father died as he was about to leave Oxford in 1952, his mother assumed the role of monitor of his achievement. She did not do so consciously: she had never interfered in Sir Keith's business affairs and would not in Rupert's, despite his tender age. When the executors of the estate decided to sell Sir Keith's share of the *Courier-Mail* in Brisbane, leaving only the *News* and the *Sunday Mail* of Adelaide in family ownership, she did not question their judgment, though Rupert would have preferred it otherwise. But when the owners of the rival Adelaide paper, the *Advertiser*, sought to buy the *News*, she resisted that out of a sense of loyalty, suppressing her doubts – inspired by Sir Keith – about Rupert's business capacity.

Rupert knew of those doubts and was determined to show them unfounded. Throughout his career, he has operated as though his mother's approval was paramount among the criteria for taking decisions. Even today, they talk by phone two or three times a week, wherever he is.

Before leaving Britain to establish himself on the *News* in Adelaide, Rupert spent a few months as a junior sub-editor on the *Daily Express*. Sir Keith had been friendly with Lord Beaverbrook, the paper's Canadian proprietor, and had

asked if his son could be "blooded". Under the editorship
of Arthur Christiansen, the *Express* had become a model
for middlebrow popular newspapers – bright and readable
but maintaining a stronger grip on sober reality than its
down-market rival the *Daily Mirror*. Beaverbrook put
Rupert in the care of Edward Pickering, managing editor in
charge of night production of the paper, who slotted the
young Australian in at the bottom end of the subs' table,
never entrusting him with any big stories. Among the other
subs, Rupert was best known as an enthusiastic gambler on
horse racing in both Britain and Australia, a frequent
visitor to the sports desk to check on the latest results.
Professionally, he impressed Pickering as a trainee of
promise, though some of his colleagues on the subs' table
were sceptical. Certainly he was the only *Express* sub-
editor who would repair home to the Savoy Hotel after
finishing his shift.

Most successful journalists will admit, if pressed, that
one figure early in their career exercised an important
influence on them, teaching them much of what they know.
There is evidence that for Murdoch the tall, lean Pickering,
the epitome of a Fleet Street professional, was that person.
It would explain why, nearly thirty years later, he plucked
Pickering from retirement and placed him in an influential
position on *The Times*, his latest and most troublesome
acquisition.

Rupert was only twenty-two when he went to Adelaide and
assumed the title of publisher of the *News*. So he had – and
took – plenty of time to establish himself. In commercial
matters he would generally defer to his elders on the board.
The journalistic side of the paper was in the hands of the
charismatic and mercurial Rohan Rivett, a liberal, campaigning editor admired by Sir Keith, who had placed him
in charge of the *News* a year before his death.

Rupert already knew Rivett fairly well. They had met
while he was at Oxford and Rivett was the London correspondent of Sir Keith's Melbourne *Herald*. The young
undergraduate would visit the Rivetts at their house in
suburban Sunbury-on-Thames. An engaging guest, he

would roister energetically with the Rivetts' children. Once he shared a motoring holiday with Rohan and Nan Rivett and a woman friend, touring the countryside in a black Hillman.

For a few years Rupert was content to watch and learn. The rival paper in Adelaide was the *Advertiser*, controlled by Sir Lloyd Dumas, one of the "white knights" who dominated South Australian society. The *Advertiser* had offered Rupert and his mother £150,000 for the family holding in the *News* just after Sir Keith's death and when this was refused they tried to run their rivals out of business by launching a Sunday paper against the profitable *Sunday Mail*, which the *News* published. After a couple of years of ferocious and expensive competition a truce was called and the two organisations decided to merge their Sunday interests by publishing the *Sunday Mail* jointly, each owning half the stock and sharing costs and profits. This went against Murdoch's competitive instinct; he agreed to it only with reluctance.

As if to purge himself, not long afterwards he made a hugely optimistic takeover bid for the *Advertiser*. Although he offered £14 million – a substantial sum in the late 1950s – there was no real hope of success. The Herald and Weekly Times group in Melbourne were the largest stockholders in the *Advertiser* and it was never likely that they would agree to sell. The eager Murdoch waited outside the *Advertiser* building while the board were having their crucial meeting. As the directors emerged he approached Sir Lloyd Dumas, the chairman, and asked him what had happened. Sir Lloyd marched on and into his car, staring through the upstart as if he were not there.

Murdoch had already plunged into what was to become the most consistently profitable aspect of his operations, television. Roy Thomson, the Canadian tycoon, had not yet made his famous remark that owning a television station was a licence to print money, but its truth was already apparent to Murdoch. In 1958 he made a successful application for the licence for Channel 9 in Adelaide and hired Bill Davies from a local radio station to run it. It was an instant money-earner and Davies became one of the solid, unflappable men who have formed a sound base for his organisation, freeing Murdoch to lead its imaginative forays.

By now Murdoch had bought his first paper in another state, the *Sunday Times* in Perth, Western Australia. He tackled the venture with the enthusiasm that has become his hallmark, travelling to Perth almost every week to supervise the paper's production and quickly improving its circulation and profitability. He was also starting to flex his muscles on the *News*, and as he did so he became increasingly irked by Rivett's restraining presence. The two differed over whether the paper should carry advertisements on the back page. Murdoch was in favour, because of the extra revenue it would generate, but Rivett wanted to keep the whole page for sport. Murdoch waited until the Rivetts were on holiday in Spain before he made the change; but he wondered to himself why he should have to indulge in such subterfuge on what was, after all, his own paper.

In 1959 the *News* became involved in a contentious issue that divided opinion in South Australia and was to have a profound effect on the young publisher. An aborigine named Rupert Max Stuart, a funfair worker, was tried and convicted of murdering a nine-year-old girl, and sentenced to death. His appeal to the South Australian Supreme Court was turned down.

As the date of the execution approached, doubts grew as to the validity of the conviction. The prosecution case rested almost entirely on a "confession" Stuart had made to the police and there were questions about how this had been obtained. New witnesses were found whose accounts suggested that Stuart could not have committed the crime. The execution was postponed several times while the Privy Council heard the case, but they too found no reason to alter the sentence.

Rivett, a socialist and humanitarian, became convinced that justice had not been done and began campaigning in the *News* for a reprieve and a commission of enquiry into the trial and sentence. Murdoch, at that time also a socialist, backed him to the hilt. At Oxford, Murdoch had been a prominent member of the Labour Club and here in Adelaide he continued his left-wing associations. With Rivett, he would attend social evenings organised by Don Dunstan, an up-and-coming Labour politician who was to become one of South Australia's most notable Premiers. Adelaide's embattled radicals would attend, and impassioned political discussions would take place. On one occasion in the early 1950s, at Dunstan's invitation, Murdoch addressed a meeting of the local Fabian society.

So although the *News* under him and Rivett did not give formal editorial support to the Labour Party, it could be relied upon to take a radical line on issues such as colonialism (it printed James Cameron's disturbing despatches from Cyprus) and human rights. The Stuart case was just such an issue. Rivett sent reporters to the remote northern part of the state and into Queensland to find witnesses who had not come forward at the trial, and the story was never absent long from the columns of the *News*. James Cameron, a leading liberal British journalist of the day, now turned his attention to the case in the *News Chronicle*, describing Rivett as "the Zola of South Australia". He commented: "Hundreds of uneasy Australians all over the nation, stirred and challenged by the Adelaide *News*, are now keenly watching the cause of a pauper black man who could so easily have gone into limbo unnoticed."

The very opposite of praise came from the "white knights", the Adelaide establishment, who viewed Rivett's campaign as irresponsible rabble-rousing. But it had its effect. Sir Thomas Playford, the veteran Premier of South Australia, announced a Royal Commission to look into the case. But even this did not still the criticism. When the names of the three commissioners were announced, it emerged that one would be Sir Mellis Napier, a seventy-seven-year-old judge who had presided over the High Court when it rejected Stuart's appeal, and another was Mr Justice Reed, the trial judge. The *News* declared that the naming of the judges and their terms of reference "arouse the gravest doubts and fears among all those who know something of the history of the case." Those doubts appeared to be confirmed when, not long after the commission began its hearings, Stuart's chief counsel, J. W. Shand, walked out because he felt they were not being conducted fairly.

The way the *News* reported this incident was later to be the subject of a long court case. The front page headline quoted Shand as saying: "THESE COMMISSIONERS CANNOT DO THE JOB." Two posters on the Adelaide streets shouted: SHAND QUITS: "YOU WON'T GIVE STUART FAIR GO" and COMMISSION BREAKS UP – SHAND BLASTS NAPIER. Two weeks later, on September 2nd, 1959, Sir Thomas Playford told Parliament that the headline and the posters were "the gravest libel ever made against any judge in this state". In particular he pointed out that the words in quotation marks in the headline were not a precise quotation from Shand. Asked why no libel action was taken, Sir Thomas said it would be considered "at the appropriate time", when investigations into the Stuart case were over.

The next day, September 3rd, the *News* ran a front page editorial which, it emerged later, had been written by Murdoch. Although it contained an element of apology, it was rumbustious stuff that showed the proprietor just as committed to his paper's campaign as his editor was. It was headlined: LET'S GET THE RECORD STRAIGHT. It read in part:

"The *News* has AT NO TIME alleged any crime by any member of the government, the Supreme Court, or even the South Australian police. However, we conceive it as our duty to report all statements in such an important matter." The editorial went on to admit its mistake in publishing as a quotation the challenged front-page headline. "Mr Shand did not use these words and the headline should never have been published and we regret that it was." It was also incorrect to suggest in the poster that Mr Shand had singled out Sir Mellis Napier for attack. But after these apologies the editorial reached a rousing conclusion: "We have never claimed that Stuart is innocent – merely that he must be shown to be guilty beyond all doubt before being hanged. The *News* sees it as its duty to fight always not only for justice to be done but for justice to appear to be done. WE MAINTAIN THIS STAND AND WILL CONTINUE, WITH PRIDE, TO FIGHT FOR THIS IDEAL."

Stuart's sentence was commuted to life imprisonment. In

January 1960 Rivett and News Ltd., Murdoch's company, were charged on nine counts of libel, including three of seditious libel – a charge rarely used, which involves uttering a libel with the purpose of bringing some part of the machinery of the state, including the administration of justice, into contempt. The penalty was a fine or term of imprisonment at the judge's discretion.

At the trial, Rivett stated that Murdoch had not only written the September 3rd editorial but had also suggested the wording for the controversial headline and for one of the two posters. He had approved the other poster, "YOU WON'T GIVE STUART FAIR GO", before it was distributed. He added that Murdoch had asked him to point that out to the court.

At the end of the ten-day trial, the jury dismissed eight of the nine charges – those of seditious libel had already been ruled out by the judge. They disagreed on the ninth charge, concerning the "FAIR GO" poster. Ten weeks passed before the state decided to drop that charge as well. Then the *News* published an editorial affirming confidence in the state's judicial system, its judges and the commission.

Five weeks later Murdoch dismissed Rivett as editor – a notable landmark in the young publisher's career for two reasons. To begin with, Rivett was the very first of what was to become a flood of editors removed from their posts by Murdoch. Secondly, the dismissal marked the end of the Stuart affair and the involvement of the *News* in it. It was significant as the last time a Murdoch newspaper entered into a human rights campaign with anything like that commitment or fervour. His proprietorial style from then on was to engage in power politics, supporting one politician or party against the other, seldom straying beyond the formal party struggle. Although the *News* had won glory in liberal circles for its Stuart campaign, its effect on advertisers and probably on most readers was negative. What was the point in bucking the establishment, especially when the establishment controlled most of the advertising and much else in the state? Where was the profit in it?

The style, too, of Rivett's dismissal was one that would become familiar later. Murdoch dictated a curt, three-line letter and sent it round to Rivett's office, where a secretary opened it. She burst into the editor's office in tears. Rivett, shaken, left immediately and was never again to occupy an executive post in newspapers. Soon afterwards he became director of the International Press Institute in Zurich.

By the time Murdoch had gritted his teeth and purged himself of the unpleasant experience, the Stuart affair was a long way from being his central concern. Adelaide was pushed into the back of his mind by his move into the big time, to Sydney, to trade blows with such heroic newspaper proprietors as the Fairfaxes and the Packers. If you sought to pick the most significant year in Murdoch's career this one, 1960, would stand out. In February he had nibbled at the fringes of the city by buying the Cumberland group of giveaway suburban weeklies for £1 million. Three months later came the really big break, when he began negotiations to buy the *Daily Mirror*, one of the city's two evening papers.

This broadening of the Murdoch interests almost certainly contributed to Rivett's downfall. There was a period when Rivett thought he might go with his proprietor to Sydney but, after the nerve-racking turmoil of the libel trial, Murdoch did not feel confident enough in him either to put him in charge of the *Mirror* or to leave him in Adelaide deprived of his own restraining influence.

The sale of the *Mirror* to Murdoch was an act of extraordinary misjudgment by the Fairfaxes, owners of the *Sydney Morning Herald* and the *Sun*, the rival evening paper to the *Mirror*. It was not long before Rupert Henderson, Fairfax's all-powerful managing director, started to regret the day he agreed to it, and in ensuing years the Fairfax group was to spend millions of dollars mitigating its effect.

Their motive was to prevent any of what they then saw as their serious rivals from strengthening their position. The *Mirror* had been owned by Ezra Norton, who had inherited a batch of decidedly racy papers from his father, John Norton. For years he had wanted to sell his papers – including low grade weekly rags in Sydney, Melbourne and Brisbane – and in 1948 had come close to agreement with the Mirror group in London (who the following year bought the Melbourne *Argus*, to their subsequent regret).

Though fierce rivals, the Sydney newspaper barons recognised a community of interest. In 1958 Norton told Henderson of his plan to sell out. Henderson and the Fairfax management were obsessed by the fear that one of their two dreaded rivals would move in. Sir Frank Packer, who owned the *Daily Telegraph* and the *Sunday Telegraph*, would dearly have loved an afternoon paper to gain maximum use from his presses – an economy that Fairfax already enjoyed with the morning *Herald* and the evening *Sun*. Henderson wanted to prevent that and was also determined that the Herald and Weekly Times group in Melbourne, which Sir Keith Murdoch had built into the largest newspaper group in the country, should not be allowed to gain a toehold in Sydney.

The simplest response to Norton's approach would have been for Fairfax to buy the *Mirror* and then close it, leaving the afternoon field clear for the *Sun*, but Henderson and the Fairfaxes, conscious of their reputation as the most respectable of the city's newspaper groups, were unwilling to face the public obloquy that such a blatantly self-interested move would have provoked. Instead, they created a new company, O'Connell Pty Ltd., to run the old Norton papers. Though nominally independent, it was controlled by Fairfax.

By 1960 it was apparent that the ruse was not working. Because of the ambiguity of its ownership, the *Mirror* lacked the stomach for the head-to-head fight with the *Sun* that was its only chance of competing effectively. Its circulation slipped – as did that of the sister *Sunday Mirror*. Murdoch, sensing an opportunity, approached Henderson, who looked on the deal with initial favour because of the respect he had had for Sir Keith. Perhaps because he had known Rupert as a boy, he could not persuade himself that he presented any substantial threat.

Henderson had already displayed his avuncular attitude to Murdoch when the young newcomer to Sydney went to ask him for help in printing *New Idea*, the women's magazine that had come with the Cumberland group. It was printed on primitive letterpress machines and as a result looked shoddy compared with its competitors. Henderson agreed to print the magazine on Fairfax's more advanced rotogravure, and to do it at bargain rates until it reached an economic circulation. Then the price of the printing would be raised to a realistic level. But before that point was reached Murdoch had put in his own rotogravure plant and printed *New Idea* on that, having established it with Henderson's cut-price help.

Others at Fairfax warned Henderson against selling the *Mirror* to Murdoch. Sir Warwick Fairfax, the chairman, was opposed and Robert Falkingham, the shrewd company treasurer, wrote a memorandum denouncing the plan in strong terms:

"I do not think we should contemplate selling to Murdoch at any price," it began. He went into details about the dangers as he saw them. Murdoch would cut advertising rates, do backdoor deals with the unions and not stick to agreements. Murdoch had already attacked the Fairfax group in one of his new suburban papers. "We would make a greater capital profit and would better protect our own operations by adhering to our original intention of reconstructing the *Mirror* as a widespread public company, with ourselves holding only enough shares to prevent another paper getting control," Falkingham wrote.

But Henderson was determined to go ahead. Falkingham went on holiday and on his first day away received a message to ring the office. "Come back right away," Henderson told him. "I've agreed to sell the *Mirror* to Murdoch."

Arriving at the office late in the evening, Falkingham found both sides supported by teams of high-powered lawyers. The negotiations were concluded at about 1.30 in the morning. Murdoch put in a jubilant phone call to his old rival Clyde Packer, Sir Frank's eldest son. One version of the occasion has him dancing a jig in Henderson's office after the deal was made.

Although Murdoch was about to slough off the influence of Rivett, he still felt the need, as he has always done, for a man of serious substance somewhere near the top of his organisation. His father had plucked Rivett from London to take charge, and it may have been a subconscious reflex action that persuaded Rupert to do something similar. Douglas Brass, a dour New Zealander, was London correspondent of the *News*. Murdoch brought him back as group editorial manager based in Sydney. In the relation between the two there were some similarities to that between Murdoch and Rivett but there was one crucial difference: while Rivett had been in place when the young Murdoch arrived back from Oxford, Brass was his own appointment. After Rivett, he was careful never to let anyone in his organisation rise to a position that was not ultimately dependent on his patronage. There were ups and downs in relations between Murdoch and Brass and in the 1970s Brass left for a while, but until he retired in 1981 he was an influential figure.

When Murdoch acquired the *Mirror* its circulation was in decline and its image uncertain. Founded during World War Two, by 1953 it had established a lead of 11,000 over the *Sun*, in a total market of just over 600,000. But the *Sun* revived after the Fairfax group bought it and it had overtaken the *Mirror* by the time Norton sold out five years later. Under the O'Connell ownership the *Mirror* wilted further and was 13,000 behind the *Sun* when Murdoch arrived on the scene. Norton's *Mirror* had been a racy tabloid. In the O'Connell period it was toned down to be closer in approach to the more sober *Sun* but this had only resulted in fudging its identity. Murdoch, influenced by Brass, at first tried to take it further in that more responsible direction, but circulation charts showed that this was not what readers wanted. So Murdoch took it back down market, though it never became as lurid as in Norton's day. Soon it was a viable competitor to the *Sun*. It was a lesson Murdoch was to put to good effect when he took over the London *Sun* nine years later.

Freed from Rivett's overpowering influence, the new Sydney press baron no longer felt inhibited from playing the role to the hilt. The *Mirror* was indisputably his paper and its executives his people, there to please him. An early victim was Robert Hughes, the *Mirror*'s cartoonist and art critic. Murdoch did not like his work and suggested he take a hefty pay cut. Hughes left and is now the highly respected art critic of *Time* magazine in New York.

Murdoch would visit the composing room almost daily, at first, to watch the metal type being placed in the page formes.

"What size is that headline?" he would ask. "Wouldn't it be better to take it down a size?" And he would scribble an altered wording to fit the smaller letters. Many found this an engaging habit, evidence that the proprietor was not too grand to roll up his sleeves and muck in with the lads. For the editors, though, it was an irritation, especially on the *Sunday Mirror*, where the weekly rhythm, leading to a climax only once every seven days, is different from that on a daily paper.

A former *Sunday Mirror* executive put it like this: "You'd slave your guts out over the paper for the first four days of the week, see nothing of Rupert, and on the fourth or fifth day Rupert would bowl in, be very nice and breezy and so on but he'd want to push you a bit, inject an idea or two of his own into it. I'd be irritated about this, frankly. I used to think that he was a bit of a dilettante. He had nothing to do with it for most of the week and then suddenly he'd show up and expect to run it."

He still likes to second-guess his editors even from thousands of miles away. In New York, it can take a week for his Australian papers to reach him, but he will telephone editors about editions they have long confined to the darker recesses of their mind and say: "Your front page headline's all wrong."

Another restraint Murdoch left behind in Adelaide was too great a care to avoid the sensational in the name of accuracy. The cut-throat competition between Sydney's two evening papers gave him, he felt, a licence to stretch the facts. The *Mirror* had, after all, always done it, and the *Sun* had few scruples that he could detect. At the end of 1961, the *Mirror* sent reporter Brian Hogben, later to climb to a senior position in the organisation, to Hollandia, Dutch New Guinea, to report a local war. The *Sun* had also sent its own man and when Hogben had not been heard of for a while his colleagues were terrified they would be scooped. So they invented the kind of story they thought he might write and kept it on ice for a while. It was a colourful piece about cannibalism and shrunken heads, stuffed with hackneyed jungle clichés. When the editors' nerve could hold no longer they published the story in the paper under Hogben's byline. There is no evidence that the decision was taken by Murdoch personally: it was probably Douglas Brass, as editorial director, who gave the go-ahead, but working, as he did throughout his career, within Murdoch's guidelines. When Hogben received a copy of the paper he sent a furious telegram to his office: "Nearest shrunken heads to Dutch New Guinea are in Sydney."

The two other Sydney newspaper groups, Fairfax and Packer, had lucrative television stations there as well. When, in 1962, the government decided to introduce a third Sydney station, Channel 10, it seemed to Murdoch that he was the logical person to own it. He found an impressive band of backers and made a plausible bid, but he was not awarded the licence, probably because of the opposition of Sir Robert Menzies, the veteran Prime Minister, the symbol of the old Australian establishment that Murdoch instinctively opposed.

Thwarted, he decided to attempt entry into Sydney television by an oblique route. Apart from the three main channels, there was a number of small stations in the suburbs whose transmission range included part of the Sydney metropolitan area. By law these could not be owned by anyone who ran a central Sydney station, so they usually belonged to groups of local businessmen. The Sydney stations saw them as potential opposition and used their muscle to prevent them getting major American programmes that were then – and still are – the staple of Australian television fare.

As Murdoch told the story in a 1967 television interview, Channel 4 at Wollongong, south of Sydney, was on the brink of bankruptcy for this reason. The big stations, he claimed, had told the American distributors: "If you sell any single programme to Wollongong you won't sell any to us. So you take the £25 for half an hour there and don't get the £2,000 from us." So the owners of Channel 4 made an appeal to him to rescue them.

"I was tempted by the thought that if it was true that the Wollongong station was too close to Sydney and could in fact one day compete with a Sydney station this might be an opportunity to get in and try out. So I went in. But I realised that to have any hope at all of doing this, of making people change their viewing habits in Sydney – they'd have to even change their antennae around – I'd have to have the most attractive programmes.

"So I went over to America and bought every new programme from every network that was available for a year and spent very nearly three million dollars to buy Australian rights. I knew we could show them in Adelaide and, through Ansett [owners of Melbourne's Channel 10], in Melbourne . . .

"Meanwhile the existing people here sat around and said they'd let me go broke, that I was making my really fatal mistake, that I would go broke. However Sir Frank Packer at some stage must have slid away because he rang me up and our paths crossed at San Francisco airport and then later he rang me – I was in Honolulu and he was in New York – and he said: 'Let's do a deal.' So I went back to New York and he agreed to sell me a 25-per-cent share interest in Channel 9 in Sydney and Channel 9 in Melbourne. This doesn't give me control or much say in it . . . but still it's a very important investment and it got me off the hook. But then I think the original thought occurred that I might really have overstepped myself in taking this gamble in Wollongong – looking back at it now I think they were probably right then."

Murdoch hates standing still. After he had owned the Sydney *Mirror* for a couple of years he could see it was holding its own in its battle against the *Sun* and he looked round for other opportunities. Along with his two Sydney papers he had bought two weeklies, both called *Truth*, published in Brisbane and Melbourne. They were as far down market as you can get without straying across the line into simple pornography. "Rapes in Nigeria, that kind of thing," was how one senior executive put it dismissively. The Melbourne *Truth* survives today, though no longer under Murdoch's ownership, making much of its profit through advertisements for massage parlours.

However dismal his Brisbane and Melbourne papers, they did mean that, taken together with his operations in Sydney, Adelaide and Perth, he had printing capacity in every state capital. He was therefore uniquely placed to try something that Australian newspapermen had regarded as an impossible aspiration for years: the creation of a national newspaper.

Because of the distances involved, such a paper could not economically be distributed from a single printing plant. But the technology of the day did allow the printing of a newspaper by photo composition. Whole pages could be photographed and converted into lightweight matrices which could be flown from a central point to printing presses in all the capitals.

It was a seductive idea and the obvious place to mount such an operation was Canberra, the purpose-built federal capital, sited between Sydney and Melbourne. The paper would, after all, be specialising in federal politics and overseas news, and Canberra was the diplomatic and political hub of the nation. The snag was that, in a small town of only 40,000 inhabitants, there was not much of a local population to provide a solid advertising and circulation base.

Moreover, Canberra already had a paper of its own, the *Canberra Times*. It was a dim little tabloid selling 16,000 copies a day but it did make a stab at covering national politics and it obviously had to be put out of business if a new paper was to get an economic level of local Canberra advertising. The *Canberra Times* was owned by Arthur Shakespeare, son of the man who had established it in 1926 when the federal government was moving into the new city.

Shakespeare had no children and was worried about what would happen to the paper when he died. He discussed the matter with Henderson in the late 1950s and they reached an understanding that the Fairfax group would be informed of any move to sell. In the meantime Fairfax were thinking of printing a Canberra edition of the *Sydney Morning Herald* which might have developed into the national daily people were talking about. John Pringle, deputy editor of the *Observer* in London, was brought out to Australia with that possibility in mind. To protect their flanks from an outsider, Fairfax made a secret agreement with Shakespeare by which ownership of the *Canberra Times* would pass to Fairfax if any rival appeared on the scene.

To strengthen his paper, Shakespeare hired a new editor

in 1962. He was Dave Bowman, who had left the Adelaide *News* and worked for six months on the *Sunday Mirror* in Sydney. Murdoch rather liked it when people left his organisation on their own initiative rather than waiting to be fired. It was evidence of sturdy independence; he would never want to close the door on re-engaging them. He was polite to Bowman at their farewell interview.

"Got a chair of your own, eh? Good. I wish you a lot of luck." Then he added something that may have been a hint of what he had in mind, though it was to be two years before the *Australian* came into being: "Arthur Shakespeare has got it all to himself down there. I wouldn't want to wake up one morning and read in the paper he'd sold it. I'd like to hear about that in advance."

Bowman's brief was to modernise the *Canberra Times*, broaden its outlook and put it in better shape to withstand the competition that Shakespeare and the Fairfax group were convinced would come. One afternoon in 1963, when Bowman had been in Canberra for less than a year, he received a message that Murdoch had arrived and wanted to see him. They shook hands like old friends. Murdoch had really called to see Shakespeare, but he was out, and in any case he seemed delighted to chat to his former employee about old times and his present position. The affable Bowman took him on a tour of the office and the printing plant and discussed the problems of the paper: it was always, for instance, being produced late because of inadequate capacity in the composing room. Murdoch was absorbed, and when the tour was over he told Bowman: "You might like to come and work with me." Bowman shrugged off the suggestion, and only several months later, when the rumours of Murdoch's plans began to harden, did the true purpose of the reconnaissance visit dawn on him.

The opening of Parliament at the beginning of the year, towards the end of the Australian summer, is an important social occasion. The Governor-General hosts a reception in King's Hall in Canberra. Newspaper owners and other prominent Australians are invited. By the beginning of 1964 it was known that Murdoch had bought some land in Mort Street, only a few hundred yards from the office of the *Canberra Times*. At the King's Hall reception, Murdoch and some of his senior men found themselves in a group that included Shakespeare. It was a large circle of about a dozen people, standing shaking their drinks idly, trying not to feel awkward. To relieve a pause in the conversation, Shakespeare, a short and peppery man in his sixties, suddenly snapped at Murdoch: "What are you going to do with that property in Mort Street?" Murdoch paused for only an instant before roaring, "Run you out of business!" and cackling loudly. Everyone in the circle joined in the laughter but at least two of them – Murdoch and Shakespeare – knew it was no joke. Not long after that Shakespeare flew to Sydney to invoke the agreement with Fairfax.

Murdoch had already begun planning Australia's first national daily. To run the editorial side, he hired Max Newton, managing editor of the *Financial Review*. This specialist paper, owned by the Fairfax group, had just made a successful transition from weekly to daily under Newton's talented leadership, but he was a volatile, plain-speaking man and he had fallen out with the Fairfax management. When Murdoch hired him for the new venture he took with him Jules Zanetti, his deputy at the *Review*, and hired a number of other senior journalists. They all met to plan the new paper in Murdoch's suite on 'Mahogany Row', the nickname given to the executive offices at his Sydney headquarters. They had endless inconclusive discussions and it soon became plain that Murdoch planned to do it very much in his own way.

The first thing they had to decide was a name. Each of the eight or nine men sitting in the room had his own idea. Names like National Inquirer, Canberra Star, National Chronicle were thrown up and considered. Suddenly Murdoch piped up: "I've had a thought. What about calling it the *Australian*?" The consensus was that it was a boring name. The others quickly dismissed it and went back to discussing their own suggestions. But it soon dawned on them that what Murdoch had said was not a passing idea at all. He had decided that was going to be the name of the paper and had chosen that oblique way of telling them.

His new employees quickly learned this as one of his techniques. At a planning session Murdoch pulled a telegram from his pocket. "I've just had a cable from this man in London offering his services. Name's Chandler. Anyone ever heard of him?" Nobody had and Murdoch put the cable back in his pocket. The talk switched to other matters and the others assumed that was the end of the matter. But a few months later Solly Chandler, formerly with the *Daily Express* and at the time with the *Daily Sketch* in London, arrived and started to sit in on the planning meetings. Neither he nor Murdoch would be specific about his role. When the paper started he became copy taster, with the job of looking at incoming news stories and evaluating them. Zanetti, whose tasks were supposed to include finding a story to lead the paper with – not easy in a country with no tradition of national journalism – would discover towards the end of the day that Chandler had been working away on a different front page lead from him and Chandler's would normally take precedence. He was an example of Murdoch's penchant for putting a "spoiler" into a newspaper's hierarchy, believing that the resulting tension keeps people on their toes. When Zanetti complained to Murdoch about how wasteful it was of resources and energy to pit people against each other like that, the proprietor would smile.

"Survival of the fittest, that's how you run a newspaper," he would declare. "You've been reading too many of your management books." Zanetti did not find a way of handling the technique and soon asked to quit his executive post. At the end of 1964 he was sent to London.

The early days of the *Australian* amounted to the most concentrated period of excitement in Murdoch's life. Starting a new paper is not something anyone gets to do very often, but this was one facing problems nobody in Australia had tackled before: how to edit one paper to capture the whole nation's interest and, more practically, how to ensure that it reached audiences separated by many hundreds of miles.

It had, too, to find a national advertising constituency. City papers attract local classified advertising and page after page of display panels for department stores, supermarkets and entertainments. At first Murdoch hoped local Canberra advertising would provide a solid financial base for the project, but the improvement of the *Canberra*

Times, charging only about 60p a line for classified ads, ruled that out. The *Canberra Times* changed from a broadsheet to a tabloid just before the *Australian* was launched. Readers did not like the change much and its effect, combined with the appeal of Murdoch's new paper, distributed free for its first few days, was to push sales of the *Times* down to around 12,000 at its worst. But then as the *Australian* began to falter, the *Times* regained health and it became apparent that it was not to be displaced as the local daily paper of the capital. Murdoch's paper had reached sales of over 200,000 in its first heady days but quickly sank to around 50,000.

Adrian Deamer, later to become the *Australian*'s most controversial editor, gave a graphic account of the early days in a lecture at Melbourne University in 1971, soon after his rancorous dismissal. The chief practical problem was flying the plastic matrices from Canberra for printing in Melbourne and Sydney. In winter, Canberra airport often gets fogbound around midnight. Murdoch would go and plead with the pilots to make the trip anyway; if they would not, the matrices had to be driven to Cooma, more than an hour's drive away, for the flight to Melbourne, while those for Sydney were taken all the way by road.

"It was exciting and entertaining," Deamer said. "Real frontier newspaper stuff right out of an old B class movie – with Mr Murdoch, in the early days, standing on the tarmac in his pyjamas egging the pilots on, convincing them and [airport] officials that the fog was really only a light mist. But it was not the most reliable way to produce a newspaper and reliability, however dull it sounds, is the first requirement of a newspaper."

In a television interview in 1967, Murdoch called the launching of the paper "the greatest challenge and the biggest task that has been put before me I think in life yet . . . the biggest and most exciting thing." In the same programme Max Newton described an evening when he was having a drink with Murdoch, who told him: "I've got where I am by some pretty tough, larrikin* methods, but

---

* Larrikin: boozy, uncultured Australian. Though the more cultivated citizens affect shock at their excesses, they secretly admire them as part of their distinctive heritage.

I've got there. And what I want to do is produce a newspaper that my father would have been proud of."

Newton, who quickly fell out with his new proprietor, said: "Throughout the planning period Rupert was excellent. I think he gets more fun out of planning things than actually the business of doing them. He's not very good at managing things . . .

"Rupert was excited and at the top of his form. He was happy. It was when we got started that he started to get unhappy because he was continually afraid that somebody – myself – was going to, as it were, take over, I think. Another thing of course was that while he had this great ability as managing director to get into the detail of the organisation he carried this to extraordinary lengths. The first four or five months, up until the time I left the organisation, Rupert would quite often be seen down on the stone making up the paper . . . Very unnerving. This is the sort of work that should be done, as you know, by a sub-editor earning about twenty-five pounds a week.

"Mr Murdoch was known around the office after a while as 'Puff the Magic Founder' . . . not a vicious or a satirical comment on him but an indication I think that a certain cynicism quickly grew up because the paper didn't live up to its own promise, and the staff who'd been quite excited at the prospect of working on a great newspaper felt that somehow they'd been cheated and the paper wasn't anywhere near so good as they'd been led to believe."

It was an uncertain start and the temperamental Newton, who has some larrikin characteristics himself, was its first victim. The production problems, combined with the differences over editorial content, made it impossible for two strong individualists to work together for long. On that 1967 television programme, which remains the best documentation of the early days of the *Australian*, Murdoch said bitterly: "It frankly proved a lot bigger job than I expected. We ran into opposition from quarters we didn't expect, heartbreaking opposition at some times. It's been a pretty buffeting two years that I've had, getting a paper established. People who've made a life out of criticising newspapers, calling for something better, have been turning on you and making a full-time occupation of looking for spelling mistakes in the one paper that's been trying to satisfy them."

And Newton took up the narrative: "When I met Rupert it seemed a very exciting thing. Here was a young bloke prepared to spend a lot of money doing something that was probably going to be very good. At least we hoped it was. One didn't realise at the time, meeting Rupert, who on first impression gives you this sort of 'I'm just a simple boy, you know – I'm a very likeable kid' thing, you don't realise that there's a great deal of iron behind the boyish exterior, and he's a very tough proprietor who I think in the course of the period of the *Australian* sacked more journalists than I think I've ever seen sacked in my whole career. He's a tremendous sacker. But of course he's also a tremendous hirer. He's always sacking them and hiring them."

The words were prophetic for Newton who, some fifteen years after he left the *Australian* following a blazing row, was hired by Murdoch as a financial commentator for his *New York Post* and now writes a Wall Street column for *The Times* as well.

Murdoch defended his record in the television interview: "Just because I haven't managed to get the right working relationship with every single editor I've appointed doesn't for a minute suggest that I'm ruthless. In fact if you'd known the precise reasoning at the time . . . and the sort of settlement these people got, I think one would consider me – a lot of people did consider me – rather ridiculously soft . . . I'm far too easy-going as a rule."

His secretary vouchsafed: "He suffered intensely with every staff change he had to make . . . There were no heads rolled before he made enquiries as to how the person would be placed . . . nothing ruthless – it may have appeared to be that outside because he has to have a face outside, otherwise he'd be taken for a ride."

In March 1956, a few years after taking over at the *News*, he had married Patricia Booker. Some twenty-eight years later people who knew him and Pat say now that the couple were not well matched. She could not cope with his dynamism and unpredictable schedule and, soon after they moved to Sydney in 1960, the marriage began to break up. It was a rancorous business. Their daughter Prudence was especially wounded, and lawyers were called in to negotiate a financial settlement.

Not long afterwards, Murdoch met Anna Torv, the eighteen-year-old daughter of immigrants from Latvia. She was a trainee reporter on the *Mirror* and one of her first jobs was to report the night-club circuit. They are said to have met first at a Sydney night-club called Chequers. Murdoch had gone there with Douglas Brass, who introduced him to Anna. Soon they were seeing much of each other, and when Murdoch went to Canberra to start the *Australian* Anna was one of the Sydney reporters sent there to help launch it.

Because Murdoch was for the next few months at least going to be spending most of his time in Canberra, Anna wanted to work there, and she went to see Jules Zanetti, the assistant editor, to ask for a job. She and Murdoch had kept their relationship so discreet that Zanetti knew nothing of it. He had already been warned against poaching staff from other papers in the group, so he turned down her request. Next day Murdoch called on him:

"I believe that girl Anna Torv was in to see you," he observed. Zanetti said she had been after a job.

"Did you give her one?" he asked, and Zanetti said he had not, that he had already been having problems with the Mirror organisation and had no plans to make things worse. Murdoch looked at him quizzically but said nothing. Later Anna went to see him again. Slow on the uptake, Zanetti did not recognise his conversation with Murdoch as an instruction to hire her. So when she asked him: "Hasn't Mr Murdoch spoken to you?" he replied that yes, her name had been mentioned, but there was still no job. That night Murdoch came to see him again and said simply: "That girl Anna Torv. Hire her." So Zanetti did. She was soon given one of the most coveted assignments for young reporters, a berth on the gossip column.

They married in 1967 in Sydney and Anna has proved an ideal wife for Murdoch – competent and self-contained, an excellent organiser and hostess, bringing order to a home life which, because of his business demands, must necessarily be erratic. She had learned these skills as a child. Her parents were separated and, as the oldest of the children, she had been almost a surrogate mother to her brothers and sisters, living with their father in the western suburbs of Sydney. There are three children from Murdoch's second marriage.

The period of Adrian Deamer's editorship, from 1968 to 1971, is regarded by many as the high point of the *Australian*'s history. Now published from Sydney, where production difficulties were fewer than in Canberra, the paper reached a circulation of 143,000 in the early months of 1970 and was making a tidy profit. But a recession and a price increase combined to push the circulation down and, under a succession of short-term editors, it has seldom looked like recovering.

Deamer was an editor of decided views, not an easy man to work with, but he did impart to the paper a clear political philosophy that it had hitherto lacked. He was, in one sense, lucky that his term of office coincided with Murdoch's thrust into Britain, so he was less subject to proprietorial interference than Newton and the early editors. In the end, though, the fact that Murdoch was visiting Australia ever more rarely was a factor in Deamer's dismissal. Just as he had not felt able to trust Rivett on his own in Adelaide, Murdoch wanted an editor whose views he could rely on. One of the results of the growing multi-national nature of the organisation has been the appointment of safe, colourless editors: yes-men may not be too strong a word – mice who can be trusted not to play irresponsibly during the cat's long absences.

Under Deamer, the paper had found a constituency among intellectuals at the universities. Deamer, admittedly a biased witness, put it like this in his 1971 Melbourne lecture: "They were intensely devoted to the paper in a way that I have never come across before. They felt somehow that the paper belonged to them and they cared about it, argued about it, disagreed with it but kept on buying it."

But Murdoch and his most influential lieutenants were not happy with what they saw as a growing leftward drift. Bruce Rothwell, a conservative formerly with the *Daily Mail* in London, had been brought in to edit the *Sunday*

Australian, launched in February 1971 and modelled on the London *Sunday Times*. The new paper had not been a success in its first months and Rothwell was keen to increase his influence in the organisation. He reported to the proprietor that, under Deamer, the *Australian* was too obsessed with liberal causes, and Murdoch listened.

Deamer said that the gist of Murdoch's complaint was that the paper had become too intellectual and too political. "It was anti-Australian, it preferred black people to white people, it wanted to flood the country with Asians. He complained it took up every 'bleeding heart' cause that was fashionable among the long-haired left. It was not interested in the development and progress of Australia. It criticised the political leaders he supported. It was dull, it was a knocking paper, and it stood for everything he opposed and opposed everything he stood for."

A year later Murdoch gave the same Melbourne lecture, inevitably seen as a reply to Deamer. "There is a tendency," he said, "for many journalists to bring their commitments with them and impose them on their work." He ended with a succinct statement of his publishing philosophy: "The public certainly has no duty to support newspapers. It is the duty of the publishers to provide the type of newspaper the public wants to read."

Looking through the files of the paper for June 1971 – the month before Deamer left – it is easy to see what irritated Murdoch. The front page was generally dominated by two issues that had become the subject of left-wing protest – the Vietnam war and the Springbok Rugby tour of Australia. The Premier of Queensland had declared a state of emergency to help his police maintain order while the Springboks played there. When the Australian Prime Minister, Billy McMahon, offered the use of an air force jet to fly the team from Perth to Adelaide, Deamer ran a front page editorial headed, "Cynical misuse of a Prime Minister's power". Other editorials urged that a proposed South African cricket tour be banned by the government – but the paper also denounced violent demonstrations against the Rugby team.

On July 24th, 1971, a short announcement appeared on the front page headed: "New posts on the *Australian*." It said that Bruce Rothwell was now editor-in-chief of the *Australian* and Evan Williams of the *Sunday Australian*. Deamer was not mentioned at all. It was as though he had never existed.

Rothwell's brief was to broaden the appeal of the *Australian* by making it less political – moving it towards the *Daily Express* model rather than the *Observer*. Business coverage was strengthened to attract wealthier readers for the pleasure of advertisers. The university audience gradually flaked away but was not replaced by an equivalent number of new readers.

Chapter 2

GO NORTH, YOUNG MAN

Rupert is a gentleman.
                                                    – *Sir William Carr*.

When you have newspapers in all the main Australian cities, as well as the country's only national daily, and you are still comfortably under forty, what next? Australia has scarcely more than fourteen million people and there is a limit to how many words they can read. Yet the other big Australian press magnates – the Fairfaxes, the Packers and the rest – had never thought seriously about expanding beyond their own hemisphere. They were content to slug it out among themselves in their existing markets, gaining satisfaction from a comparatively marginal redistribution of the spoils in their favour.

Murdoch, when he worked briefly at the *Daily Express* in London before returning to Adelaide, was impressed with the slickness, the self-confidence and the success of the operation and he thought it significant that it was all in effect the creation of a single dynamic man. Lord Beaverbrook had come to Britain from Canada armed with great energy and unrestricted by the fusty conservatism that afflicted much British commerce. Again, the most recent major acquisition in the British press had been by another Canadian, Roy Thomson. He had bought the badly-managed Kemsley Newspapers – including the *Sunday Times* – in 1959 and added *The Times* itself to the stable in 1966.

The trouble was that the family dynasties that owned much of the British press depended too much for their success on the managerial competence of whichever generation happened to be in charge. It was a hazardous business. There was nothing to guarantee that the son of an accomplished entrepreneur would inherit his father's business sense. So some of the groups had drifted and atrophied and were ripe for the injection of bold new ideas from outside. But why did it always have to be Canadians? Just because an Australian had never done it was no reason why one should not try.

The idea of launching himself into Fleet Street had been growing for years, and soon after his move to Sydney Murdoch decided to do something about it. Through his London bankers, Morgan Grenfell, he began unobtrusively to buy shares in the International Publishing Corporation, publishers of the *Daily Mirror*. Though he had worked on the *Express*, the *Mirror* was the paper he really admired. It seemed to him, as to many others, the epitome of what a tabloid should be – racy, irreverent and with a red-blooded quality. His *Mirror* in Sydney was frankly modelled on it. Like an art collector who has never been able to afford anything more than a reproduction Picasso, he longed to move up in the market and buy an original. To extend the metaphor, when his chance did come, he had to decide whether to hold out for the Picasso or settle for an original by a lesser artist.

The *News of the World* was unique in nearly every respect. It had by far the largest circulation of any paper in Britain, over six million every Sunday. It sustained this by a peculiarly British mixture of titillation and ingenuousness. Its stock-in-trade on the "news" pages was stories about sexual crimes or indiscretions among the respectable classes, with as much explicit detail as was allowed by a somewhat arbitrary and often changing yardstick of taste. Mixed with this were frequent "revelations" about prostitution, preferably taking place in seemingly innocent suburban terraced houses. The world created by the *News of the World* was one where torrid lusts and passions were acted out in unsuspecting day-to-day surroundings. The reader was supposed to wonder whether that mild man opposite in the pub was the one who lured his teenage niece to the bicycle shed and there made her do unspeakable things. And was the mousey woman shuffling down that tree-lined street going to turn in at number thirty-five, pull on black fishnet stockings, draw the chintz curtains and start her day's work entertaining a succession of furtive male customers in bowler hats and raincoats?

The paper had been more or less controlled by the Carr family since 1891. Sir Emsley Carr, editor for fifty years until he died in 1941, had created the formula that had essentially remained unchanged since. His son, Sir William Carr, had, by 1968, been chairman for sixteen years. Then fifty-six, he ran the firm as a family concern and saw nothing wrong in using its resources for his personal comfort and amusement. The family enjoyed company boxes at Ascot races and the Covent Garden opera. There were company golf courses in Surrey and Spain where Sir William played. The paper owned racehorses and a stud farm and sponsored a race at Goodwood. Carr would host regular black-tie stag dinners at the company flat at Cliveden Place – one floor below his own plush quarters. All this affected profitability and the share price, and that was compounded by an unadventurous record of expansion. While other newspaper companies had branched into a variety of profitable sidelines, Carr ran the *News of the World* conservatively. Diversification had been almost exclusively in print-related businesses and television, though there were small interests in chemicals, transport and engineering, plus the Townsend Hook paper company. But profits, at below £2 million, had dropped by nearly £1 million over five years. And the paper's circulation had fallen by a quarter from a peak of well over 8 million in 1950.

Carr drank too much and his health was a worry. He suffered from a painful and debilitating aneurism, a swelling of the main artery. He owned thirty-two per cent of the shares. The second largest block, twenty-five per cent, was held by his cousin, Professor Derek Jackson, a slightly eccentric scientist and inventor who had married six times and now lived in Paris. He was a difficult man to get on with and was not on especially friendly terms with his cousin William. The Carrs were a quarrelsome family. Sir William had only managed to gain control after the war by dint of a cleverly-executed campaign against his relatives. That was why Jackson did not consult him before announcing that he was going to sell his holding, then resisted his cousin's blandishment to change his mind.

It was alarming news for Carr, for unless the Jackson shares fell into friendly hands he could easily lose control. So he instructed Hambros, his bank, to offer Jackson the then market price of twenty-eight shillings a share. Rothschild's, handling the sale for Jackson, said it was not enough and sought another potential buyer. The family feud came to the surface here, too, because Jacob Rothschild, who ran the firm, was married to Serena Dunn. Her father, Philip Dunn, had been chairman of the *News of the World* in the 1940s as a representative of the Jackson interest – and he was the man Sir William had ousted to gain control.

Rothschild found a customer for the shares in Robert Maxwell, the ebullient, high-flying Labour Member of Parliament who had achieved great success with Pergamon Press, a group devoted chiefly to publishing scientific and technical books and journals. As the Pergamon share price climbed in the 1960s, the company expanded into other publishing, printing and overseas ventures. The ownership of a national newspaper seemed a logical next step. Maxwell bid 37s. 6d. for *News of the World* shares that then stood at 29s. 3d. A few days later they were up to 49s. 6d.

Carr and his portly editor Stafford Somerfield, close friends and drinking companions, reared back at the thought of sharing control with the abrasive, assertive Maxwell. They were not keen to share with anyone, but certainly not with this naturalised Czech who would surely try to turn the paper into a vehicle for his party. Somerfield delivered a harsh attack on Maxwell in an editorial published on October 20, 1968, just four days after his interest became known.

"Why do I think," he asked, "it would not be a good thing for Mr Maxwell, formerly Jan Ludwig Hoch, to gain control of this newspaper which, I know, has your respect, loyalty and affection – a newspaper which I know is as British as roast beef and Yorkshire pudding?"

Somerfield claimed that the paper's editorial stance was independent – though it was an independence standing very much to the right of centre. He pointed out that leaders of all parties had written for it.

"I, as editor, as those before me – there have only been six of us since 1891, we don't change very often – have been able to direct this policy because of the complete backing of the chairman of the board, now Sir William Carr, who has followed a great family tradition. Would this attitude and policy be continued by a complete stranger, as far as Fleet Street and this newspaper are concerned, a man with no newspaper experience and a Socialist MP?

"Mr Maxwell has gone on record as saying that if he gained control he would not change the policy of the paper. But what guarantee is there of this? Mr Maxwell has also said that he would cease to be a Socialist MP if he gained control . . . But is it possible for him to support the Socialists one day and become completely impartial the next? I do not think so. I believe that Mr Maxwell is interested in power and money. There is nothing wrong with that but it is not everything."

Then he went back to his point about Maxwell's nationality: "This is a British newspaper, run by British people. Let's keep it that way."

The harsh tone of the editorial alienated many who had formerly sympathised with Somerfield and Carr. David Steel, the young Liberal MP, summed up the prevailing attitude in an article in the *Guardian*: "What a revolting piece of chauvinism. Mr Maxwell is not everybody's cup of tea and he knows it, but he is as disgustingly British as anybody I know. He even has a Rolls-Royce with a telephone in it." In his book *Banner Headlines*, Somerfield defended himself by saying that, to him, the situation was akin to 1939. "I was at war and, when at war, I saw no point in throwing friendly leaflets."

Rupert Murdoch had been alerted to the forthcoming fight over the *News of the World* by his friend, Lord Catto of Morgan Grenfell. It was not easy to decide whether to get into the bidding, for he knew that if he did so he would have to give up his ambitions with respect to IPC. He thought that if he continued to buy IPC shares steadily he could be in a position to bid for the company within ten years. (In fact it was sold to Reed International in 1970.) Should he hang on, or go for the here and now? Waiting was not really part of his nature. On hearing from Catto, Murdoch instructed the London bureau of his Australian newspapers to send to Sydney all news and press comment on the rumoured Maxwell bid. When the bid became public he was in Melbourne preparing to go to the races. He flew immediately to London, pausing in Sydney to pick up his luggage and relevant documents. He arrived in such secrecy that it took his London office a day to discover he was there.

Murdoch, Catto and Harry Sporborg of Hambros had devised a clever plan to outflank the confident Maxwell. Instead of entering the contest as a third party, Murdoch would in effect shore up Carr. In return, Murdoch would become joint managing director, with Carr staying on as chairman and consultant. The plan was put to Carr at a breakfast meeting on Tuesday, October 22nd, at his flat in Cliveden Place. Sporborg convinced him that it was the only way to keep some control of the paper for his family. Next day Murdoch's News Ltd. began buying shares and it was only then that his interest became known publicly. Even Somerfield, a director of the company, had not been told. The first he knew was when, early the following morning, a friend on the *Daily Express* telephoned him and said: "Your saviour is here. It's young Rupert Murdoch from Australia."

By October 24th, 1968, Carr and Murdoch between them owned fractionally more than half the shares, but Maxwell was not finished. He complained to the City's Takeover Panel, which did not approve of companies buying their own shares to frustrate a takeover offer. Dealings in *News of the World* shares were suspended and remained so until Christmas. During that two months the battle between Murdoch and Maxwell became increasingly acrimonious, with each side accusing the other of dirty tricks. Murdoch's Australian papers launched an investigation into the operation of encyclopaedia salesmen working for a Maxwell company there. Maxwell suspected people working for Murdoch of spreading a rumour that he was bankrupt. Maxwell and his ally, the respected financier Sir Isaac Woolfson, tried to persuade Carr that Murdoch's inten-

tions were dishonourable. "You will be out before your
feet touch the ground," Maxwell told him. "Bob, Rupert is
a gentleman," Carr replied.

When dealings were suspended Murdoch had only three
and a half per cent of the shares – a stake of less than one
million pounds in a thirty million pound company. On
October 26th he revealed his clever plan in full. New shares
would be created in the *News of the World* by merging some
of his Australian properties into it. All the new shares
would go to Murdoch, giving him forty per cent of the
issued shares. His understanding with Carr contained three
safeguards: that he and Carr would be joint managing-
directors, that a member of the Carr family would remain
chairman of the company for the foreseeable future and
that he would not seek to increase his shareholding to give
himself absolute control.

Many financial commentators agreed with Maxwell that
the deal with Murdoch violated rule thirty-three of the
Takeover Code. This stipulated that companies could only
take allies to defeat takeover bids if it was not prejudicial to
the interests of shareholders. Murdoch's offer of a link with
a random bunch of his Australian papers seemed intrinsi-
cally less beneficial to shareholders than Maxwell's cash
offer. Professor Jackson arrived from the Continent to see
the Takeover Panel and to side with Maxwell: but the Panel
had precious little power to intervene even if its rules had
been breached. Anthony Crosland, President of the Board
of Trade, commented: "As there are very few sanctions at
the Panel's disposal, it will have to rely mainly on the
respect shown for its views." Maxwell remains convinced
that the Panel could and should have acted but did not do so
because the City establishment was against him, largely on
account of his politics.

The Carrs were an old-fashioned upper-class family.
Almost the first thing they had done in response to Maxwell's bid was to foregather – nineteen of them – in the
company flat and have their picture taken, to underline
their solidarity. Although Murdoch was in no sense their
kind of person, he was still to be preferred to the flash
Maxwell, the known and feared quantity. The grating
Australian accent was unfortunate but that presumably

would soften in time. The spirited Lady Carr took it upon herself to try to smooth some of Murdoch's rougher edges, to make him acceptable socially. It started well enough when she invited Dame Elisabeth Murdoch to lunch at the Cliveden Place flat. That went splendidly: there was a woman who obviously knew how to behave. But the enterprise foundered when she made the bold move of asking Rupert to lunch at the Coq d'Or, a classy Mayfair restaurant. It was the first time she could remember taking a strange man out to lunch and it was not a success. She found him lacking in small talk and a sense of humour. That need not have mattered – it holds good, after all, for many prominent society people – but the moment she knew there was to be no taming the Australian beast came early on, during pre-lunch cocktails, when he summoned the waiter to ask for a cigar and began puffing before the first course. She recognised then, before his business behaviour confirmed it, that Murdoch was not the good news the Carrs had hoped for.

Scenting victory, Murdoch now made the first of the crucial variations to his agreement with Carr. He was to become sole managing-director, not joint, and Carr would be chairman. In a letter to Carr, Murdoch said he still hoped members of the Carr family would continue to serve as chairman – an aspiration that, within a year, was dashed.

By now the contest between Maxwell and Murdoch was being given press coverage similar in spirit, if not in scale, to a soccer cup final. The match was fixed for Thursday, January 2nd, 1969, in the Connaught Rooms in London, where shareholders would vote on the Murdoch merger. The Takeover Panel had ruled that shares acquired since Maxwell's bid should not count for voting purposes. This meant that the balance of power as between the Jackson shares (twenty-five per cent) and the Carr shares (thirty-two per cent) lay with the small shareholders who had not sold out. There was never much doubt that Murdoch would emerge the winner, and although Maxwell could see this as well as anyone, he put on a show of resistance. He even thought of joining forces with Lord Thomson, the Canadian owner of *The Times* and the *Sunday Times*, to buy out

News Ltd. in Australia. Then Maxwell provoked three members of the *News of the World* pension fund, which owned 600,000 shares, to seek an injunction preventing the fund's trustees from voting in Murdoch's favour. The injunction was refused on the eve of the shareholders' meeting.

At the meeting, Murdoch made a three-minute speech claiming that great benefits would flow from a liaison between the Australian and British newspaper groups. He paid tribute to Sir William Carr, repeating his undertaking to keep him on as chairman. Then Maxwell gave a typical rough-and-tumble performance, attacking the record of the company and the tactics of their bankers. His own offer, he maintained, would provide great benefits for shareholders. After some angry exchanges Carr persuaded him to sit down. The vote by a show of hands was overwhelmingly in Murdoch's favour and after a tally according to numbers of shares held, Murdoch was ahead by more than a million votes. "The law of the jungle has prevailed," said Maxwell, but perhaps the most apt remark came from Professor Jackson: "I regard the *News of the World* board as raving mad."

Safely in charge, Murdoch did not take long to flex his muscles. On January 21st, less than three weeks after the shareholders' meeting, he sent Carr a handwritten letter. Beginning with some solicitous remarks about the chairman's health, he went on to announce that he was planning to buy some of the Jackson shares, which Rothschild's were putting on the market. He explained that if he did not take his chance now he would miss out, but stressed that his plan did not change in any way the understandings the two had reached. Since a key feature of the understandings had been that Murdoch would not seek a majority of the shares, it was hard to credit that disclaimer.

This was the first of a series of swift moves by which Murdoch secured sole control of the company. Carr remained ill and inactive for weeks after the change and Murdoch could have used that as an excuse to ease him out. Instead, he chose to make precisely the opposite argument, saying that the prospect of Carr's recovery made it imperative for him to act. The company had always been run on patriarchal rather than on formal commercial lines and Murdoch feared a more active Carr would provide a focal point for disaffection by the resentful "old guard" – chief among them editor Stafford Somerfield, already showing signs of resistance.

On March 2nd Murdoch wrote to Carr that his improved health and increased contacts with senior executives of the company left him, Murdoch, no alternative but to point out that there could be only one executive boss. While respecting Carr's position as chairman of the board, he did not intend a situation to develop where there could be confusion about the chain of command.

It took only three more months for Murdoch to get round to the logical climax of the pressure he was putting on Carr: he asked him to resign as chairman and a director and proposed to take over as chairman himself. Less than seven months earlier he had written that he would hope Carr or members of his family would remain as chairman: but now he wanted to tighten his personal control. This time he did use the argument that Carr's health had prevented him from carrying out his duties. After an acrimonious correspondence between lawyers the terms of Carr's departure were agreed, and at the annual meeting on June 19th, 1969, giving no hint in his dignified statement that he had been forced out, Carr resigned as chairman. He became seriously ill again not long afterwards and was more or less an invalid for the last seven years of his life. When Carr died in 1977 Murdoch offered to pay for a memorial service for him, but a proud Lady Carr refused.

With Murdoch indisputably at the helm, any remaining family atmosphere at the *News of the World* quickly evaporated. He was not coy about declaring his contempt for the talents and energy of many of the journalists he had inherited. Somerfield remembers breaking to him the upsetting news that Jack Miller, the paper's television and radio correspondent, had dropped dead the previous night. "Well, it wasn't from overwork," Murdoch snapped.

Because Somerfield insisted on keeping control as editor, the influence Murdoch was able to exert on the style and content of the paper was at first minimal. In any case, it was not his intention to alter its essential character and his first big row with British press critics and opinion-moulders came over a story of a traditional *News of the World* nature. Five years earlier the paper had paid £26,000 for serial rights to the memoirs of Christine Keeler, a call-girl whose liaison with War Minister John Profumo had discredited the Macmillan government in 1963. Now Keeler had written the story for a second time, with extra juicy detail revealed, and the papers were bidding for it again. It would not be such big money as last time but, six years after the event, interest in this distinctively British scandal was still high.

Somerfield read the new version, liked it and showed it to Murdoch. On July 22nd Murdoch wrote to him enthusiastically, urging him to buy it, though the "dirty" bits in the early parts should be held out. He did wonder, at that early stage, whether it might stir emotions so strongly that the paper and the company might be damaged.

The letter went on to suggest that the story was probably worth about £10,000 but that he would be prepared to go up to £15,000. The final purchase price was £21,000 and an extra 150,000 copies were printed in anticipation of demand. Murdoch's letter to Somerfield shows that he was aware of the storm likely to erupt when the series began to run. Emotions were indeed stirred strongly, particularly in those high Conservative circles that sought to forget the embarrassment of 1963 and to whom Profumo, who had now devoted his life to good works, had become a respected figure, well on the way to rehabilitation. For anyone to reopen these old sores – and especially an outsider who could not expect to appreciate the nuances of British life – was unsporting and reprehensible.

Yet even given all that, the outcry seemed out of proportion with the offence. The Press Council – inspired by Denis Hamilton of *The Times* and the *Sunday Times* – condemned the series, and Cardinal Heenan, Britain's senior Catholic, withdrew from a commitment to write an article for the paper. Somerfield, accustomed to such controversy, was a bit too blasé about it for Murdoch, sensitive about the impression he was creating in his new country and worried that he might be gaining a reputation that would inspire resistance to his making further acquisitions in Britain. Discussing Heenan's response in an interview with the *Daily Mail*, Somerfield ventured that he would have thought the Cardinal would welcome the idea of talking to fifteen million sinners. Next day Murdoch dashed off an angry, hand-written note. He said he was appalled by Somerfield's remarks and had apologised to Cardinal Heenan. In future Somerfield should either say nothing or clear his statements with Murdoch first. There was, he insisted, a lot more at stake than one newspaper.

The last observation was a reference to his negotiations to buy the *Sun*, about to be wound up by IPC. But Murdoch's own performance as spokesman, as defender of his right to publish salacious scandal, was not crowned with success. In television interviews he came across as sanctimonious and muddled.

"We can forgive Mr Profumo," he told interviewer David Dimbleby. "We can do what we can to see that he's rehabilitated because he has tried very hard. By all means forgive the individual; but you can't forget." Dimbleby quoted back at him his reported remark that "people can sneer as much as they like, but I'll take the 150,000 extra copies we're going to sell" and asked whether he was not lining his pocket with sleazy material.

"I don't agree it's sleazy for a minute," Murdoch snapped back. "Nor do I agree that it's unfair to the man. I have the greatest sympathy with him, but it doesn't alter the fact that everybody knows what happened. Certainly it's going to sell newspapers."

Murdoch's most notorious interview was with David Frost on London Weekend Television. His advisers were divided about whether he should accept the invitation from a man skilled at advocacy interviewing, at acting as barrister at the trial of his victims and persuading the studio audience to be the jury and pass sentence. He claims he was misled as to the nature of the programme. He was assured by David Frost that no other guest would be in the studio and that was true, but what Frost concealed, according to the Murdoch camp, was that a filmed interview with Cardinal Heenan would be inserted into the proceedings. Frost maintains that Murdoch was told about that and agreed to it. The trouble, according to Frost, was that Murdoch was too shrill in his own defence. Had he admitted graciously that he might be blameworthy in some respects the issue could have been shelved and the discussion broadened. His stubborn insistence that he was right meant that the interview was stuck on the one subject – and Murdoch's defence was inadequate.

It was the first Independent Television programme to go out live in colour and after a joke or two about that ("to viewers watching in colour, we hope you will both like it very much indeed") Frost asked the studio audience whether they approved of the publication of the Keeler memoirs. Only nine out of 230 did. That result encouraged Frost to maintain a high moral tone throughout.

Murdoch first sought to defend publication of the series by saying that the early part of the book, containing much explicit sex, had been largely excised from the serialisation. The articles would concentrate on Miss Keeler's role as a scapegoat and "the parliamentary side of it, the behaviour of the Labour Party in it: very interesting indeed". Frost was able to point out how unfortunate it was that the only episode to have appeared thus far was taken entirely from the first part of the book and that the front page trailers for ensuing weeks had concentrated on titillation rather than on any redeeming social message.

Then Murdoch was caught out in claiming that the new work represented the first time the affair had been put into proper context. Frost referred him to a book by Wayland Young, from which the Keeler work had quoted extensively. Murdoch had to confess he had not read it, and fell back on the alternative argument that it was possible to tell the same story several times. Frost was quick to point out the inconsistency. Then, in response to Murdoch's revised claim that some facts may be new to some readers, Frost asked: "But what new facts? Like this: 'Stephen brought Bill round and we spent a very amusing evening, Bill running after us and trying to pinch our bottoms'?"

That was only the first segment of the programme. It would scarcely seem possible for things to go downhill for Murdoch from that low point, but they did. Frost next showed the interview with Cardinal Heenan he had filmed earlier in the day. The contrast with the live section of the programme was startling. Here was Frost cosy and respectful, giving Heenan the chance to expound at length his moral principles and his reason for withdrawing from his agreement to write for the *News of the World*. Heenan's main concern was for Profumo, a sinner who had worked hard to rehabilitate himself. He pointed out that many of the people Profumo was working with in the East End probably read the *News of the World*. "I think they were profoundly wrong in raking up the past of this excellent man Profumo and putting it in the homes of the people whom he is now trying to help."

When the time came for Murdoch to comment on this he confessed to being "incredibly shocked". He said angrily: "This easy glib talk that the *News of the World* is a dirty paper is downright libel and it is not true and I resist it completely." People only said it, he maintained, because the paper was so successful.

John Addey, Murdoch's public relations man, was in the audience applauding these sallies, and now Frost turned on him. "Your PR man's doing a wonderful job over there. He's made more noise than the other 230 people put together . . . Still, that's what he's paid for."

By now Frost had dropped any pretence of being an impartial moderator and was assuming the unambiguous role of prosecutor. When Murdoch sought to defend the Keeler series as a "cautionary tale", Frost retorted: "A cautionary tale about the best way to make £21,000?" Murdoch came back: "You make that every week. Don't show horror about that. Come on, let's be grown up about it." And Frost declaimed, to the applause of the audience: "What money I make I don't make by means of exposing a man like John Profumo in that way."

Frost now had the bit between his teeth. He described a visit he had made to Toynbee Hall, Profumo's charitable settlement in the East End, where ex-prisoners, drug addicts and the needy were given a helping hand. "If . . . you were to damage that man and that work, could you forgive yourself? Because you're a decent man . . . There is a man doing a fantastic job of work and you are threatening that work by this story and you still haven't given us one good reason for taking that risk."

Murdoch tried valiantly to keep his end up. He said the fuss had been "whipped up by members of the sort of establishment that don't want to be seen with Mr Profumo anywhere." He added that as long as Profumo was alive people would associate his name with the scandal, and Frost snapped back: "If everybody knows, you don't need to tell the story again, do you?" Then, reading from the page one promotion for the series in the *News of the World* ("a night with the Russian huggie bear"), Frost stormed: "It's pathetic to say that that's a social document of our time." And he ended the interview on a scarcely impartial note: "Your PR man's going mad again. Your PR man is the only person who's applauded. You must give him a rise."

Reading the transcript of the interview after a gap of thirteen years, Frost's tendentious needling comes across as sharply as Murdoch's equivocation, confusion and sophistry. But it is easy to see how damaging it was to Murdoch at the time, and why for years he regretted agreeing to appear. That he did agree speaks for his confidence in his ability to defend what, probably sincerely, he felt to be utterly defensible.

He believed he had been framed. In an Australian television interview two years later he said: "I was damned upset because I had been told by him and everyone else that it was going to be a nice pally talk. It didn't turn out quite the way I had expected. I'd been lulled into a state of unpreparedness."

Anna, who was with him, is said to have turned on Frost in the hospitality room after the programme and hissed: "We've had enough of your hospitality." And as he strode out of the building, according to people who were with him, Murdoch vowed: "I will buy this company – and Frost will be out." Not long afterwards he fulfilled that promise, and those who know him are convinced that the incident, which wounded him deeply, was a factor in his decision.

There were other attacks, and he responded to them with spirit. When the *Observer* criticised his paper as being dirty, he hit back by describing as salacious an *Observer* article on how women get sexual fulfilment from riding horses. He went to see David Astor, then editor of the *Observer*, for peace talks, but relations stayed cool. Again, a few years later, he was to make a strong bid for Astor's paper, but it is possible to make too much of the element of vengeance in his attempted acquisitions. He is, after all, a man who has often felt himself slighted, and who makes a habit of bidding for whatever paper is going.

Murdoch believes today that it was a tactical error to publish the Keeler memoirs, so far as his personal standing in Britain was concerned. He has no doubt it was the right decision for the paper: it was a mainstream *News of the World* story, it increased circulation and he saw nothing ethically wrong with it himself. But he knew that if he was to become an accepted and respected newspaper proprietor he would have to come to terms with the British establishment that, rightly or wrongly, believed him to have behaved caddishly in raking over Profumo's anguish. In public he affected a swaggering disregard for such matters. What did acceptance into the inner circles of power matter to him? he would ask rhetorically. But to his friends it was clear that it did matter. It was in many respects the Rupert Stuart case all over again: he was being ostracised for a quite legitimate piece of journalistic enterprise by one of his papers, and he hated it. As he told Somerfield, "There is a lot more at stake than one newspaper." After his clear humiliation at the hands of Frost the furore died down but for some time afterwards there was a stiffness when he entered polite society and Anna, according to friends, was wounded by a few social rebuffs.

The clash with Somerfield over his Heenan remark was not their first. Relations between the two had always been uneasy and neither made much effort to improve them. An early row, that set the tone for subsequent ones, came in May 1969, when Somerfield broke a holiday in Spain on being told by a colleague that, in his absence, Murdoch was making radical changes to the paper. The two men's versions of the dispute conflict. Somerfield says Murdoch had wanted to take the leader page out of the paper altogether and only agreed to replace it when Somerfield arrived in the office during the print run, but in a letter to Sir William Carr on May 22nd, two days after the event, Murdoch wrote that the editor's version was seriously inaccurate in detail.

Murdoch's letter was in response to a pompous memorandum that Somerfield had sent to all directors about editorial responsibility: "The Editor is the servant of the board, and contractually answerable to the board and the managing director. But this does not mean that the chief executive, acting independently of the board, can take his chair, seek to discharge his functions or introduce fundamental changes in the paper, without consultation."

Unused to receiving notes of this kind from his editors, Murdoch suspected that Somerfield was seeking a showdown that would end in a handsome payoff. But the two men patched up their relations and tolerated each other uneasily for the rest of that year. The affair of the Keeler memoirs thrust them together temporarily, despite the Heenan incident, and for the last months of 1969 Murdoch was engrossed in his purchase of the *Sun* from IPC. With that under his belt, he returned to Australia for two months round Christmas. Before leaving, he gave a lunch at the Ritz for senior colleagues and asked Somerfield to sit next to him. During the meal he thanked Somerfield for what he had done. The now wary editor wondered if anything sinister lay behind that friendly remark.

He had to wait until Murdoch's return to find out. Arriving in his office on a morning in February 1970, Somerfield was told that Murdoch wanted to see him at noon. In a short interview, he asked for his resignation. Somerfield fled to a pub round the corner, told his friends, and in a couple of hours it was headline news in the evening papers. The remaining seven years of his contract were paid off – a lump sum of around £100,000. Somerfield, then 59, was never to work in Fleet Street again, though he later bought a magazine about pedigree dogs which he edited from Ashford, Kent.

One characteristic of the *News of the World* that damaged its profitability was that its presses were used only once a week. Nearly all its rivals had daily sisters to share overheads. Soon after taking control of the paper Murdoch had spoken of launching a daily, to use the presses more economically. He believed in saying things like that, often and with conviction, simply to put the wind up the opposition, but few doubted he would some day carry out the threat. As it was, the chance to start a new daily came faster than he had anticipated.

The *Daily Mirror* had, in 1961, bought Odhams Press, publishers of the *Daily Herald* and the *People* – the main Sunday rival to the *News of the World*. The motive for the purchase was not to acquire the two newspapers but the string of profitable magazines that went with them. The *Herald* had the largest circulation of any daily paper in the 1930s, but had declined steadily since – weighed down, many thought, by a formal commitment to support the policies of the trade union movement. In 1964 Hugh Cudlipp, Chairman of Mirror Newspapers, had masterminded a revamping of the still sagging *Herald* as the *Sun*, a paper aimed at affluent young people and, as the publicity said, "born of the age we live in". The commitment to the unions was dropped and optimism ran high, but the paper was not a success. Starting with the *Herald*'s old circulation of about 1,500,000, it never rose consistently above that and by the middle of 1969 it was down to 850,000. IPC had lost £12,702,000 on the *Herald* and the *Sun* since 1961.

One of the architects of the *Sun*'s marketing concept had been Bert Hardy, deputy advertising director for the *Sun* and the *People*. Market research had indicated that the better-educated and more sophisticated working class were growing out of the traditional, wham-bang tabloids and wanted something a bit more intelligent. The size of the paper symbolised that – midway between a tabloid and a broadsheet. There was an emphasis on youth and leisure, especially in a twelve-page weekend supplement. They even had a name for their target audience: the growth generation. But either the market research was wrong or the concept was inadequately fulfilled, for the twelve weekend pages dwindled to almost nothing and the paper languished. Bert Hardy left IPC at the end of 1968, after twenty years, to join Rupert Murdoch – the first British executive he hired. The second, also from IPC, was Alex McKay, an Australian who had worked for Murdoch's father.

In the summer of 1969 the board of IPC decided to sell the *Sun* or, if they failed, to close it. The first person to declare an interest was Robert Maxwell, thwarted over the *News of the World* and still keen to break into Fleet Street. Maxwell's idea was to keep the paper's commitment to Labour and run it on a lower budget than was customary, not aiming for a mass circulation that would make it a rival to IPC's *Daily Mirror*. On this understanding, and because some jobs at least would be saved, IPC were prepared to give him the title for nothing, but the unions, to nobody's surprise, were less than enthusiastic, not just because of the precedent lower manning levels would set but because they did not think Maxwell was a proprietor they could rely on. Scouting for an editor, Maxwell was rejected by a number of top Fleet Street men before he gained a highly qualified commitment from Mike Randall, once editor of the *Daily Mail* and then assistant editor of the *Sunday Times*. Randall accompanied Maxwell to a meeting with the editorial staff of the *Sun* where they were both given a hard time, with hostile questioning. It seemed clear that he was not going to make it work.

Murdoch kept himself informed about all this and in August he felt the time was right to stake his claim. First he flew to Rome to see a holidaying Richard Briginshaw, head of NATSOPA, one of the most difficult of the print unions. Assured of his support, he wrote to IPC asking to start negotiations to take over the *Sun*. Hugh Cudlipp wrote back saying that as long as the discussions with Maxwell had not formally come to an end he could not start talking with anyone else – leaving the unstated implication that as soon as Maxwell pulled out he would start doing business with Murdoch. Most of the IPC directors did not see much of a threat in a Murdoch purchase: like the press barons of Sydney nine years earlier, they were convinced he would be letting himself in for a heavy loss. A few – notably Frank Rogers, the managing director – had their doubts but Cudlipp could not see that he had any alternative. To close the paper when a buyer was ready to take it might on the face of it assure the commercial future of the *Mirror*, but it would be unacceptable to the unions, who could take revenge on the *Mirror* and its sister papers, even though IPC's formal commitment to keep the paper going, made when they bought Odhams, had expired in 1968.

Maxwell pulled out and Cudlipp started talks with Murdoch. At first Murdoch was pressing to be given the title for nothing, as Maxwell had been offered it. But Rogers went to see him at the *News of the World* office in Bouverie Street and told him, first, that he did not personally favour any deal at all and, secondly, that he would certainly not agree to giving it away. The final modest price was under a million pounds. The rump of the editorial staff joined Murdoch, although most senior executives stayed with the Mirror group.

Murdoch knew precisely what kind of paper he wanted the *Sun* to be. He was convinced that the *Mirror*, by far the best-selling tabloid, was not as good as it had been when it was the object of his most fervent desire. Now, he felt, it was the soft underbelly of the popular market. It was suffering to an extent from the affliction that had led to the demise of Cudlipp's *Sun*. It was getting above its readers, trying to push them up-market against their will. To do this it had introduced special sections – the Inside Page, Mirrorscope – that sought to deal with serious issues in a way its readers could comprehend; but they were out of tune with the rest of the paper. You turned a page and it shouted at you: "This is the serious bit." Murdoch thought readers must resent this and would enjoy the chance of buying a tabloid that did not keep reminding them how little they knew – a tabloid modelled on the *Mirror* of the 1940s and 1950s, before it had become seized by ideas above its station. Moreover, he thought Cudlipp's reputation as the guru of tabloid journalism greatly exaggerated. In Murdoch's view, Cudlipp's abilities had peaked when he edited the *Sunday Pictorial* in the 1940s.

Murdoch is never shy about seeking advice – even if sometimes an inquiry about what *you* think is simply a pretext to test his own opinion. When he asked around Fleet Street whom he should appoint editor of his new paper, two names kept cropping up, both ex-*Mirror* men. Larry Lamb, a Yorkshireman of forty, had been a protégé of *Mirror* editor Lee Howard, who saw him as a future editor. But Cudlipp did not at that time share Howard's view: he thought Lamb a little too self-confident, too ambitious for comfort. Sensing that this could bar his way to the top *Mirror* job, Lamb had accepted an offer to join the *Daily Mail* as Northern editor in Manchester. Bernard Shrimsley, another who had felt shunted aside in the jostle of senior *Mirror* executives, had spent the previous year revamping the *Liverpool Daily Post*. Murdoch invited Lamb for dinner at Rules in Covent Garden, where they sat for nearly four hours swapping ideas for the new tabloid. Then they moved on to the *News of the World* office. It was 1 a.m. before Lamb left. Murdoch told him he still had a few more people to see and would be in touch.

Three hours later Murdoch phoned Lamb at home and told him the job was his. They met again later at Murdoch's flat in Sussex Gardens, Paddington. By coincidence, Lamb told Murdoch he would like to hire Shrimsley as his deputy.

The first issue of the new *Sun* appeared on November 17th, 1969, and Murdoch invited senior people from Fleet Street and elsewhere, advertisers and politicians, to a celebratory party, to watch Anna push the button to start the presses. The ceremony was timed for 9 p.m. but because of production delays it was after 11 when the button was pressed and the run began. It was an exciting evening, with a flushed Murdoch in his shirtsleeves and his friends congratulating him raucously. But it was only his friends. Hardly any of the invited VIPs had turned up. Murdoch guessed that this was partly to do with the Keeler business a few months earlier but, more practically, because Cudlipp had chosen to throw a rival party at the *Mirror* at the same time. If you were an advertiser or a person who needed Fleet Street's goodwill, and you were being made to choose sides, it was no contest. Far more important to butter up Cudlipp, the established star of the Street, than this gauche newcomer, this unknown quantity.

Around midnight some copies of the *Sun*'s first edition were delivered to the Cudlipp party, smudgy and full of misprints. Cudlipp cast a professional eye over what Fleet Street regards as the salient parts of a tabloid: the front page, the back, page three and the centre spread. He hurled it down on the table and shouted to Howard across the room: "Lee, we've got nothing to worry about." Howard replied: "I haven't read it yet, Hugh." Within a year the *Sun*'s circulation had doubled and soon after that it passed two million, chiefly at the expense of the *Mirror*.

The feature by which the *Sun* became best known was the daily picture of a bare-breasted woman, usually on page three, but that did not begin until nearly a year after the launch. It was not Murdoch's idea, nor indeed a conscious stratagem at all. Lamb simply decided to do it one day and the reaction was so positive he thought he should carry on with it. The *Mirror* felt obliged to do the same for a while.

People on the *Mirror*, and others of the Fleet Street establishment, were bitter about the *Sun*'s success. They felt wounded not so much because their circulation was suffering but because they had been obliged to come down market to stop the *Sun* driving them off the street altogether. Mirrorscope and the Inside Page were quickly killed off and the *Mirror* was competing stridently on the *Sun*'s terms. It had dozens of capable tabloid journalists on the staff and it competed effectively. It was not until 1976 that the *Sun* caught up with the *Mirror* in circulation. Many felt and said that the *Sun*, by its success, had set back responsible popular journalism by years. In a radio interview an embittered Cudlipp said: "Someone will always be found to scrape the bottom of the barrel," but later he was able to take a more philosophical view. He told Simon Regan, a biographer of Murdoch: "Murdoch is in the tradition of Beaverbrook and Thomson – rustling 'colonials' who could in fact teach their grandmothers how to suck eggs. There was room at the top for a new force in Fleet Street: Rupert's it."

It was not just the editorial content that made the *Sun* a commercial success. Murdoch is a frugal publisher, resenting unnecessary expenditure as though it were all his own money. For years Fleet Street had grown used to extravagant practices, particularly the employment of many more people than were needed to produce the papers. Some journalists on the popular tabloids were paid comfortable salaries and generous expenses for writing perhaps only one article a week. Murdoch introduced more rigorous scrutiny. And he did not see fit to waste money providing luxurious working conditions: the staff of the new daily

paper were crammed into the *News of the World*'s existing
Bouverie Street premises. He does not stint, though, when
it comes to promotion. Many attribute the *Sun*'s success in
large measure to expensive but effective television advertising.

Murdoch's next expansion in Britain was into television. In
1966 a consortium of big-name television stars and
businessmen, with David Frost prominent among them,
got together to bid for the licence to operate London's
commercial television from Friday night to Sunday. They
won the contract on the strength of their names and of a
programme prospectus that assumed an unsatisfied taste
among British viewers for weekend fare of a more cerebral
nature than they had hitherto been offered, emphasising
plays, documentaries, news and interview programmes.
   It was a laudably ambitious notion but it was illusory.
The creative people put into management jobs – such as
former BBC man Michael Peacock and current affairs
specialist Aidan Crawley – proved weak in organisational
and commercial skills. London Weekend Television was
over-staffed, under-organised and losing a packet of
money. The traditional view of programme planners had
been correct: what people wanted to watch on Saturday
night was light entertainment. As audiences dropped so did
advertising and by 1970 the company was on the brink of
collapse, seeking a saviour.
   Whether or not the threat he made after his disastrous
Frost interview was a factor, Murdoch became interested in
the travails of London Weekend and in 1970 bought a block
of shares owned by Arnold Weinstock's General Electric
Company. His foothold established, he was approached by
the directors – led by financier David Montagu and Sir
Jock Campbell of Booker Brothers – and asked whether
he would inject some capital and his company's management skills. They proposed a new issue of shares which
Murdoch would buy, giving him about forty per cent of the
share capital: a replica of the *News of the World* deal.
   Murdoch has never been too lucid about his precise
motive for accepting this offer. If he saw it as yet another
British media company throwing itself into his arms, he

must have been unfamiliar with the rule of the Independent
Broadcasting Authority that makes it impossible for any
single shareholder to gain effective control of a commercial
TV station. But by now Murdoch had come to enjoy the
actual challenge of reviving failing institutions. And in
LWT he saw some parallels with Cudlipp's *Sun*, an information outlet that had gone astray through making
over-optimistic assumptions about the intellectual level of
its audience.

Not that he ever sought to bring London Weekend as far
down market as his British newspapers. Indeed, one other
attraction of the deal was that it irked him to be identified in
Britain only with those two papers. He was not ashamed of
them: far from it. But he saw himself as someone who could
operate across the cultural board. The *Australian* was his
token of respectability but to him it was more than a token.
It was just accidental that most of his papers operated at the
popular level: he was not exclusively a purveyor of opium
to the masses.

Because of the rules limiting the extent to which newspaper owners could control television companies, Murdoch
could play no formal executive role in London Weekend.
But for some months at the end of 1970 he effectively ran it
and seconded his best British manager, Bert Hardy, to
restructure the commercial side, especially advertising
sales. In his familiar style, Murdoch dismissed those executives he felt to be responsible for the mess the company had
got into. That was easy, but what he now needed was
someone who could take over and guide London Weekend
into calmer and more prosperous waters.

When the consortium had been formed in 1966, John
Freeman had been asked to join it. A protégé of the
socialist writer Kingsley Martin, Freeman had succeeded
him as editor of the weekly journal the *New Statesman* in
1961. Then he had become renowned as a remorseless
television interviewer, most famous for driving the crusty
personality Gilbert Harding to tears. Soon after Harold
Wilson became Prime Minister he appointed Freeman
High Commissioner to India in 1965. Since he was still in
that job in 1966 – and would in 1969 become ambassador in
Washington – Freeman turned down the initial approach

from LWT. But he did say, in what now seems a fit of prescience, that if they would ask again when he was free, he might be ready to consider it.

Less than a month after Freeman's return from Washington in early 1971, Frost and Sir Jock Campbell asked him whether he would be interested in coming to LWT as chief executive. Freeman said he might well be, but would want to be assured that the move had the approval of Murdoch who had, he knew, the real power. He did not want to go in as the nominee of one faction in an internal squabble. Murdoch – whom Freeman had met only once before, at dinner with the Carrs in 1968 – telephoned from Australia and Freeman accepted.

The two quite quickly became friends, despite their obvious differences of temperament. While Murdoch is impetuous, Freeman had a calm, diplomatic mien even before he became a diplomat. He solves problems by conciliation and discussion. When he arrived at London Weekend he saw it as a casualty clearing station after a major battle. Senior people had been dismissed and only some of them replaced. Nobody was certain what was going to happen.

Murdoch, very much in charge, held Freeman's hand for the few months it took him to learn the ropes, then left him to his own devices. Freeman proved a shrewd choice as chairman. The company's health improved dramatically and it kept its franchise, until now it is one of the strongest ITV licence holders. Murdoch quit the board when he began to get involved in the United States and nominated Bert Hardy to represent his interest. In 1979, when he needed cash to acquire a television station in Sydney, he sold nearly all his shares in LWT, at a comfortable profit.

And David Frost? He switched his allegiance to the BBC not long after, and sold his shares in 1976. Now he is back with the commercial channel – a shareholder and presenter with the morning company, TV-AM.

Chapter 3

THE USES OF POWER

Rupert Murdoch will probably never be played by Jason Robards.

> – *Ron Powers, CBS press critic.*

If you sit around long enough under an apple tree in autumn, a ripe apple will fall either into your lap or on your head. Like Sir Isaac Newton, Rupert Murdoch could probably benefit from either eventuality but in the case of the Sydney *Daily Telegraph* and *Sunday Telegraph* in 1972 the fruit fell painlessly within reach.

For some time the Packer organisation had been worried about the Telegraph newspapers. The problem was that their chief competitor, Fairfax, was getting maximum utilisation of its presses by printing the *Sydney Morning Herald* in the morning, the *Sun* in the afternoon and the *Sun-Herald* on Sundays. Sir Frank Packer was growing old and control of the group was moving to his younger son Kerry, who did not share his father's sentimental attachment to the papers that had made him a power in the city. Kerry could see that the only way to make money out of the *Telegraph* was to start a new evening paper to share its overheads. But even had he wanted to enter the cut-throat contest between the *Mirror* and the *Sun* it was simply not feasible to distribute an evening paper from the *Telegraph* plant, sited in Sydney's congested commercial centre. The Packer television and magazine interests made a comfortable profit on their own. The sensible if agonising course was to get rid of the newspapers altogether.

The future of the *Telegraph* papers had for months been

the subject of excited speculation among Sydney newspapermen. Angus McLachlan, then the managing director of Fairfax, found himself sitting at a dinner next to Rupert Murdoch, who told him: "Frank's not going to last all that long and you're going to have the Melbourne *Herald* in there." He was playing on the Fairfax horror of competition from his father's old group – an obsession that had led them to sell him the *Mirror* papers in 1960.

A few weeks later McLachlan, Murdoch and Sir Frank Packer were in London at the same time and met on that neutral territory to discuss what was to become of the *Telegraph*. One scheme was for Murdoch and Fairfax to buy it jointly, and McLachlan undertook to raise it with the Fairfax family on his return. But in the end Sir Frank could not stomach the thought of doing a deal with his fiercest rival. Murdoch was the less painful option.

Sir Frank arranged an evening with Murdoch at a championship boxing match, preceded by dinner. When the time came the old tycoon did not feel up to it, so Kerry went with Murdoch instead. Telling the story later, Kerry gives the impression that the subject of the *Telegraph* came up simply by chance in a general discussion of the newspaper scene, but it is clear that there was a strong element of forethought. Kerry's first proposition was to sell a half share in the *Telegraph* newspapers to Murdoch and have them printed at News Ltd.'s headquarters, where they would share overheads with the *Mirror* and the *Australian* – a deal similar to the one Murdoch had made years earlier over the Adelaide Sunday paper.

But Murdoch was loath to share. If he was to print the *Telegraph* titles, he wanted to own them. By the time the dinner and boxing were over he had agreed to buy the goodwill of the papers – nothing more – for fifteen million dollars. The staff were to remain employed by the Packer group, though Murdoch did eventually hire many of them. By not buying the whole staff he avoided responsibility for redundancy payments – a ruse he must have wished he could call on when buying *The Times* and *Sunday Times* in London nine years later. The Packer group did not want to be faced with a heavy bill, either, and Kerry took it on himself to persuade key men to accept Murdoch's terms.

Given that Murdoch had to set up essentially a fresh printing and editorial operation from scratch, it was remarkable that the transfer went as smoothly as it did.

Murdoch was now the biggest newspaper proprietor in Sydney. Fairfax had a morning, evening and Sunday paper, while Murdoch had an extra two Sundays as well as the *Australian*. The *Sunday Australian*, never as successful as Murdoch had hoped, was a casualty of the *Telegraph* acquisition, being merged with the *Sunday Telegraph* a few months later. The *Sunday Mirror* was eventually to go the same way.

The editorial floor of the Murdoch building at the corner of Holt and Kippax Streets, near Sydney's Central Station, is mightily impressive. His four Sydney papers share an open-plan office so large that signs are hung above each section to assist navigation. They are like the labels above shelves in supermarkets but instead of COOKED MEATS and FROZEN VEGETABLES they say AUSTRALIAN NEWS DESK or MIRROR SPORT. It is surprisingly quiet. The background sound is the seductive click of scores of video display terminals. And it is run with rigid economy. People who work there call it "Shoestring International".

Murdoch's growing empire gave him increasing political influence. The remnants of his youthful radicalism, which he was fast growing out of, ensured that his papers supported the Labour Party under Gough Whitlam during the election campaign of 1972. Indeed Billy McMahon, the Liberal Prime Minister, believed the sale of the *Telegraph* newspapers, his most influential supporters in the press when owned by Packer, was a critical factor in his defeat later that year.

Murdoch admired Whitlam, identifying in him many of his own qualities. He was forthright, he had presence and style. He was the very opposite of the cliquish old politicians, the Menzies gang – and, going back to his Adelaide days, the white knights he scorned so. Whitlam was not an establishment man. Moreover, Murdoch could tell that the country was restless after twenty-three years of stifling conservative rule.

He and Whitlam became close friends in the years leading up to 1972. Murdoch even suggested some planks of
Labour's election platform, including the plan to commission an Australian national anthem to replace "God Save
the Queen" – a typically symbolic enthusiasm they shared.
In a country where Labour had been so long out of office
there was a clear need for them to be promoted as a credible
governing party, and Murdoch readily allowed his papers
to be used to that end. The theme he developed was that
under the Liberal-Country coalition Australia had slumped
into comfortable, idle middle age. A reviving dose of
radicalism was needed to halt a slide into early senility.

Murdoch's support for Whitlam continued through the
next election, in 1974, but very soon after that he turned
against him as fervently as he had supported him hitherto.
The following year Murdoch was a key figure in the man-
oeuvring that culminated in the unprecedented dismissal of
the Prime Minister by the Governor-General, Sir John
Kerr.

In an election speech in December 1975 Whitlam
claimed that an important reason for Murdoch's switch of
loyalty was the government's refusal to grant him a bauxite
development licence in Western Australia, in partnership
with Reynolds Aluminium, an American company worried
about the long-term future of their existing bauxite supplies
from Jamaica. Whitlam vetoed the licence because his
government was opposed to a major extension of foreign
investment in Australia's key industries, as well as on
environmental grounds.

But there were other reasons for Murdoch's disillusion.
He felt that since attaining office Whitlam had deliberately
turned away from him. Murdoch likes to be made much of
by the powerful. He likes to consult and be consulted, to
have easy access. Whitlam had scruples about getting too
close to a newspaper proprietor, aware of the danger of
being compromised: so he distanced himself.

Murdoch's own explanation is simply that Whitlam in
office appeared to be making a mess of things. The dollar
was devalued by twelve per cent after the 1974 post-
election budget. There were scandals over some unortho-
dox negotiations for government loans through the offices

of a Pakistani financier named Tirath Khemlani, and over a relationship between Jim Cairns, the deputy Prime Minister, and a Chinese-born aide, Junie Morosi.

The climax to this period of growing confusion came when the opposition, led by Malcolm Fraser, used its Senate majority to block the supply of funds for the day-to-day running of the government. In the resulting stalemate Sir John Kerr, egged on notably by the Murdoch papers, dismissed Whitlam, appointed Fraser as temporary Prime Minister and called a December election that Fraser won in a landslide.

The role of the Murdoch papers in this affair is on record, but whether Murdoch played a part personally in influencing Kerr to take his constitutionally controversial action is a subject of debate. Much has been made of a weekend party Murdoch gave for his senior journalists at his ranch at Cavan, near Canberra, in November, 1974. Late on the Saturday afternoon Sir John arrived for a drink. The host and guests sat round the swimming pool and discussed affairs of state. One guest recalls that Sir John wondered aloud how Whitlam could run the country when the Senate was controlled by the opposition, and what would happen if the Senate refused to pass the budget. In fact the 1974 budget had just been approved by both houses and people later pondered Kerr's ability to foresee so clearly the difficulties that did materialise the following year.

The *Australian* led the Murdoch papers in urging Kerr to act. Not for them the agonised doubts that affected other journals about whether he had the constitutional power to dismiss a prime minister who could not engineer the provision of essential government funds. Some of Murdoch's senior people were uneasy about the proposition but he would not be budged.

Because journalists on the *Australian* would later protest about what they saw as the newspaper's biased coverage, it is important to stress that while the paper was editorially uncompromising in its opposition to Whitlam, some of its commentators, notably Paul Kelly in Canberra, were writing material from the other standpoint and, at least early in November, were still getting it in the paper. On November 5th, for instance, an editorial blamed Whitlam for rejecting a compromise settlement offered by Fraser, who would have agreed to allow the budget to pass in exchange for a commitment by Whitlam to hold an election after six months. If Whitlam were allowed to win this conflict, the editorial said, he would have wrought an enormous extension of the Prime Minister's powers. Yet in the same paper Kelly was discussing ways in which *Fraser* could emerge without utter humiliation, and writing confidently that Kerr would definitely not intervene on either side to swing the balance.

Two days later Kelly stuck to this view, while the leader-writers were becoming more blatant in their appeals to Kerr to act. It was "not a situation he can view with equanimity," they wrote. Whitlam's "determination to tough it out regardless of the consequences . . . [is] fraught with danger for the national body politic."

On the morning of November 11th, the *Australian* was explicit in its advocacy of "positive intervention" by Kerr, despite the risk that he would be seen to be taking sides. It is hard to conceive that Murdoch did not have advance knowledge of Whitlam's dismissal, for that was the day it happened. Mark Day, then editor of the *Daily Mirror*, recalls that as the only time Murdoch ever gave him a specific instruction about what to write in his editorial.

"Write a leader for tomorrow more in sorrow than in anger," he was told. "Whitlam's got to go. You know, talk about the brave experiment failing." Although the *Mirror* has a much higher circulation than the *Australian*, the editorial opinions of Australian tabloids have never counted for as much as those of their British counterparts.

The partisan passions aroused by the dismissal made the 1975 election campaign among the most heated in Australian history. An enraged Whitlam characterised Fraser as "Kerr's cur". In an emotional speech to his supporters outside Parliament House he urged them to "maintain your rage," adding: "Well may they say 'God Save the Queen', for nothing will save the Governor-General."

In a chapter on the 1975 campaign in her book *The Politics of the Press*, Patricia Edgar of La Trobe University concluded that there was "quite clear bias" in the *Australian*'s coverage. After a close analysis of the content of four major papers, she found that the paper "published no comment article which was not either neutral or supporting of its editorial line . . . No articles appeared in which opinion disagreed with editorial policy." However, more bylined news stories were favourable to the Labour Party than the Liberal-Country coalition, indicating that many reporters were out of step with the paper's policy.

Coverage can be slanted in a number of ways. Reporting that election for *The Times* of London, I noted that the choice of pictures in Murdoch's papers seemed to favour Malcolm Fraser, who invariably looked firm and gritty, while Whitlam looked miserable and unimpressive. In the book *Fixing the News*, edited by Keith and Elizabeth Windschuttle, there is a revealing comparison between the front pages of the first and second editions of Murdoch's *Daily Mirror* on November 26th, 1975. The headline on the first edition is GOUGH'S PROMISE: CHEAP RENTS. By the second edition this has been changed to GOUGH PANICS: CHEAP RENTS. And in the same paper on December 3rd, a front-page splash on the loans scandal had a colossal headline GOUGH GUILTY! And in letters a quarter the size underneath A LIE! SAYS WHITLAM.

In the event, Labour was defeated comprehensively and it is doubtful whether the pro-Fraser campaigns of the Murdoch papers had a really decisive influence. But Whitlam was so angered that he delivered a savage attack on Murdoch at a lunch at the Brisbane Press Club on December 4th, nine days before the election.

"Anybody who works for his papers knows how odious Mr Murdoch's control is," he said. "Some of his employees have gone around Australia with me and they are finding it very difficult to get their stories published. When stories have not suited him, others have been published . . . Some of the people on the *Australian* have courage and it requires courage because the editors of the *Australian* have the shortest duration of anybody . . . This expatriate tycoon lives in various places on either side of the North Atlantic."

Whitlam went on to predict that the *Australian* might not survive many more weeks. "Circulation is dropping and the readership is, of course, losing faith. The newspaper is inaccurate and has lost whatever standards and integrity it ever had." He added an appeal for Australian television reporters to "cut up" newspaper owners as David Frost had cut up Murdoch in the interview on British television in 1969.

Next day Murdoch responded in kind. "Mr Whitlam's comments are highly irresponsible and entirely false. They are scurrilous and defamatory." An editorial in the *Australian* declared, in a misquotation: "Whom the gods destroy, they first make mad. Mr Whitlam is going out not with a stance of dignity but with a whimper."

Influenced no doubt in part by Whitlam's outburst, journalists at the *Australian* went on strike on December 8th, complaining about unacceptable bias in the news pages. The strike lasted only twenty-four hours, yet it was destined to become one of the most celebrated causes in Australian journalism, the subject of numerous reports, hearings, analyses and inquiries.

It had been building up before November, so it cannot be put down entirely to the passions aroused by Whitlam's dismissal, though they were surely a factor. In evidence before a hearing over one of Murdoch's television licence applications in 1980, Robert Duffield, a leader-writer who had been with the paper since its foundation, said it had become clear from the start of 1975 that Bruce Rothwell and Les Hollings, the editor, had been instructed by Murdoch to campaign against Whitlam. He cited cases where he had been told to write anti-Whitlam leaders he thought unreasonable, and picked out some news stories from the *Australian* and other Murdoch papers that were, in his view, unfairly biased.

In August 1975 Duffield asked to be relieved of leader-writing duties and in October he and Barry Porter, a sub-editor on the *Australian* and president of the New South Wales branch of the Australian Journalists' Association, drafted a memorandum to the proprietor that became the basis for what was known as the "Murdoch Mutiny". Written in a self-important, maudlin style guaranteed to enrage Murdoch, it began:

"Our loyalties to yourself, to the *Australian* and to the profession of journalism have made it essential that we approach you urgently. For the three loyalties, which could and should be fused to make a great paper, have become intolerably incompatible.

"We do not dispute your prerogative to decide the editorial policy of the paper; that point is not at issue.

"But we would not be loyal to you if we failed to say that, among the influential Australians with whom we come into daily contact – including and especially the intelligent mid-dle-income earners it is the paper's policy to attract – the *Australian* has become a laughing stock. Reporters who were once greeted with respect when they mentioned the *Australian* have had to face derisive harangues before they can get down to the job at hand. It is not so much the policy itself but the blind, biased, tunnel-visioned, ad hoc, logical-ly-confused and relentless way in which so many people are now conceiving it to be carried out, both in the editorial and news columns.

"We can be loyal to the *Australian*, no matter how much its style, thrust and readership change, as long as it retains the traditions, principles and integrity of a re-sponsible newspaper. We cannot be loyal to a propaganda sheet."

The memo went on to specify what it was complaining about: slanted headlines, imbalance in news presentation, political censorship, the distortion of what journalists wrote, the stifling of dissent and impartial opinion. "Many of us are near breaking point," it declared, and asked Murdoch to name an early date for a round-table meeting.

The letter was signed by seventy-five journalists on the *Australian* and delivered to Murdoch on November 2nd. When he had not replied after two weeks, Duffield and Porter wrote saying they were about to publish the letter and to announce his refusal to answer it. By now the election had been called and the campaigning was under way. Murdoch did reply this time, saying: "If you insist on providing ammunition for our competitors and enemies who are intent on destroying all our livelihoods, then go ahead."

After a further exchange of letters the staff met and agreed to take up specific examples of bias with the man-agement. That evening Duffield and Porter were inter-viewed on television about the issue.

Murdoch clearly saw that as another act of disloyalty and refused to discuss the matter further. The editor, Les Hollings, reacted in a curious way: on the morning after the TV interview, he ordered Duffield to move out of his private office to a desk in the features section.

On December 6th, a Saturday, printers of the *Sunday Mirror* and *Sunday Telegraph* went on strike in protest against anti-Labour editorials in both papers, but returned to work when Murdoch agreed that a letter expressing their views should be published in the *Daily Mirror*. That weekend demonstrators burned copies of the *Australian* outside the Holt Street offices. All this unsettled the journalists who, at a meeting attended by over a hundred of them, agreed on a two-day strike at all three of Murdoch's daily papers. Their statement spoke of "very deliberate and blatant bias in the presentation of news", and added: "We have therefore felt it necessary to dissociate ourselves entirely from the desecration of the traditional and historical ethics of journalism."

The papers were brought out by non-union labour that night. The next day an industrial tribunal recommended a return to work in exchange for a promise by Murdoch to meet Duffield and Porter the next morning. It was a heated meeting. Murdoch pushed towards the two journalists a copy of that morning's *Australian* and asked: "Any objections to today's paper?" Porter replied that he had, that the strike had not been covered properly, because it was said to be about objections to *editorial* policy rather than slanted news coverage.

Duffield then pushed a copy of the *Sydney Morning Herald* towards Murdoch and said: "See, the *Herald* got it right." Murdoch was disgusted. "You dare to show this paper to me?" he rasped. "These people are our enemies, trying to destroy us." Then he turned on Duffield personally: "You do this to me after all I've done for you, how I've protected you?" Duffield, as he admitted in public at a later inquiry, had a history of a drinking problem.

But the meeting did not continue in that rancorous vein. Duffield and Porter were able to tell Murdoch that part of the trouble, as they saw it, was that his key executives were over-enthusiastic in interpreting the company line, sometimes indulging in excesses that Murdoch would not have approved of had he been told in advance. Murdoch said he expected his staff to abide by the code of ethics of the Australian Journalists' Association, which rules out deliberate distortion. And he added that any future complaints of that nature should be taken directly to him.

Several of the paper's senior political writers resigned within months of the election – one of them, Bruce Stannard, during the campaign itself – but Murdoch persisted in trying to minimise the importance of the dispute. In an interview with *The Bulletin*, a Sydney weekly magazine, in December 1979, he attributed the strike to two agitators who did not work for his papers inciting the night shift of the *Australian* to call the strike. "There were about forty people and they whizzed a vote through on them and we lost that night's paper out of it. Nothing else. They were back within twenty-four hours, as soon as they could get a full vote. It was a put-up job."

That is an understatement, both in terms of numbers (he had halved the actual number of people taking the strike vote, and the leaders were not outsiders) and in the sense of the importance of the action. Yet his opponents have equally over-estimated its significance, because of later controversies in which Murdoch was involved and because of the emotions aroused by the circumstances of the 1975 election.

Two months after the election, Murdoch turned his hand to an unfamiliar skill, reporting: and the effect was sensational. In February 1976 John Monks and Barrie Watts, in the Melbourne office of the *Australian*, were told to stand by for a call from Murdoch in New York. For three nights they waited until, on February 24th, the call came through. Murdoch spent nearly an hour dictating to Watts.

That morning Brian Boswell, the news editor, had gone into the daily conference with several possible ideas for the front-page splash story. "Don't worry," Bruce Rothwell told him. "We don't need a splash. We've got one." Boswell knew better than to ask what it was. He would wait to read it in the paper.

It was a tremendous story, bearing in mind the previous year's fuss over foreign loans to the Labour government. It appeared in the issue of February 25th and carried the by-line BY A SPECIAL CORRESPONDENT. It began:

"Secret payments of many hundred thousands of dollars have been promised to the Australian Labour Party to pay for last year's election campaign by the extreme left-wing government of Iraq.

"The leader of the Federal opposition, Mr Whitlam, and the party's Federal secretary, Mr David Combe, told the Federal president of the party, Mr Hawke, and the Federal vice-president, Mr Egerton, of the promises."

It went on to tell how Iraqi dictator Saddan Hussein al Takrati had "readily agreed" to respond to the appeal and had sent two important emissaries to Australia to see Mr Whitlam. They were Takrati's nephew and the head of the secret police. The story continued with a detailed description of how the two men's failure to get Australian visas from the British embassy in Baghdad had forced them to travel to Tokyo and obtain them from the Australian embassy there. Staying under false names at the Travelodge in North Sydney, they met Whitlam and Combe before the 1975 election in a block of flats at McMahon's Point in Sydney. Both Iraqis wore machine pistols.

Whitlam, the story continued, had told them he was certain to be re-elected. When he was not, the Iraqis felt sore and had not paid the money, though there was talk of a plan for Whitlam to meet them in London soon.

The detailed reporting must have been Murdoch's own work, although the staff of the *Australian* deduced from stylistic evidence that Rothwell had rewritten at least part of the story. Murdoch has not revealed his source, although many supposed it to be Henry Fischer, the owner of the McMahon's Point flat where Whitlam and Combe met the Iraqis.

In strident editorials, the *Australian* called for Whitlam to resign but he did not do so, remaining party leader until the following year. All the same, Murdoch had for the time being reached the limit of his political power in Australia, on good terms with the new government of Malcolm Fraser and able to claim plausibly that he was to a significant extent responsible for putting it into office. Fraser did not share Whitlam's scruples about the danger of getting too close to the controllers of the media: so Murdoch could, had he felt so inclined, have relaxed a little and enjoyed the fruits of his politicking.

But relaxation is not in his nature. For him, the contest is as sweet as the spoils. Having completed this campaign, his instinct now was to begin another. And in America, where he had been waiting with uncharacteristic patience for his breakthrough for three years now, things were beginning to happen at last.

Chapter 4

RUPERT IN WONDERLAND

Clay Felker is the best editor in America.
                                    – *Rupert Murdoch.*

There was no simple, single reason behind Rupert's and Anna's decision to go to America in 1973. Part of it was that they still felt out of things, socially, in London. For sure, they were asked to more functions than they could possibly attend, but there remained the coolness left over from the business of the Keeler memoirs. The English establishment is slow to forget and forgive. Polite smiles were laced with a hint of frost. Murdoch came as close as he could to admitting all this in an interview with Alexander Cockburn in the New York *Village Voice* in 1976, although his powerful defence mechanism enabled him to turn the facts round to make it seem as if it were he who was rejecting society.

"I just wasn't prepared to join the system . . . Maybe I just have an inferiority complex about being an Australian. My wife accuses me of this sometimes. But you've got some money and you tend to send your kids to the school you can most afford; you join the old-school-tie system and you're going to be dragged into the so-called social establishment somehow. I never was. Just as we were being invited round to places we'd catch Lord Lambton in bed or something, and then we'd be barred from everything . . . It's very difficult not at some point to be sucked into the establishment. The last thing I wanted was to be a bloody press lord. I think when people start taking knighthoods and peerages it really is telling the world you've sold out. I've never been offered one. Well, I've been offered a knighthood a few times but no, I wouldn't take one."

He mentioned, too, the frustration of dealing with the Fleet Street unions. And Anna was still unsettled by the kidnap and murder in 1969 of Muriel McKay, wife of Rupert's senior executive in London. She was unable to erase from her mind that, according to the court evidence of the kidnappers, she had been the intended victim. But these were negative reasons. They would not in themselves have been enough unless reinforced by Murdoch's strong positive impetus. Though certain he had not finished his expansion in either Britain or Australia, he saw no immediate opportunities there. America was the only large English-speaking market left to conquer and he was sure he could do it. From what he knew of Americans, he spoke their language in more than merely the literal sense. These were people with his approach to business, single-minded for producing profits, believing hard work to be more important than social prominence.

But in other respects he does not conform with the image of the high-flying American businessman. He is neither extravagant nor expansive. Certainly he has more – and more costly – homes than most, because splitting his time between three continents means he has to have a convenient base in each. But he spends little, for instance, on clothing. "He has thirty-three editions of the same suit," said a colleague. "Dark grey with a thin light red or white stripe and an undemonstrative tie."

He finds expensive restaurants convenient for discussing business but does not scorn more plebeian places. A few years after his arrival in New York he asked George Gordon, then an executive on his weekly tabloid the *Star*, to lunch at Sloppy Louie's, a raffish old fish restaurant on South Street in New York, near the office of the *New York Post*. Though justly famous for its food, it cultivates an air of crowded discomfort and does not serve alcoholic drinks. "Want a drink?" Murdoch asked Gordon. When he said yes, Murdoch pushed five dollars into a waiter's hand and said: "Go get us a six-pack of beer from the supermarket." At the end of the meal a few cans were left over. "You've not finished your beer," Murdoch told Gordon. "Don't waste it." So Gordon went back to his midtown office in Murdoch's limousine, his overcoat bulging with beer cans.

Although Murdoch has a chauffeur-driven car he sometimes prefers not to use it. Edward Koch, the mayor of New York, is impressed that when he and Murdoch go out to dinner at a restaurant Murdoch usually arrives by taxi and, if the restaurant is fairly near his Fifth Avenue apartment, walks back rather than accept a lift in the mayor's limousine. While nobody would accuse Murdoch of being an ascetic, he certainly has no taste for the high life for its own sake.

Surprisingly few foreign publishers have tried to muscle in on the American newspaper market. Roy Thomson, who bought a string of provincial papers in the United States, was a Canadian, and that scarcely counts as foreign. But Murdoch has never been deterred from doing something just because nobody has done it before. Taking a gang of his Australian and British executives with him, he went to America to shop around.

Quite quickly, like a batsman nudging a comfortable single to get off the mark, he acquired three newspapers in San Antonio, Texas, in the expanding sunbelt of the southwestern United States. There is no special significance in his choice of city: it was not in truth a choice at all, just where a likely-looking property happened to be on the market. At $19,700,000 he thought he was paying too much for them – certainly more than he would have paid in Australia or Britain based on the ratio of price to earnings. It was a start, though. With his innings under way he could take the measure of the bowling, survey the field placings and get on with building a useful score.

He could scarcely have lighted upon a better place because Texas has some qualities of the Australian outback. The city was the site of the defence of the Alamo in 1836, when Davy Crockett and his Texas patriots had died heroically in a brave stand against the Mexicans, and it had kept some of its rough-riding properties. Not far from the Mexican border, it had long been a prosperous ranching centre, and he knew about those from back home. Enough was familiar here for him to get to grips with.

The papers he bought were the San Antonio *Express*, a

morning paper, and the *News*, its afternoon stablemate and their combined Sunday editions. He gave most of his attention to the *News*, the weaker of the city's two evening papers, competing with the *Light*, owned by the Hearst chain. (By an irony, the Hearst papers had, in the early part of the century, gained the reputation for lurid sensationalism that was shortly to follow Murdoch here.) He applied to the *News* the formula that had worked so well in Australia and with the *Sun* – banner headlines, crime, sex and trivia, with a minimum of weighty news. Some of his talented tabloid men were brought from Australia to effect the transformation. In the first year he spent a million dollars on promotion, chiefly on television advertising but also on contests for readers, devoting to them generous amounts of front-page space.

Murdoch has never been inhibited about using his front page to boast of the success of his newspapers. He would print charts showing how he was gaining readers at the expense of the opposition, provoking the *Light* to respond with a full-page announcement in their paper suggesting that the figures were not altogether accurate, that they "jump around like a kangaroo." Murdoch could have been forgiven a quick smile. This was just the sort of insult-trading he was used to from Australia. There were some who had told him he would find America very different from anything he had known: but when it came down to it, the opposition anywhere always acted in the same, predictable way.

Even at this early stage, before he had gained any position nationally, Murdoch was beginning to fall foul of the media critics who saw in the jazzed-up *News* sensationalism of a different order from what they had been used to. One headline that caught their imagination, to be quoted against him time and again over the years, was KILLER BEES HEAD NORTH. The story was of a special kind of bee with a fatal sting, sighted in south and central America. The arousal of alarm in readers on the thinnest of pretexts is a trusted tabloid technique.

Murdoch was to claim, in his 1976 interview with Cockburn, that what he had done with the *News* was simply to strengthen its coverage of hard local news. "We wondered about it and wondered about it and thought, what are people doing for news, where are they getting it? – certainly not from the Hearst papers. We studied the TV programmes. The leading channel by a mile was a station that put on two hours of local news every afternoon and was just following the cops around with mobile cameras . . . blood and guts. And we turned the *News* pretty sharply, with lots of crime reporting and the courts. It's a pretty violent city, San Antonio.''

The result of all that was to push up the paper's circulation from 61,000 when he bought it to 75,000 by the middle of 1975. That was as much progress as he could make, though. Despite the continued use of prize contests and promotions, the *News* stayed on that figure and the *Light* kept to about 120,000, still the substantial market leader. Worse, his circulation increase had not resulted in any notable improvement in advertising. Although he claimed to have figures proving that the new readers were from the upper end of the market, the advertisers, judging simply by his product, decided that his audience was not the one they were trying to reach. Murdoch learns fast. By 1976 he was moving the *News* subtly up market, trying to cream the upper end of the *Light*'s circulation, and it began to repay his investment. As for the *Express*, it is a morning paper, much less racy, which turns a reasonable profit at a circulation of 80,000. He was content to leave it alone.

Nobody doubted that all this was essentially a training workout, that he was limbering up for more crucial acquisitions to come. San Antonio was small potatoes. He yearned for more and, since there are no national dailies in the United States (except the specialised *Wall Street Journal* and now *USA Today*), he would have to do it through magazines. He took Bert Hardy with him to weigh up some publications whose owners wanted to sell, or that might be obtainable even against their owners' wishes. They looked at *Redbook*, *McCall's*, the *Ladies' Home Journal*, and even the *Village Voice*, though his stable as yet contained no paper catering to anything comparable with its specialised radical and intellectual market. Among newspapers with national clout, he looked at the *Washington Star*, number two in the nation's capital.

He had always preferred acquiring existing publications, no matter how poor a shape they were in, to a so-called "green-fields start", starting something from scratch. It saved money and, important to a man as keen to get on with things as he, it saved time. But he was taken aback by the prices American titles were fetching. In Britain and Australia a rough rule of thumb was to pay ten times a paper's annual earnings. In America they were asking – and getting – up to forty times. It was too much. He would have to go for the green-fields start after all.

The concept of the *National Star* went through several changes. Murdoch's first idea was to create a tabloid news magazine, a down-market *Time* or *Newsweek*. He thought he detected in those two successful publications the same vulnerability he had exploited in the London *Daily Mirror* – they were flying above the heads of their readers. All that polished prose about the arts, society, science, diplomacy and even literature meant very little to middle Americans who had not been to college, he guessed. There must be a market for a paper that would keep them informed, certainly, but would do it in a more accessible way, using the presentational skills of his racy tabloids.

So convinced was he of the logic of this argument that Murdoch, usually careful to be on his best behaviour in company, made a rare social gaffe in his enthusiasm to put it forward. At the time of the *Star*'s launch he was taken by a friend to a dinner party at the Park Avenue apartment of Thibault de St Phalle, an economist whom he was to meet a few years later in more publicly controversial circumstances. Among the guests was Andrew Heiskell, the chairman of Time, Inc. Over cocktails, de St Phalle remembers, Murdoch began to round on Heiskell, telling him he did not know how to run his magazine. Heiskell, who can get sensitive about criticism, reacted angrily, and the scene became so heated that de St Phalle wondered whether his party would break up before the diners had time to be seated. Heiskell was threatening to leave, until reminded that he was de St Phalle's guest and persuaded to stay. "I found him singularly abrasive," the host recalled of Murdoch later.

In the end Murdoch and his advisers decided not to take

on the soft underbellies of the news weeklies but to go instead after a market they thought they understood better. One of the most successful publications in the country was the *National Enquirer*, a weekly tabloid packed with scandalous gossip about film stars and celebrities, recipes, diets and household hints, stories about the occult and emotional domestic dramas, advice for the lovelorn, all packaged so as to appeal to housewives and sold where they were easiest to reach – at the checkout of their local supermarket. It was selling five million copies a week and had no really effective opposition. Many of the staff were British, veterans of Fleet Street, where that kind of journalism, or something near it, thrived. The idea was to go into direct competition with the *Enquirer*, but the *National Star*, first sold only in the north-eastern United States, proved a difficult launch. It was harder than Murdoch had imagined to get supermarkets to allot space to the paper. Editors came and went in rapid succession, nearly all British and Australian, as were the editorial staff, hired for their skill in stretching a story further than would seem possible without lapsing into plain untruth.

After a year the *National Star* became the snappier *Star*. Murdoch was still casting around for the right formula but stubbornly rejected the advice of some of his associates to cut his losses and wind it up. It took another three years for it to get established as a profitable enterprise with a confident grip on its market, attracting advertisements for miracle cures, mail-order astrology schools and those other services that rely on the custom of the credulous. Printed in colour, it runs headlines such as LOSE UP TO 35 LBS IN 4 WEEKS, HOW TO TURN YOUR HESITANT HUSBANDS INTO WONDERFUL LOVERS and TIPS TO KEEP YOUR PET EMOTIONALLY CONTENT WITH PATIENCE AND LOVE. By 1984 it was selling four million copies in an average week, only a million fewer than the *Enquirer*.

However successful the *Star* was to become, it was still not the American breakthrough Murdoch was looking for. This kind of periodical, devoted to entertainment, is scarcely part of the news business at all. Certainly it was a distance from his original concept of a poor man's *Time* and

Newsweek. But though he could not yet call himself a significant force in American journalism, he was confident that the time would come if he could only contain his impatience. By now he had moved his family to New York and was methodically making his entry into smart society. He rented an apartment on East 79th Street, a fashionable enough address in itself but not quite the *most* fashionable. Where you live is of prime importance if you plan to hold elegant dinner parties or ask friends and potential enemies round for a confidential drink. So he bought himself a duplex – an apartment on two floors – right on Fifth Avenue, overlooking Central Park, a few blocks north of the famous Plaza Hotel.

He worked at getting himself invited to the right parties, mixing with the right people, especially those who might know of newspapers for sale or be thinking of selling their own. As a substantial overseas newspaper owner, he felt it legitimate to telephone American proprietors out of the blue and ask if he could see their plant. This was how he first came to meet Mrs Dorothy Schiff, who had owned the *New York Post*, the city's lacklustre evening paper, for nearly forty years and who was known to be looking for ways to give up the reins while assuring the paper's future. He met the redoubtable Katharine Graham, owner of the *Washington Post*, still glowing from its success over the Watergate affair, where its insistent investigative reporting had forced the resignation of President Nixon.

It was at a weekend at Mrs Graham's home in Virginia that the Murdochs first met Clay Felker, the editor, publisher and indeed the creator of *New York* magazine, one of the publishing success stories of the 1960s and 70s. It had begun as the free magazine section of the Sunday edition of the *New York Herald Tribune* but when the paper closed down Felker, the editor of the section, and Milton Glaser, its designer, found financial backing and decided to continue it as a separate publication. It developed into a survival guide to New York for the young and affluent. It was scarcely possible to imagine living in the city without it – how would you know what to see, what to buy, how to decorate your apartment? It pioneered what became known as the New Journalism, a style of writing fact in the manner of fiction, practised by such as Tom Wolfe, Norman Mailer and Gail Sheehy. *New York* set a pattern for city magazines throughout the country and Felker, tall, sleek, impulsive, impatient and full of creative energy, became a social and journalistic celebrity.

During the Virginia weekend, Mrs Graham asked Felker to take the Murdochs under his wing, to introduce them to the rich and influential, to ease their way into society. He was glad to help. They would dine together at the restaurants patronised by those with pretensions to celebrity. They would visit each other at home. They went to a championship boxing match at Madison Square Garden. He would ask Felker's advice about journalists he was thinking of hiring for his papers. He is always asking questions. Once he telephoned Felker and asked: "What do people do here in the summer?" Felker said they went to East Hampton, on Long Island. So he acquired a house not far from Felker's and they would exchange visits. Felker had begun what was to prove a long-lasting relationship with Gail Sheehy, one of his writers, and she got on particularly well with Anna. By the end of 1976 the four of them were even talking about taking a skiing holiday together in Switzerland.

The trip was never made, for now Murdoch, after beginning to despair of ever finding a suitable American property to buy, was suddenly confronted with a rush of likely prospects. In less than four months he was to add a New York evening paper and three weekly journals to his American holdings, and to be within a whisker of owning one of the most historic newspapers in Britain.

Dorothy Schiff had for three decades been the most colourful newspaper owner in New York but by 1976 the *New York Post* had become the drabbest of the three papers surviving from the plague of closures in the 1960s. Although it had the afternoon field to itself, it had never succeeded in establishing a clear identity. It fell between the authority and style of the *New York Times* and the tabloid brashness of the *Daily News*. It was packed with page after page of features and columns, many of them repetitive, taking space from the news. The solid core of the readership were middle class, liberal Jews, and the columns and editorials reflected their attitudes, worthy but dull: a pale bowl of chicken soup.

The *Post* had survived where so many of its more illustrious contemporaries had failed partly because of a cunning move by Mrs Schiff during the long and debilitating city-wide newspaper strike of 1962/3. She then made a separate deal with the unions, so that the *Post* was able to return to the streets while the other papers stayed closed. A wealthy socialite, she had been given the paper by one of her husbands in 1939 and had kept it after their marriage ended. She ran it as a personal fiefdom, keeping it rigidly to its traditional liberalism (it was an outspoken critic of Senator Joseph McCarthy and his Committee on Un-American Activities) and maintaining an ever tighter personal grip on its finances, until in the end it was hard to get her agreement for even modest editorial expenditure.

Over the years, numerous suitors had come to inquire whether she wanted to sell her paper, but she had always refused. She was ever-conscious of its political tradition and anxious that any new proprietor should undertake convincingly to sustain it. She could never extract such a promise from chains such as Hearst, Newhouse and the Los Angeles Times group, which had made serious inquiries.

Murdoch, when he first came to New York, had looked over the *Post*'s plant but had not maintained contact with Schiff. They were reintroduced a year or so later by Clay Felker. This time the friendship proved more lasting and they began entertaining one another to meals.

In September 1976 Mrs Schiff invited Murdoch to lunch in her suite on the sixth floor of the *Post*'s dowdy old building facing the East River, overshadowed by the inelegant bulk of the elevated FDR Drive, interfering with the river view. They did not begin to talk about the *Post* until quite late in the meal – after the coffee, Murdoch was to maintain later. When they did, the conversation was remarkably similar in tone to the one he was to have with Kenneth Thomson at Kennedy Airport four years later.

"I sensed she was very tired," he told Alexander Cockburn afterwards. "She said she was very tired. She knew what was necessary to turn the paper and get it done right but she felt she just didn't have the energy left. She really made the opening, though she didn't really mean to, I think."

It was not simple tiredness, although at seventy-three Mrs Schiff had every right to think of quitting. What weighed on her more pressingly as 1976 progressed was that on January 1st a complex new inheritance law was due to go into effect. She was advised that it might make it difficult for her to pass the newspaper to her heirs, that it would be better to have the cash in hand.

Murdoch asked her to think of him if she was planning to sell.

"Oh, you'd be interested, would you?" said Mrs Schiff, according to his account. "Everyone told me you were but you've never said it. Now you've said it." She liked him. Perhaps he, an outsider anxious to make an impression, could be trusted to nurture the child with care and respect.

The wheels were in motion. But he did not have to wait idly in his Third Avenue office, scarcely able to contain his impatience to move downtown to South Street. For already another offer had appeared out of the blue, this time from London. It came in a telephone call from Lord Goodman, a respected and influential lawyer and public figure, whom Murdoch had counted among his acquaintances, if not exactly a friend, ever since they met in 1969.

Lord Goodman had an office in the *News of the World* building when Murdoch bought it. His law firm had been involved in the establishment of Television Wales and West. Sir William Carr, from whom Murdoch had bought the *News of the World*, had a large stake in TWW (the commercial television company for Wales and the west of England) and had offered Goodman office space. Working in the same building, Murdoch and Lord Goodman met. Occasionally Murdoch would ask the corpulent lawyer to act for him in cases where it seemed important to be represented by somebody of such national standing.

Among his public responsibilities, Lord Goodman was chairman of the board of trustees of the *Observer*, one of Britain's oldest newspapers, traditional Sunday reading for intellectuals of the left and centre. The paper was owned by a branch of the aristocratic Astor family, prominent on both sides of the Atlantic. (A different Astor had owned *The Times* until Lord Thomson bought it in 1966.)

David Astor edited the *Observer* until the end of 1975 – the last of the owner-editors. Then he stepped down and the job, after a uniquely democratic process of consultation with the journalists, went to Donald Trelford, a man of thirty-eight who had edited a newspaper in Malawi, Central Africa, before joining the *Observer* and becoming assistant to Astor in 1969.

For some time it had been obvious to Astor and his senior colleagues that, with labour and newsprint costs soaring, it would not much longer be possible to finance the paper through his family fortune. Newspapers, especially those operating at the top end of the market, are notoriously vulnerable to fluctuating economic conditions. They need reserves to see them through bad periods and injections of capital for their development. Astor had just about run out of resources. The paper was being operated out of the income from a family trust, the capital of which had been vested in his children and was unavailable to him.

The *Observer* languished for want of financial nourishment. Circulation was down to 667,897 from 730,832 the previous year, lower now than the *Sunday Telegraph* and almost exactly half the figure for the *Sunday Times*. Astor, like Dorothy Schiff, recognised that the days were gone when papers could be run on personal or family capital: they needed the resources of a large corporation.

Lord Goodman, informally, began trawling for possible buyers. The most obvious candidate was Lord Rothermere's Associated Newspapers, long searching for a Sunday paper to keep the *Daily Mail*'s presses busy on the seventh day of the week. But Rothermere's papers were Conservative politically and the *Daily Mail* was engaged in intense competition with the *Daily Express*. It was fairly certain that, if they acquired it, Associated would bring the *Observer* down-market to compete directly with the thriving *Sunday Express*. Moreover Goodman, who knew the business through his chairmanship of the Newspaper Publishers' Association, was unimpressed with Associated's management. The other main groups had Sunday papers that more or less competed with the *Observer*, with the

exception of the Mirror group. Their two Sundays operated
in a different market and they were suitable politically, but
they showed no interest in the *Observer*.

That left Murdoch, whose newspapers' politics fluctu-
ated according to circumstances and who owned no quality
Sunday newspaper in Britain. Goodman, who could see
clearly what was coming, had discussed with Murdoch
earlier the possibility of buying the *Observer*, though it was
a tentative sounding and no firm offer or promise was
made. Murdoch's mind was more on his American adventures and he dismissed the idea. The *Observer*, a clear
second best in its contest with the *Sunday Times*, did not
seem an attractive prospect. After that first talk with
Goodman, Murdoch discussed it with some of his senior
people in London. Larry Lamb was against taking it any
further but Bert Hardy was enthusiastic, making the point
that a revitalised *Observer* could become a serious rival to
the *Sunday Times*, which he felt had passed its peak. As for
Murdoch, he had long been trying to clear up in his mind
what he would do if *The Times* and its desirable stablemate
the *Sunday Times* came on the market. Those really
appealed to him: and he realised that if he acquired the
Observer he would put himself out of the running for the
Sunday Times.

A firm decision to look for a buyer for the *Observer* was
reached by Goodman, Astor and Roger Harrison, the
managing director, at a meeting at Goodman's Portland
Place flat in August. Harrison said Murdoch was the most
likely buyer and, he thought, the most desirable. Unaware
of Goodman's previous discussion with Murdoch on the
subject, Harrison was surprised that the lawyer seemed so
certain that the Australian would not be interested, and
urged an inquiry. Goodman agreed, went to his study and
phoned Murdoch right away. "That's a surprise," he said,
returning to the drawing-room some minutes later. "He *is*
interested." Hardy's enthusiasm had persuaded him it
might be worth a long look.

In his heart of hearts, Goodman was none too happy
about the prospect. He had conflicting attitudes to Murdoch. He enjoyed his company. In their dealings in the
NPA he admired the Australian's openness, his lack of

cunning. He would say what he thought and stick to it, in contrast to many other newspaper owners who, Goodman would tell friends, he found unreliable and opportunistic, with a low regard for business ethics.

Yet it could not be denied that Murdoch's record in publishing was scarcely one to sustain the belief that he would respect the *Observer*'s sober traditions. British readers knew him only through the *Sun* and the *News of the World* and they stood a cultural chasm from the high-minded liberal values of the country's oldest Sunday paper. Murdoch's only paper with much pretension to seriousness was the *Australian*, and that was neither particularly distinguished nor successful. There was the public relations aspect to consider. The government, through the Monopolies Commission, might want to rule on the sale and it would be hard to persuade members of parliament of Murdoch's suitability. From that viewpoint it would be better to find someone who had a track record with serious newspapers or, failing that, no record in newspapers at all.

There was, too, a more tangible objection. Early in the negotiations Murdoch signalled clearly his intention of appointing new editors if he were to acquire the paper. The two names mentioned were Bruce Rothwell, a former Washington correspondent of the *Daily Mail* who had edited the *Australian*, and Anthony Shrimsley (brother of Bernard), an assistant editor on the *Sun*. Rothwell would be editor-in-chief and Shrimsley editor, with Trelford occupying an undefined middle role as editorial director. Both Murdoch's men professed political views substantially to the right of the *Observer* but it was not that which worried Goodman chiefly. It was the fact that Trelford had been chosen editor less than a year earlier by a widely-publicised exercise in participatory democracy. For Murdoch to jettison him as his first act on buying the paper would, Goodman could see, seriously alienate the staff. As chairman of the trustees it was his prime responsibility to see that the tradition of the paper was upheld. Murdoch's stated intention was a threat to that.

Goodman put all this to Murdoch but he was unmoved. To the argument that Rothwell was not an intellectual, he snapped sharply and incontestably: "Nor's Trelford." He

believed that there were serious flaws in the *Observer* as
then edited and that only a change at the top could correct
them. Goodman and Astor, sensing a threat to the success
of the deal, asked Trelford to fly to New York to see
Murdoch. All the negotiations for disposal of the paper had
so far been conducted in secret and Trelford told none of
his colleagues why he was going to America. He said he had
to give a lecture and was trying to buy Dr Henry Kissinger's
memoirs. When he arrived at Murdoch's office on October
6th, Trelford found his potential new owner none too
pleased to see him, feeling that editors should not get
involved in these business deals. In their two meetings,
Murdoch told Trelford what he had told Goodman, that he
did not have a high opinion of the *Observer*'s editorial
quality and would want to put his own man in.

On the flight back to London, Trelford was distressed.
He wondered what he could do to head off the threat
Murdoch posed. It was not just his personal position that
concerned him, although as a new occupant of the prized
editor's chair he certainly did not intend to surrender it
tamely. He was only just starting to enjoy it. It was the
wider implication of Murdoch's attitude that worried him
more and he was surprised that Goodman and Astor had
not seen through it. For how could Murdoch say with a
straight face that he respected the paper's tradition and
then bring people from a totally different tradition to run
it? It did not seem to him that it had been thought through.

Returning to London, Trelford summoned two of his
closest confidants on the *Observer* to a meeting at his
Wimbledon home on Sunday evening. They were John
Cole, the Ulster-born deputy editor (later political editor of
the BBC), and Lajos Lederer, the specialist in East European affairs. Trelford reported on the negotiations and on
his meetings with Murdoch and found both men opposed to
any deal. He was sure that represented the views of most of
the staff. The following week Trelford took Rothwell to
lunch at the Garrick Club and tried to persuade him not to
accept the post of editor-in-chief, arguing that it would
provoke hostility among the journalists and would not
work. For Trelford, it was a thoroughly depressing lunch.
Rothwell dismissed his arguments out of hand and it was

clear that if they ever had to work together it would be a strained partnership. Trelford found Rothwell fast-talking and jumpy, perhaps a bit neurotic. He could not conceive how he would fit into the calm, scholarly atmosphere of the *Observer*'s headquarters at Blackfriars.

Trelford told Astor that he and his close associates on the paper were unhappy, and this in turn left Astor depressed. Two weeks after the New York visit news of the Murdoch negotiations reached first the *Daily Mail*, then the other Fleet Street papers. Murdoch was convinced that Trelford had engineered the leak so as to whip up public opinion against his purchase. Trelford denied this. He believed the story had surfaced because Shrimsley had been in New York and had to be summoned back to London to discuss his becoming editor. Contact had been made through the New York office of the *Sun* and the news had inevitably reached the ears of other British journalists, who maintain close contact in the bars around Third Avenue and 44th Street.

Now things moved quickly. On the morning the first stories appeared, Trelford summoned a staff meeting in the news room and told the whole story. Almost without exception, the reaction to a Murdoch deal was hostile. It was true that Trelford had not tried to put any favourable gloss on it. He told the journalists of an exchange he had with Murdoch over the *Observer*'s meticulous and conscientious coverage of Africa and Asia. "The Third World doesn't sell newspapers," Murdoch had declared. "Giving the *Observer* to Rupert Murdoch is like giving your beautiful daughter to a gorilla," said one journalist, according to a report in that week's *Sunday Times*. And Clive James, the Australian poet and television critic, pointed out: "Rupert Murdoch was one of the main reasons that people like me have come twelve thousand miles to work in Britain."

Later Lord Goodman gave the staff his version. He stressed the assurance Murdoch had given that the nature of the paper would not be changed. As he was doing so Trelford was pointedly, though he claims involuntarily, shaking his head. It was clear to everyone what he thought of Murdoch's assurances. It was clear he would try to prevent the deal if he could.

When news of these developments reached Murdoch in New York, he was furious. He felt abused. He had not, after all, sought the *Observer*: its trustees had come looking for him. He was not even sure that he wanted it much. As it had been put to him, he would be doing them a favour by coming in with sufficient reserves of cash to put the paper on its feet. He issued a petulant statement:

> Several weeks ago News International was approached by representatives of the *Observer* to take over the newspaper's business and continue its existence. Friendly and confidential talks were held and advanced to the point where News International expressed willingness to proceed on condition of mutual good will by all parties concerned. At no time did News International seek the *Observer* or any other newspaper. The pre-eminent motive was to preserve the *Observer* itself and the maximum diversity of the British press in general. In view of the breach of confidence that has taken place, together with the deliberate and orchestrated attempt to build this into a controversy, News International is no longer interested.

That seemed final enough but, almost as soon as the statement had been issued, those who knew Murdoch were expressing doubts as to whether it really meant what it said. Goodman was quickly in touch to ask if he might, in the last resort, be prepared to reconsider. Murdoch did not say yes, but neither did he say no. Only two days after the statement the *Sunday Times* reported that Murdoch was "thought to be still in the running". But formally that was that, so the search had to begin again.

Whenever newspapers come up for disposal in London there is a cast of consistent suitors whose names enter the reckoning. Sir James Goldsmith, the grocery millionaire, is one. Lord Rothermere of Associated Newspapers is another. There is the controversial publisher Robert Maxwell and the equally unpopular "Tiny" Rowland, head of the conglomerate Lonrho, once described by Mr Edward Heath as "the unacceptable face of capitalism".

All these names cropped up this time, as well as more

exotic ones. Sally Aw Sian, owner of a thriving newspaper in Hong Kong, was taken so seriously for a while that representatives of the *Observer* flew to see her. Woodrow Wyatt, the flamboyant ex-Labour MP and owner of a group of provincial newspapers, was also in the hunt, or on the fringes of it, as was Olga Deterding, an heiress who appeared often in the gossip columns, and Victor Matthews of the conglomerate Trafalgar House, soon to buy the *Daily Express*. In the end, although the actual price asked for the titles was a nominal £1, none could contemplate staking a million pounds, the minimum investment thought then to be required to give the declining paper a chance of returning to prosperity – although it turned out a substantial under-estimate.

Within a fortnight, Murdoch was again the front runner. For the record he was still protesting that he had withdrawn, but was now willing to add: "If they kick the door down that is another matter." Goodman and Astor were kicking the door with increasing desperation. There seemed no other hope for the paper's survival. Even the staff were coming round, for in the final analysis Murdoch was better than no employer at all. Goodman, though still ill at ease, thought he could persuade Murdoch to keep Trelford as editor, even if nothing was going to dissuade him from bringing at least one of his own men to play a senior role.

Goodman was worried that if they delayed things much longer Murdoch would lose interest again. By Friday, November 12th, the board were on the brink of a decision to invite him formally to be the new owner. They planned to meet the following week to wrap up the details, with the aim of having papers ready for signature by midweek. Trelford was convinced, as he left the office that weekend after seeing the paper on to the presses, that by the time the next issue appeared it would be under Murdoch's ownership. What he did not know was that Kenneth Harris, a senior journalist on his staff, was dining that evening at Rules in Covent Garden with someone who was about to spark a rapid change of plan.

Douglas Cater, an American intellectual, helped run the Aspen Institute. This think-tank in the Rocky Mountains is

funded by Atlantic Richfield (Arco), a large oil company
based in Los Angeles. It is characteristic of wealthy American corporations to support such endeavours in the arts
and sciences. As well as cutting their tax bill, it is thought to
soften their sometimes rapacious image.

Cater was passing through London on his way back from
a conference in Europe and was at a loose end for dinner on
Saturday. He phoned his friend Phil Kaiser at the American embassy but he was not free. Next he tried Harold
Evans, editor of the *Sunday Times*, who was unavailable.
(It is intriguing to speculate how Evans would have
changed his own professional future had he been free that
night; for if Cater had not dined with Harris, Murdoch
would have acquired the *Observer* and would have been
unable to bid for the *Sunday Times* four years later.)

Harris, then, was Cater's third choice and he was available. When he told Cater what was about to happen to the
Observer, the American was horrified. He was of the
generation that had known the paper's great days in the
1950s. As a liberal, even an American liberal, it had been
part of his cultural education. "Who decides these things?"
he asked Harris, and Harris said Goodman did. "Let's go
and see him," said Cater.

They arrived at the Portland Place flat just as Goodman
was beginning a late supper with a friend. He was not too
pleased to see them, but showed interest when Cater
suggested a viable new potential buyer for the *Observer*.
Cater had already phoned Jo Slater, a former journalist
who was head of the Aspen Institute, and he had under-
taken to raise the matter with Robert Anderson, Atlantic
Richfield's president. Goodman, who had scarcely heard of
Atlantic Richfield or Anderson, found the suggestion far-
fetched, but Cater was so persuasive that he agreed to talk
on the phone that very evening to Anderson, weekending
in New Mexico. Anderson was taken with the idea. The
estimated investment needed was paltry by the standards of
an international oil company. He asked Goodman to send
someone to Los Angeles to talk, and inquired how long he
had to decide. "Till Wednesday," Goodman said.

Goodman phoned Roger Harrison at 3 a.m. and asked
him to fly west on Monday. Later that Sunday he phoned

Astor, who decided to go too. The pair met Anderson for breakfast in Los Angeles on Tuesday and the deal was in motion. That week, unbeknown to Murdoch, the alternative negotiations went ahead. The hard-headed Harrison had grave doubts about handing the paper to a company with no experience either of the communications business or of the peculiar world of British newspaper publishing, with its archaic industrial practices. As a businessman, Harrison did not believe in the efficacy of last-minute miracles. Astor, though, was a romantic. What is more, the passionate opposition to Murdoch from the editorial staff had rattled him. Here seemed a heaven-sent chance to do the decent thing after all. He liked the brisk, confident syle of the Americans and, more tangibly, he was taken with their pledge that they wanted to leave the paper as it was, with Trelford in the driving seat. It was, after all, his paper to sell.

The prize, if Murdoch ever saw it as that, was slipping from his grasp, and for several days he was unaware of it, until Goodman broke the news in a phone call to New York. Although he had never been as totally committed as in most of his attempted purchases, he could not avoid a feeling of rebuff.

"When I heard, I went right through the gamut of emotions," he told the *Sunday Times* that week. "My first reaction was one of tremendous relief; second of personal grievance and annoyance, partly at myself for being sucked into the thing; and, lastly, I've got to admit that it's all for the best."

It seems an honest enough assessment. Certainly, according to his friends, his sense of personal grievance was apparent. He had long had a suspicion of the British establishment, even before the Keeler affair. He thought they were out to get him; they saw him as a brash kid from the outback, cheeky and bright but not finally of the substance needed to run one of Britain's most important cultural institutions. The outcome seemed to confirm that. An oil company with no experience of publishing had been preferred to someone of his proven expertise. For a man who detests losing anything, this was a painful defeat.

There was a postscript. When Anderson and his executives from Los Angeles came to London to sign the papers for the *Observer*, Goodman gave a celebratory dinner at his rooms at University College, Oxford, where he was Master. The eighteen guests included Anderson and Cater, Astor, Trelford, Harrison and a few people from the college. Harold Wilson, the Prime Minister, was guest of honour, having his first meeting with the new owner of one of the few papers that sometimes gave its support to his Labour Party. Goodman thought it would be nice to have Murdoch along, too. He had behaved quite decently throughout, had been willing to risk his company's funds for what might have been a thankless purpose and had, at the last minute, been ditched without ceremony. Goodman does not like impoliteness and thought he and his colleagues had been brusque with Murdoch. An invitation to the dinner would be a thoughtful gesture.

Murdoch accepted, although he was not sure what role he was supposed to play. It was a genial and civilised affair and he enjoyed, as he always does, the company of Goodman and the academics among the guests. Everybody was on his best behaviour. The Americans were determined to impress on Wilson and the *Observer* people the seriousness, not to say the nobility, of their intentions towards the paper. The others were treating the Americans with the reverence due to rich and powerful people who have virtually materialised from nowhere to effect a last-minute rescue. The atmosphere remained fairly formal and low key – a jet-lagged Anderson was even dropping off to sleep – until near the end, when Goodman invited Wilson to say a few words about the British press. Wilson can be pompous on these occasions and rose solemnly to start his oration. "I have always," he began, "had a considerable regard for the British press." Murdoch, in a clearly audible stage whisper, retorted: "Well, you had me fooled." Laughter swept the table, Anderson woke with a start, and Wilson's speech was never to attain the dignity he had intended.

The pain of the rebuff in London was mitigated by its coming almost simultaneously with Murdoch's long-

awaited triumph in New York. On the Friday after the
miracle at Rules, it was announced that he was to buy the
New York Post. It had taken only ten weeks for his tentative lunchtime conversation with Dorothy Schiff to be
translated into a firm agreement that the paper would be his
for around thirty million dollars. He thought it was a little
high but, as he explained in the Cockburn interview, it is
impossible to value a paper that is not making money. In
that year it was on its way to a loss of half a million dollars.
He had to guess how much he would make if he made it a
success, then allow "for the fact that you're bloody keen to
get it and a certain amount of sense goes out of the window
and you do the deal".

It was kept secret until late on the Friday – too late for
the *New York Post* to get the story into that night's paper.
Paul Sann, a polished newspaperman of the old school, had
been executive editor for twenty-seven years. He had first
joined the *Post* in 1931. On Friday afternoon Mrs Schiff
called him to her office and gave him the news, adding that
Murdoch was keen for him to stay on. Sann, who had been
thinking of retiring the following year, said he was not sure
whether he wanted to. Mrs Schiff replied that Murdoch had
expressed a desire for him to stay and that the deal might be
jeopardised if he left. Sann was too canny to believe that. It
may have been what Murdoch had told her, to assure her
that he did not intend any radical change in the paper's
character, but it did not square with what he told Cockburn
only a few days later. Then he was scathing about American
newspapermen in general and those on the *Post* in particular.

"They can't even bloody write . . . on and on and on and
on. Importing English sub-editors is dangerous, but I wish
to God the Americans would learn the techniques of
English subbing. The stories in the *Post* are not very well
written and they go on too long. There's no subbing.
There's no one writing headlines down there. I don't know
who the news editor is and who are organising the stories.
It seems to me they're not covering the basics of New
York."

On the evening of the announcement Murdoch went to
Elaine's, the city's most fashionable restaurant for the

media set, to celebrate with Clay Felker and Larry Lamb, who had come from London to be in at the conclusion of the purchase. Felker had invited some powerful and glossy guests. Felix Rohatyn was there, the banker who had organised the city's escape from bankruptcy by means of the Municipal Assistance Corporation. So was Shirley MacLaine, the actress, with her boyfriend Pete Hamill, a trenchant and emotional columnist. They were all giving Murdoch excited advice about what to do with his prize. "I may have paid too much for it," he confided in Felker, "but it was the chance of my lifetime."

Two weeks later Murdoch telephoned and asked Sann to lunch at Christ Cella, a sombre but excellent steak house where the well-padded atmosphere resembles that of a gentlemen's club. "Do you know it?" Murdoch asked. "Hell," thought Sann, "I knew it before you were born."

The lunch lasted several hours and Sann found he liked Murdoch, admiring his obvious newspaper expertise. But he was curiously reluctant to discuss the kind of paper he was going to turn the *Post* into. He was much more interested in the staffing, how he could make the journalists more productive without falling foul of the Guild, their trade union. He knew a shake-up would be needed if he was to make the *Post* a tightly-run paper and foresaw that this, rather than the actual journalism, would dominate his initial months as owner.

Murdoch asked Sann what time he arrived at the office of a morning – between 4 and 5 a.m. He said he would be getting in at the same time. For the first few days he was as good as his word, but he knew he would not be able to keep that up for long and quickly brought one of his own people over to keep an eye on things. This is a favourite Murdoch technique, to appoint someone to work alongside an existing senior executive with no clear distinction between their areas of authority. Either they work out an accommodation or the weaker party gives up and moves aside.

The man he chose was Peter Michelmore, a deceptively self-effacing Australian with a ferociously independent spirit. He had been the New York correspondent of the *Sydney Morning Herald* until 1975, when Murdoch asked him to be bureau chief in New York for his Australian publications. Next he was one of the many people moved to the *Star* to try to effect a breakthrough there.

When Murdoch bought the *Post* he asked Michelmore to go in and make an initial appraisal of the staff. Michelmore would arrive at the office shortly after Sann at dawn. He would sit and watch and help out and be genial, seldom venturing to suggest any alteration in the way Sann had been doing things over the years. Sann, though, knew he was Murdoch's ambassador and was careful not to cross him. For that reason there were only a few clear-cut differences of opinion between them. The first such provided Sann and the old *Post* people with a signal of the way things were going, confirming their worst fears. It concerned the execution in Utah of Gary Gilmore, the first murderer to be put to death in the United States for nine years. Opponents of capital punishment held a candlelight vigil outside the prison. The reporter's story stressed that it had been a low-key affair but Michelmore insisted on a headline that had the protesters "storming" the prison. Sann objected and the headline survived for only one edition, but for him it was an ominous sign.

After a few weeks Murdoch's pre-dawn appearances in the news room grew less frequent, not because he was in any way growing tired of his new plaything but because he now had yet another acquisition to cope with. *New York* magazine and the *Village Voice* are two weeklies serving different sections of New York society. Although they do not compare in importance with the *New York Post*, his purchase of them was more controversial because it was done without the consent of their owner – and he was Murdoch's old friend and a pillar of New York's café society, Clay Felker.

Felker had inadvertently given Murdoch the idea of buying his publications on the night of that celebratory dinner at Elaine's, after the purchase of the *Post*. In the taxi home he confessed to Murdoch that he was having trouble with his board of directors. In fact he had been quarrelling with his backers since shortly after he became the magazines' owner. Like many journalists, Felker was naive in money matters and had little patience with those who thought them more important than editorial quality. In 1969 the company he had created went public at the suggestion of Alan Patricof, one of his most important backers, who became president. Felker and Patricof feuded constantly. In 1974 Felker wanted to buy the *Village Voice*, a weekly serving a mainly student and intellectual readership, less affluent than the readers of *New York* but numerous enough for the paper to attract plump advertising and make a profit.

Patricof was unwilling to borrow money for the purchase, so in the end it was effected by an exchange of stock. Carter Burden, a socialite and aspiring politician, had owned the *Voice* in partnership with his friend Bartle Bull. Between them they were given thirty-four per cent of the stock in the new merged company, diluting Felker's own stake.

In 1976, at Felker's urging, the company launched *New West*, a California version of *New York*. Its initial losses exceeded estimates. Felker claims this was because it was so successful that simply printing it cost more than had been anticipated. Patricof, Burden and Bull began to manoeuvre against Felker and Glaser.

That was the position as Felker told it in the taxi home. It was natural that he should turn for advice to Murdoch, a friend and experienced businessman. He was not astute enough to recognise that what he was doing was like asking an alcoholic to sniff your drink. Murdoch said he would think about it and they agreed to meet in a few days. Nine days later they had lunch together. Murdoch expounded his philosophy that it was no use being a minority shareholder in anything – you had to own fifty-one per cent even if it meant borrowing money. "Then you don't have to take any crap from anybody." He also observed, in what Felker should have seen as a prophetic warning: "You and I could never work together."

Felker had been trying to sound out Burden about selling his stock but Burden refused to discuss it. Now Murdoch, on the day after his lunch with Felker, instructed his investment bankers to make inquiries of Patricof and the other shareholders. Within a week he was satisfied that he would be able to buy a majority shareholding, but first his conscience dictated that he should try doing a deal with Felker. He phoned him in California.

Felker hurried back to meet Murdoch and Stan Shuman, an investment banker. The proposed deal was that Murdoch should buy the company and sell Felker a third share in *New West* alone for a million dollars. Felker said he could not afford that and asked Murdoch and Shuman whether they could help him get a loan. The answer was no. "I knew then," Felker recalled later, "that they were trying to screw me." At the end of the meeting Murdoch said to him: "I realise that wasn't a very good deal," and added: "I'll let you know what I'm going to do." Felker replied: "I'm going to fight you with anything I can." He detested the idea of working for someone else. What is more, he felt that anyone who could violate a friendship, as he believed Murdoch had done, would not be a satisfactory business partner. He began to make use of his international contacts to seek finance to ward off the bid: Sir James Goldsmith said he might be able to help.

Having disposed of Felker to his satisfaction, Murdoch set about acquiring his majority shareholding. Burden was the key man, the last holdout, playing hard to get. When the negotiations reached their climax in the last days of 1976, Burden was skiing in Sun Valley, Idaho. The Goldsmith talks had come to nothing but Felker, back from spending Christmas in the Bahamas with his friend David Frost, had persuaded Katharine Graham to make a counter-bid to Murdoch's on behalf of her *Washington Post* company. She was offering $7.50 a share – fifty cents more than Murdoch – but Burden would not for some time come to the phone to discuss it. When he did, he demanded a role for himself in the company. Felker said he could have no such thing and that Murdoch would not give him one either. Over the years Felker had taken no trouble to conceal his contempt for Burden; now he was paying the price. Felker thought he had the legal right to first refusal of the Burden shares but the fine print of that agreement made it void if the company was making a loss – which it was, due to the start-up costs of *New West*.

As his revenge on Felker, Burden agreed to sell to Murdoch at the lower price of seven dollars a share.

Murdoch flew to Idaho to finalise the deal. The company formally changed hands on Monday, January 3rd, at a meeting at the Park Avenue law office of Theodore Kheel, the labour lawyer and power broker who represented *New York* magazine. It began in the evening and lasted through the night. Murdoch lurked in the entrance hall, making occasional forays into the lavatory for conspiratorial talks with his advisers. He was like a small boy pressing his nose against the window of a cake shop, but knowing he had in his pocket enough cash to buy up the stock. Patricof announced that Murdoch had proxies for more than half the shares. Murdoch and Shuman were elected to the board and Kheel was dismissed as the company lawyer. A group of the magazine's writers were waiting in an anteroom and five of them were invited to the boardroom to talk to the new directors. Passions were high and tempers flared. Gail Sheehy, one of the writers present, described the event in detail in *Rolling Stone* magazine a few months later. She reported that only Murdoch stayed calm. "This is very unfortunate," he said. "Can't we get together, Clay?" When Felker pointed out that they had once agreed they could never work together, Murdoch answered: "I meant we could never work together as publishers. We could work together if I were publisher and you were editor." He was now anxious for Felker to stay on. He flattered him as "an editorial genius" and "the best editor in America". He wanted a private discussion between the two of them. Felker said he would take the advice of his staff.

For Murdoch, having the *New York* journalists gathering and holding protest meetings, vowing never to work for him, ridiculing him for being foreign and for publishing (as they saw it) low-grade tabloid newspapers, was essentially a reprise of what had happened with the *Observer* a few weeks earlier. There were two important differences, though. This time he had already secured the deal. Short of a successful legal challenge, which he thought unlikely, there was nothing these pompous intellectuals could do. And this time he genuinely did want the editor to stay, though on his terms. He was not planning, as he was with Trelford, to emasculate Felker by slotting his own man above him in the hierarchy.

By now the takeover bid was the biggest news story in New York. Columns of print were devoted to it in the newspapers and most of the comment was hostile to Murdoch, the interloper doing down the hometown boy. Television cameras were waiting outside every meeting place. The magazine's writers were expressing in public their determination to resist Murdoch, and attracting general sympathy. But on Wednesday, at a preliminary court hearing on the question of Felker's option on the Burden shares, the judge ordered Felker and Murdoch to meet. They did the next day, together with Shuman and Roger Wood, a British newspaperman briefly the youngest ever editor of the *Daily Express* in London then editor of Murdoch's *Star*. Felker and Glaser reiterated that they could not work for Murdoch, who declared: "I can't back down. After losing the *Observer* I'd be a journalistic untouchable around the world. I can't lose."

He did not. The lawyers confirmed that Felker's first option clause, on which his case rested, was unenforceable because of the company's losses. On Friday the staff, refusing to work, held a sombre gathering at a restaurant opposite the *New York* offices, when Felker made his tearful farewell. Murdoch and his senior executives had to bring the magazine out themselves. Some forty staff members and writers eventually resigned. *New York* was never to regain the polish and inspiration Felker gave it, but it survives and makes a tidy profit.

Many have suffered at Murdoch's hands but few have had their career destroyed so comprehensively as Felker, or can so justifiably feel a sense of friendship cruelly betrayed. True, he took nearly a million dollars with him from the settlement, but he was never again to achieve the dazzling success he had with *New York*, the unique and ideal vehicle for his self-expression. A few months after the débâcle he embarked on a new venture with the British newspaper magnate Vere Harmsworth, later Lord Rothermere, heir to the wealthy Associated Newspapers group.

Harmsworth was one of those who had volunteered assistance to Felker in warding off Murdoch, but by the time he arrived on the scene it was too late to halt the sale of Burden's shares. Now he bought control of *Esquire*, a declining glossy monthly magazine for men, and put the team of Felker and Glaser in charge. It did not work and after two years it was sold. Then in 1980 Felker was hired by the *Daily News* to shape their new evening paper *Tonight*, aimed at driving Murdoch's *Post* from the streets of New York. But he could not adapt his magazine techniques successfully to daily newspapers and the evening edition closed after less than a year, with multi-million dollar losses. Another Murdoch victory. Felker is still a popular and wealthy man, living with Sheehy in a splendid co-operative apartment in the fashionable Sutton Place area of Manhattan; but in the cruel world of the New York media those two failures count for more than his one astounding success. And he has been forced to re-evaluate his naive illusions about friendship.

Meanwhile, downtown, the staff of the *Village Voice* had given their formal support to the *New York* protesters, though with less enthusiasm. Felker was still pretty much an *arriviste* at the *Voice*, not overwhelmingly popular. His appearances on the editorial floor and his interference in policy went down poorly with journalists who, through all their changes of ownership, prized their tradition of rugged independence. So although they had reservations about Murdoch, and had heard alarming stories of the way he operated, they felt that in many ways he could scarcely be worse than their former owner. Anyway, had he not made a pledge that he would not try to move the editors of any of the three magazines, assuming they wanted to stay, for at least two years, or for the duration of their contracts? Surely that was a sign of noble intentions?

Well, no, as it turned out. On the *Voice* the first thing Murdoch did was to try to replace the editor, Marianne Partridge. She had been editor only since August and was not, actually, too popular among her staff. Yet the other journalists, grasping quickly that if he was allowed to get away with this there would be no long-term hope for them, mounted an effective counter-move.

The story has become part of the folklore of New York journalism. Partridge first heard from Murdoch one Sunday a couple of weeks after the takeover was completed. In a brief call, he told her he would be wanting to talk to her.

The following day his secretary tracked her down to the compositors' plant at Mount Kisco, New York, where she was supervising the last stages of production of that week's issue. An appointment was made for her to see the new proprietor on Tuesday evening.

Only a few days after his formal acquisition of the *New York Post* he had already installed himself in Dorothy Schiff's green and gold sixth-floor office, a sickly interpretation of the style of the French Empire. (An unflamboyant man, he was later to have it done in a more sober caramel shade.) Partridge remembers the interview as being highly civilised. Murdoch did not actually say she had to go but told her he would be hiring an editor-in-chief to supervise things – the Trelford/Sann technique. They chatted about where she had come from and her previous experience in journalism. He kept responding "Oh, oh," as though surprised by what she was saying, or not really listening. He gazed across the East River at the lights just beginning to flicker on in the dusk. "Manhattan's a beautiful town," he sighed. "That's Brooklyn," she snapped.

"How can you do this?" Partridge asked, as the news sank in. "Didn't you say you'd keep editors on?" Murdoch replied that she could stay, or he would honour her contract by paying her off. "That's not honouring my contract," she said calmly. "This is all very surprising. I'm going to have to talk to my lawyer. Perhaps you weren't aware of what was reported as your promise?" Murdoch made soothing noises and said he was sure it would be sorted out. He thanked her for being so civilised and asked how she was getting home. She said she would take a taxi.

"Call her a cab, call her a cab, call her a cab," Murdoch repeated in a mechanical, preoccupied fashion to his secretary. To stem the flow, Partridge employed an old music-hall line. "OK, I'm a cab," she shouted. Murdoch, not known for his sense of humour, gave the impression he was unfamiliar with the joke and laughed uproariously. With no cab obtainable he ordered his driver to take her home in his limousine. As she left, he did not really think she was going to give him much trouble.

On the Sunday that he made his first call to Partridge, Murdoch had also approached the man James Brady, the new editor of *New York*, had advised him to hire to replace her. Michael Kramer was a smart, fresh-faced young writer, a coming talent. He had worked for *New York* and was now editing *More*, a monthly magazine devoted to journalism with neither a wide nor a profitable circulation: but it did reach important people in the media and to edit it was therefore a high-profile job. Kramer was in his office on West 57th Street, putting the final touches to that month's issue, which had as its main feature a long article about Rupert Murdoch. At the same time, he recalls, he was watching the Super Bowl, the American professional football final, on the office television.

The initial phone call came from Brady, speaking from Murdoch's apartment. Could Kramer go to see them? Arriving not long afterwards, he was met in the lobby by Brady and they spoke for ten minutes. Brady said he was to be offered the editorship of the *Voice*. "What about Marianne?" Kramer asked. "She's leaving," Brady replied. "She'll be paid her contract." Kramer assumed it had been agreed with her. He was not to know that Murdoch had not even spoken to her yet.

He was ushered into Murdoch's presence in the living room, where the offer was formally made. They had a brief discussion about the direction the paper would take. Kramer said he wanted a free hand editorially and would try to make it more political, as it had once been. "As long as it's making money I don't care," Murdoch said.

Kramer asked again about Partridge. "She's leaving," Murdoch said. "Didn't Jim talk to you about that?" Kramer said he would go away and think about it.

On the Tuesday afternoon, shortly before Marianne Partridge went down to South Street, Murdoch summoned Kramer to see him, saying he needed a decision that day. They talked about changes in style that Kramer wanted to make and Murdoch wondered whether they would put him in conflict with Jack Newfield, the talented but abrasive investigative reporter who was one of the *Voice*'s stars. Kramer said they probably would. He had never got along with Newfield or, for that matter, with Alex Cockburn, a mercurial Englishman who wrote a brilliant column of press criticism in the paper. (He is the son of the radical

journalist Claud Cockburn, who died in 1981.) Murdoch
discussed with equanimity the prospect of his new editor
clashing with two of the paper's established writers. That
was, after all, the way several of his publications were run.
It never did any harm to give people a prod if they seemed
too comfortable, too entrenched.

It was not to work out like that, though. Kramer, while
prepared to tackle Newfield if need be, was too clever to
declare open war from the beginning. The first thing he did,
as he got back to the *More* office after dusk, was to phone
Newfield at the *Voice*. He told him he was to be the new
editor and that he wanted Newfield to stay as his chief
political correspondent.

"I don't see how you can do this," Newfield retorted.
"What about Marianne?" Kramer explained what he had
been told about Partridge. Newfield said it was not true. He
claims to have ended the conversation by saying: "I will kill
you with my bare hands" – a remark widely reported in
contemporary accounts. Kramer does not remember that
specific threat, but certainly the tone of the exchange was
such as to make him worry about whether Partridge was
really leaving of her own volition. He tried to phone her but
there was no answer. She was down at the *Post*, seeing
Murdoch.

As soon as Newfield put the phone down after talking to
Kramer, he contacted Alex Cockburn. Though the two
were not on the most cordial terms, this was an emergency.
Internal differences had to be buried. In any case, Cockburn had access to Murdoch, having done that long interview with him a few weeks earlier. Cockburn rang Murdoch, told him of their concern, and arranged that he and
Newfield should go and see him at his apartment. They met
in the lobby of the Plaza Hotel and walked the short
distance up Fifth Avenue. Murdoch came to open the door
and announced: "I'm going to take the wind out of your
sails. We're back to square one. Marianne has been reinstated. Come in and have a drink." They did. They re-
minisced about Alex's father. Murdoch told them how he
had been known as "Red Rupert" at Oxford because of his
left-wing views. "It was," Newfield recollects, "a relatively
charming hour."

Things had moved quickly after Partridge left Murdoch's office. She went home in a state of shock to her apartment on 59th Street and Second Avenue. She did not want to phone anyone at the *Voice* because it would seem as though she was asking them to put their own jobs on the line for her. As she sat, Murdoch telephoned. He wanted to know how she was feeling and suggested a further talk. While she was on the phone to him the doorbell chimed. It was Kramer. He had been trying to contact her for an hour or so and had finally decided to make an unannounced visit. Murdoch said he would ring back. Kramer's and Partridge's memories of his visit differ. He says that as soon as he heard that she had not agreed to quit he decided to pull out, and this was what he came to tell her. She claims he spent some time trying to persuade her to stand down. Both agree it was a difficult and embarrassing meeting. Kramer paced the room nervously and Partridge offered him something to eat. He declined so she made herself some soup, and he helped.

Kramer was still there when Murdoch phoned again, this time to tell Partridge that it had all been a terrible misunderstanding, that he had not properly understood the situation at the *Voice*, that she could keep her job after all. "But don't talk to anyone until I've told Michael," he added. "He's still here," she said, and passed the phone over to him. Kramer, feeling sore and abused – a familiar state of mind for a new Murdoch victim – says it was he who formally ended the short-lived courtship by telling Murdoch that he had accepted the offer only on the understanding that Partridge was leaving willingly, and that now he had found she was not he was not interested. "I'll get back to you," said Murdoch. That was the last he heard from him.

By his graceful, or at least speedy, withdrawal, Murdoch was starting to absorb the lesson of recent weeks, that outside Australia editors need to be treated with a bit more tenderness and respect than those he was used to. By underestimating Trelford he had lost the *Observer*. Now he had risked an unnecessary row at one of his most recent acquisitions by trying to make a change motivated not by any perceived need for improvement in the paper's quality but simply by the desire to make a dramatic announcement of his arrival, a show of strength. He could not tell whether Partridge was a good editor because he did not understand the *Voice* or the concerns of its readers. He understood from its balance sheets that it could turn a modest, steady profit, but its journalism was not of a kind that interested him and he could see now that it was wrong of him to have blundered into alien territory, firing without taking careful aim.

After that nasty shock and his enforced climb-down, Murdoch was content to let the *Voice* go its own way, changing his relation to it from that of an interfering parent to a kindly uncle, smiling tolerantly if sometimes thinly at its misdeeds. On the day after the Partridge drama he went down to the *Voice*'s office in Greenwich Village, uttering consoling words to the staff. After that, he watched from a distance, only occasionally picking up the phone to complain vociferously about stories, nearly always stories about himself or his papers. He was angry when Cockburn wrote an article scoffing at Paul Rigby, the Australian cartoonist and an old friend, then working at the *Post*. Next day he apologised to Partridge for his outburst through Bill Ryan, his publisher at the *Voice*. Later he heard that Nat Hentoff, one of the paper's sharpest writers, was preparing a critical article about the *Post*, so he phoned and said he did not see why he should be vilified in his own newspapers. Partridge said surely this was proof that he did not interfere editorially in his publications, as his critics charged. He has since used this argument quite often in interviews, citing the *Voice* as an example – almost the only example amongst his holdings. The Hentoff article did not in fact appear, although Partridge says it was nothing to do with Murdoch's complaint.

Some eighteen months later, with six months of her contract to run, another attempt was made to dislodge Partridge, this time by Ryan. He had already hired David Schneiderman, from the *New York Times*, to take over, but again the staff rallied round Partridge, who would not go, although she would have been paid to the end of her contract. About fifty of them rounded on Ryan in the office. "What do you know about the paper?" Joe Conason, a young reporter, shouted at the sleek-suited Ryan. "I've never seen anyone who looks like you buying the paper." Schneiderman sat in an office uptown for six months, skimming through back issues and mapping his strategy, until Partridge's contract was up. He has been editor of the paper since 1979 and Murdoch is obviously happier with him, although the two do not agree politically. Murdoch knows that it would be wrong for the *Voice* to be edited by someone of his conservative views and he appears to enjoy his infrequent meetings with Schneiderman, when they argue about the city's politics. Occasionally the new editor has been on the receiving end of criticism for individual stories, mainly about Murdoch. In 1981 he printed a thinly-veiled suggestion that the *Post* was getting a tax reduction on its South Street office building because of its support for Edward Koch, the mayor. After the piece appeared one of Murdoch's senior henchmen phoned Schneiderman to tell him how badly Murdoch viewed it, but there was no hint of reprisals. As long as the paper makes a profit, Murdoch lets it be.

Since Schneiderman became editor, the *Village Voice* has entered a period of stability. Its circulation holds steady at around 160,000. "Schneiderman, like all editors, has become the ally of the staff against the owner," says Newfield. "The flies always capture the flypaper." Schneiderman does not quite see it like that: he regards himself as a buffer between Murdoch and the rest. Murdoch clearly trusts him as much as he trusts anyone working for a paper that does not relate to anything he knows about.

While the *Voice* makes money he is prepared to let it do its own special thing, but his real effort in New York is spent on the *Post*. Here, many changes were needed to cast the paper in his image. He lost no time in initiating them.

Chapter 5

"SOCK, SOCK, SOCK, DAY AFTER DAY"

> No one ever went broke underestimating the taste of the American public.
>
> – *H. L. Mencken.*

Soon after he bought the *New York Post*, Murdoch called the editorial staff to a meeting in the news room. As they milled shoulder to shoulder, or sat on the edge of desks for their first glimpse of their new proprietor, he told them: "I want you to forget all you have ever heard about me." After a few months, those who took him at his word wished they had remembered.

A quality of Murdoch's that impresses those who deal with him is his ability to compartmentalise his affairs. When he switches his attention from one of his enterprises to another he can appear completely absorbed in the new subject. Yet he keeps the latest state of play on the old one in the front of his mind, ready to switch back. It is an intercontinental facility. After taking off his jacket and writing the front-page headline for the Sydney *Mirror*, he can go back to his office, get on the phone and decide how to deal with an impending industrial dispute at the *Sun* in London, with no discernible shift of gear.

   That is how, in the midst of the round-the-clock drama over his acquisition of *New York* magazine, he could still keep track of his more important recent purchase, the *Post*. One morning in early January, arriving at the *Post* before dawn as usual, Paul Sann had a call from Murdoch, who had been up all night in a lawyer's office wrapping up the

details of the *New York* deal. He wanted Sann to go in for a
talk. Murdoch had borrowed a cramped room and ordered
hamburgers and coffee. He told Sann that his new purchase
meant he would have less time to spend at the *Post* so he
was appointing an executive editor to look after things. The
man he chose was Ed Bolwell, an Australian who had
worked when a teenager for a paper owned by Murdoch's
father. But he was not one of the Australian tabloid artists.
His record in American journalism had been on its more
sober side: he had worked at the *New York Times* and was
now a senior editor at *Time* magazine. He was an interesting choice, an indication that so far Murdoch had no
intention of pulling the *Post* down market but sought to
serve the existing middle-brow readership better.

Murdoch told Sann he wanted him to stay on and was
offering him a two-year contract. He had a pad of yellow
paper on the desk and pulled it towards him as if to start
drafting the document. He offered Sann a cold hamburger.
Sann declined both the food and the contract. He was
getting close to retirement and was uncertain of what
direction the paper would take. He did not want to be
tied.

Bolwell, a short, slim man wearing built-up shoes, arrived a week later. Almost right away Sann could tell he
was not going to like him. He had an unsettling manner,
shouting at his staff in a way the gentlemanly Sann would
never countenance. In an interview with *Time*, Bolwell
described his philosophy of man management: "Running a
newspaper is a little like conducting a symphony orchestra.
Some people have to be badgered and some coddled to get
the best out of them. And you have to stretch. Not to
stretch is not to live. I am very competitive."

As Sann remembers it, there was scarcely any coddling
and a great deal of badgering during Bolwell's first weeks at
the *Post*. The new editor was convinced that the best
market for expanding circulation was the commuters who
spend an hour or so on the trains of an evening, going home
to Westchester or Long Island. Bolwell was one of them
himself and insisted on detailed coverage of commuter
train delays. One morning he read a reporter's story of a
delay that included no explanation for it. "Have you got the

president of the line out of bed yet?" he shouted at the reporter. "Have you done that yet?"

Sann hated this style of exerting authority and on occasion would tell Bolwell as much. Always, in front of Sann, Bolwell was deferential, admitting the error and apologising. The final break between the two came over a matter of professional judgment. An actor, Freddie Prinze, who starred in a popular television series called *Chico and the Man*, had killed himself in California playing Russian roulette. It had happened too late for the morning papers and Sann saw it as a natural front-page lead. He began to work on it and to get reporters to prepare background articles. When Bolwell came in he was unhappy about the scale of the coverage. He did not want the story to occupy the whole front page, as Sann had planned. He may have thought that, because it was about a Puerto Rican, it was directed too far down market. It would not be of absorbing interest to the suburban commuters whose attention he wanted to attract.

Looking through the pile of stories, Bolwell found one about a big power blackout at Utica, in upstate New York. What about letting that share the front page lead with Freddie Prinze? Sann was appalled. It would destroy the impact of the dramatic layout he had drawn. Moreover, Utica was nearly 250 miles away, outside the *Post*'s circulation area. What did New York readers care?

Bolwell was insistent, so Sann found room on his front page for the power cut. Still furious, the veteran editor went to see Bolwell after the second edition had been locked up. "Look," he told him, "I'm going home now. I won't be back." According to Sann, Bolwell was worried, knowing that Murdoch respected the older man. He thought Sann might have second thoughts by the morning.

Next day Sann went in to clear up his things. Murdoch called him in and they spoke for two hours, interrupted only by a call from Murdoch's daughter Prudence in London, excited at having secured her first job. He said he would call her back and resumed what appeared to Sann an attempt to persuade him to stay on. He apologised for Bolwell, again offered Sann a contract and, when that was rejected, asked him to write a regular column. Sann could not be budged. "I had four respectable decades as a newspaper man," he said later. "I didn't want to go out as a guy putting out this kind of newspaper." To save face he agreed to serve as a "consultant" but was consulted only once.

Sann's version of events, of Murdoch's reluctance to see him go, does not square with the recollection of others. On the day of the resignation, Peter Michelmore passed Murdoch in a corridor in the *Post* building. "Paul Sann has just done us a favour," said Murdoch. "He's resigned." It was January 31st, exactly a month after the takeover.

Robert Spitzler, Sann's deputy, left a few months later, followed one by one by most of the old executives. Of the most senior journalists who had run the paper under Mrs Schiff, only James Wechsler was to remain in the long term. A veteran liberal who had led the paper's fight against the McCarthy committee, he was coming to the end of his career and of his energy to fight. His name appeared on the masthead as editorial page editor for two years before the increasingly conservative tone of the leading articles became a clear embarrassment to him. The title went to Bruce Rothwell, who had effectively been in charge of the page for a long time. Within four years the list of senior editors printed daily was to contain not a single American name. Murdoch could rationalise this. "The poor old broken-down *New York Post*," as he described it once, had been brought to that condition by a gang of tired newspapermen drained of inspiration. The only hope for success was to import a new slate of people. While he would have liked to find Americans to do the job, in the end he worked best with the Australian and British journalists he knew.

Bolwell did not last long. Murdoch could have lived with his short temper and his unpopularity with his staff. In general, he thought editors who did not get on well with their underlings were more effective than those that did. But Bolwell was not producing the paper Murdoch wanted. He had not been trained in the tabloid tradition. It was still afflicted by the lack of professionalism he had detected before he bought it. In July Murdoch asked Bolwell to resign and appointed Roger Wood as editor.

Just after Wood took over, New York became obsessed

with a news story of a violent and sensational character that was to become identified in the minds of readers and critics as characteristic of the changing style of the *New York Post*. Since July 1976 the city had been shaken by a series of motiveless murders of young men and women in middle-class areas of Brooklyn and Queens. They were all shot with a .44-calibre revolver late at night as they sat in the back of parked cars. In eight attacks, six people were killed and seven wounded.

As the attacks continued and the gunman remained at large, the tone of the coverage in both the *Post* and the *News* became increasingly hysterical, reaching a pitch that had not been experienced in the city since "yellow" journalism had gone out of fashion several decades earlier. Nobody, they shrieked, was safe from the fiend. The *News* vied with the *Post*, sensation for sensation, but received less criticism because it was perceived that the *Post* was dictating the tone of the coverage and the morning paper, rattled, was simply trying to keep up, as the *Mirror* in London was seen to have reached into the gutter to ward off the *Sun*. It was the *News* that first dubbed the killer "Son of Sam" – the name he used in a letter he wrote to the paper as well as in a note found beside the body of one of his victims.

The last attack came on July 31st, 1977. Wood was away and Murdoch was editing the paper day-to-day, helped by Steve Dunleavy, a young Australian for whom he had a high regard. Dunleavy, brisk and well-built, has a liking for the lurid and little patience with considerations of good taste and restraint that might hinder him from writing a story to the very limit of its worth and, some maintain, beyond. "Dunleavy decides what he wants the story to be and then sends reporters out to get it," is how one *Post* reporter puts it.

As Murdoch and Dunleavy rolled up their sleeves to produce fresh sensations daily, Murdoch would say: "There's only one game in town and that's Son of Sam." The *News* had an initial advantage over them in the person of Jimmy Breslin, their much-read Irish-American columnist, a specialist in heart-tugging prose. Son of Sam wrote to him and Breslin quoted from his letters. In one column Breslin forecast that the killer would strike again on

July 29th, the anniversary of the first murder. This was one of the aspects of the reporting that angered the *New Yorker*, that mouthpiece of respectable liberal opinion. In a comment published in early August, the magazine maintained that by printing such speculation and making the killer into a celebrity, the two tabloids were encouraging him.

"The Son of Sam has killed six people and wounded seven and he has sold a lot of newspapers," the *New Yorker* wrote. Such solemn knuckle-rapping did not in the least deter Dunleavy from writing an open letter to the killer, in the hope that he, like Breslin, might receive an answer. On August 10th, as the latest of its breathless exposés, the *Post* reported that the Son of Sam wore a wig. NEW WITNESS SAW SAM CHANGE WIG, shouted the headline.

Early the following day that and similar speculation proved false when David Berkowitz, a twenty-four-year-old postal worker, was arrested and charged with the killings. He had not worn a wig, nor had he invariably adopted a two-handed combat pose before firing, as had also been reported. All these discrepancies were forgotten in the excitable coverage the papers gave to the arrest. The *News* and the *Post* devoted twelve pages each to the story that day, with twenty separate news items in the *News*, nineteen in the *Post*.

The arrest did not interrupt the flow of the story. Breslin and Dunleavy received new letters from Berkowitz in prison. The *Post* published some old letters he had written to a girl-friend under the front-page headline: HOW I BECAME A MASS KILLER, by David Berkowitz. Murdoch later apologised for that, characterising the headline as "inaccurate and wrong". The *New York Times* joined the *New Yorker* in wondering whether the persistently high-pitched coverage by the two tabloids would make a fair trial impossible. (In the end, Berkowitz was judged unfit to plead through insanity.)

Sometimes controversies arose for reasons Murdoch found baffling. It seemed there were people in New York who would seize on any small detail, any apparently inoffensive headline, and use it as evidence against him. In the summer of 1977 a major power failure in New York was followed by a night of looting in many areas. Production of the *Post* was lost for a day because of the lack of electricity, and when it returned its front-page headline was: 24 HOURS OF TERROR. The city administration, under Mayor Abraham Beame, thought it a sensational and exaggerated account of the night's events, perhaps a subtle attempt to discredit Beame in a year when he was up for re-election. Beame's deputy mayor for economic development was Osborn Elliott, a former editor of *Newsweek*, later made Dean of Columbia University's school of journalism. He wrote an angry open letter, published in the *New York Times*, accusing Murdoch of cheapening American journalism by importing crude Australian methods. Murdoch, who never ducks a fight, wrote a full-page editorial equally rude about Elliott. A couple of years later the *Columbia Journalism Review*, published by the school Elliott ran, printed a startling editorial entitled: DOING THE DEVIL'S WORK. It described the *Post* as "appealing to the basest passions and appetites of the hour" and seemed to suggest some kind of protective legislation against it. It exploited social passions, terrorised the fearful and incited the wrathful. "It is no longer enough to judge the paper solely by journalistic standards . . . Here we enter a moral universe in which judgments are of a different order altogether, suggesting, as they do, that the matter ought not to be allowed to rest after the press critics have pronounced their anathemas. For the *New York Post* is no longer merely a journalistic problem. It is a social problem – a force for evil."

Murdoch and Dunleavy had long ago learned to dismiss such pomposities as coming from effete Martini-sipping intellectuals, too refined to soil their hands by engaging in the kind of journalism the bulk of New Yorkers actually wanted to read. "I don't give a damn what the media critics say," Murdoch told *More* magazine. In May 1977, three years before that *Review* editorial, he had given a cogent defence of his philosophy and of lowest-common-denominator journalism in a speech to the American Newspaper Publishers' Association in San Francisco. He accused the publishers of going above the heads of their audience, catering to an idealised market, pretending the interests of readers were as lofty as their own and their writers'. "Élitist journalism," he dubbed it, adding: "A press that fails to interest the whole community is one that will ultimately become a house organ of the élite engaged in an increasingly private conversation with a dwindling club . . . I cannot avoid the temptation of wondering whether there is any other industry in this country which seeks to presume so completely to give the customer what he does not want."

Yet many of the *Post* reporters shared the "élitist" opinion of their paper. They saw the new brashness and brutalism infecting not just the coverage of crime but also political reporting. Many were offended by what they saw as the insensitivity of Paul Rigby, the cartoonist. They found two cartoons in the early summer particularly hard to take. The first was about Andrew Young, the suave black southerner President Carter appointed ambassador to the United Nations, where he offended traditional American conservatives by his outspoken support for the Third World. Some felt the cartoon was racist. Not long afterwards another cartoon provoked the staff to action. It was a comment on a decision by the city to introduce one-woman police cars. It showed a policewoman luring a gang of robbers into her car by showing a seductive pair of thighs. A few dozen reporters signed a petition against it, calling it "sexist and offensive". Joy Cook and Barbara Yuncker, officials of the office branch of the Newspaper Guild, a trade union for journalists and clerical workers, sent the petition to Murdoch.

He replied with a terse note: "Personally I have known Mr Rigby and his work for many years and have never found him to be either sexist or racist. But then, perhaps I am insensitive! Mr Rigby's cartoons add brightness and humour to the paper. It could do with more of both!" And he added this hand-written postscript: "Andy Young enjoyed the other cartoon so much he has asked for the original!"

The main political event in the city that year was the election for mayor. Beame, who had held the office for four years, was running again but faced several opponents in the September Democratic primary. Newspaper endorsements are important for candidates running for city office.

Traditionally, the candidates present themselves for interviews with senior editors of all the papers and submit to questioning, as if they were applying for a job. Early in the summer Murdoch had been inclining towards Mario Cuomo, an Italian-American who had the support of Hugh Carey, the Governor of New York State. The *Post*'s coverage of the early campaigning reflected this preference. Murdoch was disinclined to support Beame, whom he blamed for the city's near-bankruptcy two years earlier. He thought he was too weak in dealing with the unions representing city workers. When a report by the federal government on the fiscal crisis appeared that summer, the *Post* put it on the front page with the uncompromising headline: BEAME CONNED CITY. Beame responded crisply by calling Murdoch an "Australian carpetbagger".

In the interviews with the candidates, Murdoch was unimpressed with Cuomo, but was much taken with Edward Koch, a Jewish congressman who had entered the race with little support, as measured by the opinion polls. It seemed to Murdoch that Koch shared his own pragmatism, especially his realistic attitude to the limits of the city's ability to pay for welfare and services. He seemed determined to stand up to the unions and vested interests. He was a Democrat of a conservative stamp – a category in which at that time Murdoch placed himself.

Koch learned he was going to get the *Post*'s endorsement just after seven one morning in August, as he was waiting for the bus that would take him to begin his day's campaigning. The phone rang. "Hallo, Ed, this is Rupert." For an instant Koch was at a loss. "I don't know any Ruperts," he thought. Rupert was not a common name in his social set. Then he recognised the Australian accent and said quickly: "Yes, Rupert?" On hearing the news Koch said: "It's very important to me." Murdoch replied patronisingly: "All we ask is that you do a good job." Koch was endorsed by the *News* two weeks later and believes that he would not have won the primary, nor the election itself, without the support of both. And he doubted whether he would have been backed by the *Post* had the more liberal Dolly Schiff still been in charge. Koch and Murdoch have remained friends. The mayor admires the publisher's modesty ("he never comes with an entourage") and relishes the paper's brash, campaigning approach, especially when it is campaigning for him. "Sock, sock, sock, day after day," is how he sees it.

What many of the paper's staff objected to was that the "sock, sock, sock" was not confined to the editorial opinion column. Suddenly, with the endorsement, the extensive and generally favourable news coverage given to Cuomo was turned off and Koch replaced him as the star contender. Barbara Yuncker drafted another petition to Murdoch speaking of the "great disquiet" of the staff, and some eighty journalists signed it:

"We are dismayed," it said, "at the kind of puff journalism which has followed your endorsements. We believe that it will ultimately help neither the newspaper nor your candidates.

"You have lost good writers over this and related issues. You should be aware that editorial people of stature and integrity whom you ought to value are very unsettled and also may be lost to the paper.

"All of us signing below accept the basic premise that independent reporting produces the best results for public welfare. Journalists did not become the Fourth Estate and Thomas Jefferson did not put us ahead of courts and legislatures in anticipation that narrow partisanship would guide us.

"Political stories should be written by the best intelligence good reporters can bring to the facts – and not homogenised afterwards to fit an editorial position. Space should be even-handedly divided among viable contenders; not to do so cheapens the support for the paper's choices and destroys our credibility.

"There is a subtle but important additional danger. When the coverage seems skewed, conscientious reporters may feel constrained from writing certain legitimate stories lest they appear to be pandering to an editorial bias. That is insidious . . .

"We are afraid the *Post* is gaining the reputation of being a sheet where facts don't much matter. The *Post*, as the oldest daily continuously published in this country, is a heritage we cherish and so should you. We are dismayed to be manipulated into becoming pamphleteers."

This could have been precisely calculated to infuriate Murdoch, and so it did. Pretentious twaddle. Who did these people think they were? All that nonsense about Jefferson confirmed his prejudices against American journalists. If only they would come down from the clouds and get stuck in to some proper reporting, learn to write a half-decent headline, he might be able to sell a few more papers. If they didn't like it why didn't they leave? It was all too like that irritating business with staff of the *Australian* in 1975.

But he knows too much to rant like that in front of his reporters. When he summoned Yuncker to discuss the petition he tried hard to remain his measured self, though clearly angry. "If anyone on the staff thinks I lack integrity, if he had any integrity himself he'd quit," he said. Yuncker said she had signed it. Did he want her to quit? "Let's not get personal," Murdoch said. Yuncker persisted. "It's our newspaper, too," she affirmed, and at this Murdoch very nearly blew his top. "Oh no, it's not," he snarled. "When you pay the losses you can say it's your paper too. It's *my* newspaper. You just work here and don't you forget it."

Had he taken the trouble to go back over some of the old files of the paper, to remind himself how it had looked just before he took it over, Murdoch would have been able to deploy a more telling argument. For it was disingenuous of the reporters to claim that slanting and selecting news stories for political purposes was something Mrs Schiff's *Post* never did. In the run-up to the presidential election of 1976 the paper carried several front-page headlines calculated to damage President Ford's chance of re-election. HOW FORD BLOCKED FIRST NIXON PROBE screamed one, raking over the coals of Watergate. NEW QUESTIONS ON FORD'S MONEY read another. The anti-Ford campaign reached its climax on October 29th with a banner headline that even Murdoch would have found it hard to improve upon: FORD AD MAN LINKED TO PORN. The story told how Michael Goldbaum, who was helping promote the Ford campaign, also made pornographic films. When the *Post* presented Goldbaum with the evidence he was fired by Ford's staff. Readers were spared no details of the pornographic films he had made:

"Principal actors must perform their own fellatio and cunnilingus." And for good measure the same day's paper carried another story headlined: FORD FILES DON'T ADD UP. The vital difference between this and the *Post*'s campaign for Koch was that most *Post* reporters were liberals who, like their paper, had supported the Democratic presidential candidate, Jimmy Carter. Not many were similarly committed to Koch.

Barbara Yuncker, as head of the Guild's office branch, saw much of Murdoch during his first two years of ownership. Towards the end of 1977 she began to hear from senior executives that he was trying to get rid of the "dead wood", including many who had signed the pre-election petition. In February 1978 he presented a list of 148 Guild members he wanted to dismiss – about a third of the membership on the paper. On March 9th he announced: "The *Post* proposes, on a one-time basis, the right to terminate members of the staff, with appropriate severance pay, who in its judgment are incompatible with the new management's publishing concept." The shell-shocked staff dubbed it the "Auschwitz clause". Since it conflicted with the existing Guild contract it had to be negotiated.

Discussions continued for two months, partly under the auspices of the federal mediation service in Washington. In the end Murdoch achieved as much as he could reasonably have hoped. The 148 listed people would be asked, not forced, to leave and attractive redundancy terms were offered to help persuade them. They were called in one by one and told they were no longer required. Nearly half agreed to go, and several who were not on the "hit list" took advantage of the improved terms and left of their own accord, bringing the number who left to eighty. After that, the management announced dismissal of a further eighteen employees who had been with the paper for less than two years and thus had no protection under the Guild contract. Sixteen of them went but seven were later re-engaged.

While that dispute was important for the evidence it gave of Murdoch's attitude to his journalists, it was soon overshadowed by much graver labour troubles involving all three New York papers. With new contracts due to be negotiated with the work force that year, there had been talk for months of a likely strike. The managements were known to be determined to reduce the manning levels in their pressrooms, and the unions just as determined to resist them.

A successful negotiation with the printers four years earlier had encouraged the publishers to think that this time they could solve once and for all the problems of over-manning in the pressrooms, where the newspapers are produced. In American newspaper terminology, the prin-ters are the men who operate the Linotype machines and then fit the metal type into the page. When newspapers introduce the new technology of photocomposition, their role becomes redundant. In 1974 the printing unions had agreed, without a strike, to the introduction of the new machinery. They ceded to the proprietors the right of deciding how many men were needed to operate it. In return the publishers agreed to keep on the payroll every-one then working as a printer, even if there was virtually nothing for them to do.

This agreement did not include the men who worked the printing presses. They are represented by a different union. To complete their programme of modernisation and reduc-ing labour costs, the proprietors sought to alter the system by which manning levels were decided. The existing system was known as "unit manning": the publishers agreed to deploy a fixed number of men to every press or unit. They wanted to go over to "room manning" where they, the publishers, would decide how many people were needed to perform the overall printing operation and would bring the staff down to whatever figure they arrived at. As with the printers, they were prepared to give lifetime job guarantees to existing employees. The New York City proprietors argued that radical surgery was the only way they could bring their costs into line with suburban papers, operating at lower manning levels than they and competing more and more effectively for circulation and advertising on the fringes of the city.

The *Post* had not negotiated in concert with the other two papers since 1963, when Dorothy Schiff quit the Publishers' Association and made her own settlement with striking printers. There was diffidence on both sides before the three decided to make common cause in 1978. Executives of the *News* and the *Times* were suspicious of the newcomer. As for Murdoch, in a worse financial position than the other two, he feared they would do a deal with the union so expensive that he would not be able to afford it and would be forced to close down. But at a dinner with the proprietors of the two papers in the summer of 1977 he became convinced that they were determined to force manpower cuts on the pressmen and were prepared to take a strike if necessary. At the dinner they reached no firm agreement to negotiate together but they could see they were headed in the same direction. In November that year the *Post* rejoined the Publishers' Association.

The other two papers did not give Murdoch any support, though, in his "hit list" battle with the Newspaper Guild. A long account of the 1978 strike was written for the *New Yorker* by A. H. Raskin, a veteran labour reporter. In it, he recounts how he met Arthur Ochs ("Punch") Sulzberger, publisher of the *New York Times*, during the Guild dispute at the *Post*. "The man is wild," Sulzberger said of Murdoch. "We'll support him on the things we have in common but not on the crazy kind of things he's after with the Guild."

The *Times* and the *News*, still negotiating without the *Post*, told the pressmen's union in the summer that they would unilaterally introduce new working conditions and manning levels on August 8th unless an agreement on cuts had been negotiated by then. This would inevitably mean a strike. Murdoch, before formally joining them, wanted to convince himself that they were committed to holding out for room manning – especially the *Times*, which had historically taken a softer line with the unions than the other two. On July 18th, 1978, he had dinner at Christ Cella with Joe Barletta of the *News* and Walter Mattson of the *Times* – the two who were to play with him the leading roles in the negotiations on the publishers' side. Barletta was a lawyer sent to New York by the Chicago Tribune Company, owners of the *News*. He came with a reputation for ruthless bargaining. Mattson is the executive vice-president and general manager of the *Times*, Sulzberger's most important adviser. Both men, like Murdoch, were in their forties.

At the dinner they agreed to hold out for room manning, although even at that stage Murdoch was worried about Mattson's resolve. He feared he would in the end settle for slightly reduced manning but still on the unit basis. Yet when the day of the deadline came, and negotiations were still in progress, it was the *Times* that took the lead in introducing the new work rules without agreement from the union, inevitably provoking the strike that began on August 9th, 1978.

A few days later, Mattson and Barletta came up with what seemed a masterly idea to serve the twin functions of improving the public image of the proprietors and ensuring that Murdoch did not do what Mrs Schiff had done and break away from the alliance. They invited him to become spokesman for the Publishers' Association, with the title of President. They still by no means trusted him and felt that as nominal leader he would be less likely to make a hasty exit when things looked gloomy, as from time to time they surely would. They recognised, too, that his brisk confidence went over well on television. As with many strikes that affected people's way of life, it was important for each side to convince the public that it was being reasonable. Murdoch would prove the most persuasive spokesman of the three: and since his paper was in the worst shape financially, he could most effectively plead the case for substantial cuts.

He did not immediately accept the offer, and his decision whether or not to do so marked the introduction into the dispute – or at least on to its sidelines – of Theodore Kheel, the labour lawyer and power broker who had acted as mediator in many of New York's most notable strikes, including that at the newspapers in 1962/3. Kheel and Murdoch had been on different sides in the *New York* magazine takeover struggle, but a few months later Murdoch accepted Kheel's help in solving a dispute with the Guild stemming from his takeover of the circulation list of the *Long Island Press*, a suburban evening newspaper that had sold 150,000 copies daily before its closure. During the dispute Murdoch had been impressed by the work of

Martin Fischbein, a young assistant to Kheel, and he hired him for his own organisation in April 1978.

Fischbein was the only one of Murdoch's advisers to oppose his accepting the presidency of the Publishers' Association. He thought the risks outweighed the advantages. If Murdoch was going to hold out for a tougher settlement than the other two, he would be in a stronger position if he could make them worry all the time about his breaking away from them. Fischbein telephoned Kheel, his former boss, to ask him to persuade Murdoch to refuse. The three – Murdoch, Kheel and Fischbein – agreed to meet for breakfast next morning at the Regency Hotel on Park Avenue, only a few blocks east of Murdoch's flat and the place where many powerful city people meet to start the day: the Elaine's of the breakfast hour.

Not long after the meal began it became apparent to Kheel that Murdoch had all but made up his mind to accept. He harboured a suspicion about the other two publishers similar to theirs of him, that they would leave him in the lurch and do a more expensive deal with the union than he could afford. That would be harder if he were their nominal leader. He had more personal reasons, too, connected with his *amour propre*. "It will give me international projection," he enthused to Kheel. And later he was to tell Raskin: "Aside from the temptation of flattery, I knew I'd be the lightning rod. There was a chance to be seen arguing a case other than Son of Sam or some dumb headline in the *Post*." He formally accepted the role at a lunch at Christ Cella on August 18th.

It was not long before Fischbein's warning proved justified. After a study into the cost of moving to room manning, in terms of job guarantees that would have to be given to presently employed pressmen, the *Times* and the *News* decided to drop it from their negotiating position and move instead to substantive cuts in personnel under the existing unit-manning system. Murdoch saw this as a weakening and was reluctant to acquiesce. Only his newly strengthened commitment to collective bargaining persuaded him to accept the change. The proposal was that the existing twelve qualified pressmen on each machine should go down to eight and there should be cuts in subsidiary

operations in the pressroom, resulting in a staff reduction
of some fifty per cent. William Kennedy, president of the
pressmen's union, responded with a plan to reduce the
number at each press by only one. Negotiations trickled to
a halt and the prospect of an early settlement receded.
Kenneth Moffett, the mediator appointed by the Federal
Arbitration Service, found himself powerless and returned
to Washington.

By now three strike papers had appeared in New York to
take up some of the spare advertising with hardly anywhere
else to go, and to provide rudimentary news coverage for
New Yorkers. They were professional jobs in the sense that
they were staffed by journalists from the three regular
papers made idle by the strike, but they were poorly
produced and, because printed outside the city, had im-
possibly early deadlines. The best of them was the *Daily
Metro*, launched by a young businessman named Frederick
Iseman. There was indignation amongst some of its staff
when they discovered that the paper was financed chiefly by
Murdoch, whose organisation helped with advertising and
distribution. The *Metro* was sent to *Post* subscribers, and
when Murdoch's involvement became known after a few
weeks some, still suspicious of the unpredictable Australian, believed he might keep it in being as the morning
newspaper he had often said he wanted to launch in New
York. Some of the journalists quit in their anger but the
other two papers were also giving discreet if less substantial
help to strike sheets – the *Times* to one called *City News*
and the *News* to the *Daily Press*. It was a prudent move to
protect their circulation from too great an incursion from
the suburban papers still being published normally.

With negotiations effectively deadlocked, Murdoch,
Barletta and Mattson discussed how they could get them
moving again. To bring in Kheel was one obvious way, but
none of the three was keen, feeling that past settlements in
which he had been involved tended to favour the unions at
the expense of management. Kheel himself was pawing the
ground on the sidelines, scarcely able to believe that this
major city dispute was going on without him. On September 2nd, Labour Day weekend, he wrote an article in the
Daily Press suggesting that the fate of the strike might hinge

ultimately on the attitude of the other printing unions not involved in it, and how long they would refuse to cross the pressmen's picket lines.

The print unions are linked in a co-ordinating body, the Allied Printing Trades Council. After the article appeared, the council president, George McDonald, invited Kheel to enter the talks as his adviser. If, as Kheel hoped, he was to act as a mediator – one with better contacts and greater depth of experience than Moffett – he had to get the approval of the still reluctant publishers. He was invited to Murdoch's apartment to meet him, Barletta and Mattson. Barletta, as he recalls it, was strongly opposed to letting Kheel play a role. "His way of settling is to give in to the unions," he told the other two, before Kheel arrived. But, again according to Barletta, Murdoch was keen to have Kheel, remembering his useful part in the earlier dispute at the *Post*. He saw the appointment as a way of getting things moving. As the owner of the most vulnerable of the papers, he needed a settlement more urgently.

Kheel passed his audition, and told the three men that he would need ten days to marshal the facts. He stressed that he would not be making any firm recommendations for a settlement, just clarifying the points at issue. Soon after his arrival on the scene the mistrust between the publishers, always dormant, almost came to a head. Murdoch suspected that Kheel was having a secret meeting with Mattson. He had Fischbein check it by asking friends in Kheel's office. When he learned beyond doubt that it was true, Murdoch was furious. He had always feared that, despite Mattson's protestations, the real aim of the *Times* was to do a deal with the union that would be too expensive for the other papers to live with. The secret meeting seemed to confirm it. Relations between the three publishers were never to recover fully.

Kheel's attempt was allowed to proceed but it was not long before Murdoch regretted he had given any support to it. Kennedy was none too happy, either, knowing that Kheel had met the publishers and fearing a plot to persuade the other print unions to cross his picket lines. Mistrust abounded. Murdoch, without consulting the other two, made things tenser by appealing on television to the Allied unions to go back to work. Next day Kheel countered by making a public request to be allowed to investigate whether both sides were acting in good faith. The publishers, Murdoch especially, thought Kheel was taking too much on himself. Murdoch phoned Barletta and, repeating himself as he does when under stress, blurted: "Joe, you were right, you were right, you were right, you were right." Barletta said later: "He'd let the camel into the tent and he recognised it."

Murdoch issued a further statement, this time agreed with the other two, denouncing Kheel. But within a few days Barletta and Mattson had persuaded Murdoch – or they thought they had – that Kheel represented the best, almost the only hope for a reasonably fast solution. Their alliance was patched up and the negotiations resumed both in New York and in Washington, whence Moffett had summoned the parties in a fruitless attempt to promote some real give-and-take. In New York, Kheel finished defining the issues, but that did not seem to get anyone very far.

By now Murdoch was at the end of his patience. The strike had lasted six weeks and there was no prospect of an early deal. How could he be sure that, when he had sweated through the remaining weeks, he would not after all have been conned by Mattson, that the settlement would not be too expensive for him to bear? He was growing convinced that this was just what would happen and he found himself thinking more and more of Dorothy Schiff and the 1962/3 strike when she had broken ranks with the other publishers. They had found it despicable. Well, they would, but it had worked, hadn't it? The *Post* had survived, while most of the other papers, those that had loyally stayed in harness, had gone out of business within a few years. For sure, the people at the *Times* and the *News* would be outraged if he left them and did a separate deal, but he was fairly certain they had a contempt for him already. And in the final reckoning, they would have more respect for a skipper who steered his ship to survival than one who let someone else take over the navigation and guide it on to the reefs.

On the morning of September 27th he called his advisers

to his office and announced, according to Raskin's account:
"We have to blow this up and get out of it." He phoned
Barletta and arranged lunch at Windows on the World, the
restaurant on the 103rd floor of the World Trade Centre in
Lower Manhattan, close to the federal mediation office
where a round of negotiations was due to be held that
afternoon. Each took his senior legal adviser. Murdoch
complained about Kheel and the seeming endlessness of
the dispute, although Barletta insists he gave no hint of
what he was about to do. "What's the alternative?" Barletta asked him, and within minutes he had his answer. The
four men went down in the lift and walked the few blocks to
the office of the mediator. As they neared the entrance
Murdoch said to Howard Squadron, his lawyer: "Go on in
and throw the bomb, throw the bomb." Squadron went in
and told the other negotiators that in Murdoch's view
Kheel's role was now too dominant: "He has become the *de
facto* mediator and seems to be moving towards becoming
the *de facto* arbitrator." The *Post*, he went on, could not
accept that and was pulling out of the negotiations. The
meeting ended in confusion.

While the other two publishers huddled to assess the
damage his defection would cause them, Murdoch began
that evening an attempt to do a separate deal with Kennedy
and the pressmen. His withdrawal had been a gamble
because he had no guarantee that they would agree to settle
with him alone – indeed Kennedy had walked out of the
meeting as Squadron was announcing the *Post*'s decision.
What Murdoch was seeking, again drawing on the Schiff
precedent, was a "me-too" agreement, under which the
Post would resume publication quickly and eventually go
along with whatever settlement was reached by the other
two papers. There was, he knew, still a risk that the
agreement would be more expensive than he could afford,
but at least if it was he would have had a few weeks of a
virtual monopoly of the New York press in the prosperous
autumn advertising season.

The union leader had his doubts but in the end saw it as a
useful weapon against the other two papers. It took five
days to negotiate the "me-too" deal. In the small hours of
the morning of Monday, October 2nd, Murdoch left

Squadron's office with the agreement under his belt and said wryly: "I'll be even less popular in this town in certain quarters." It was not long before that prediction was fulfilled. "His actions are reprehensible and unconscionable," said John Thompson, a senior executive and spokesman for the *Daily News*. On Thursday the first plump edition of the post-strike *Post* appeared, eighty-four of its 128 pages crammed with advertising. WELCOME BACK! its banner headline shouted, like a man shaking hands with himself. "The *Post* is a piece of junk," said John Pomfret of the *New York Times* when he saw that first edition. "Just another strike paper," said Barletta. Kheel was more personal, calling Murdoch "an immigrant heady with power." And Kheel was to add later: "Rupert committed the arch-crime of collective bargaining: he walked through the publishers' own picket line . . . He may have me-tooed himself to death."

Murdoch was quick to cash in on his initiative. For the next month, before the other two settled, the *Post* printed more than a million copies a day – nearly double its former circulation. He started a Sunday edition, declaring that it would continue even after the strike at his rivals had ended – it did, but only for a few weeks. He announced plans to start a permanent daily called the *Sun* but this was scotched by the unions. They did not mind helping Murdoch make money so long as their own position did not decline, but he had declared his intention of making the *Sun* a low-budget paper with a bare minimum of staff: why should they let him thus jeopardise the future of the *News*, where so many of their members worked and where more generous staffing arrangements were in operation?

Murdoch and his people were strident in justifying what the other publishers saw as their treachery. "They made a complete fool out of me," he said, and Squadron elaborated: "They were definitely trying to do a number on Rupert. We were scared stiff. They were playing footsie with each other and we thought they might try to get on the streets before us. That would have killed us." But Murdoch was understandably chirpy. "Monopoly is a terrible thing – till you have it," he told Raskin. Kheel, meanwhile, was suspected of being the source of photocopies of a Robert

Browning poem that were scattered over the room where
the negotiations with the other papers were continuing:

> "Just for a handful of silver he left us,
> Just for a riband to stick in his coat."

Murdoch's opponents cite his abandonment of the publishers' alliance as proof of his treachery and unrelia-
bility. It is the most famous incident in his early American
career, exceeding even the battle for *New York* magazine.
His exact motives may be as unclear to him as to the others
who took part. There are no grounds for thinking that the
move was premeditated, that he joined with the *News* and
Times simply to increase the impact of his break with them
later, or that he urged them to stand firm so as to lengthen
the time he could enjoy his monopoly. With Murdoch it is
often best to take him at face value, to stick to the simpler
explanation. He knew that, since the Felker incident, the
city establishment held him in low regard, so he could
justify to himself the suspicion that the other papers were
bent on reaching an agreement that would damage him
mortally, hoping to run him out of town. The *Times* had a
history of making soft deals with the unions. There was a
risk that at any moment the city's wealthiest paper might
revert to type. In retrospect, it seems clear that this was not
Sulzberger's intention, but with a tender, newly-acquired
property to nurture, Murdoch did not want to take the
chance. His experience in Australia had taught him that
there are seldom good reasons for trusting anyone.

On November 6th, a month after the *Post* resumed, the
Times and the *News* were back on the streets. The eighty-
eight day strike had not produced the savings the publishers
originally sought – only one fewer pressman was to be
assigned to each machine, though there were more significant reductions in apprentices, maintenance men and supporting personnel. Murdoch insisted that what he feared
had come to pass, that the other two had been insufficiently
vigorous in their pursuit of savings; but he paid up all the
same.

Meantime, as he had predicted, personal attacks on him
increased. Richard Reeves, earlier among the most vocifer-

ous opponents of the *New York* takeover, wrote an article in *Esquire* (then edited by Felker) that quoted A. M. Rosenthal, the executive editor of the *New York Times*, as calling Murdoch "a bad element, practising mean, ugly, violent journalism," adding that he hoped he would disappear from the New York scene within two years. At the *News*, advertising executives instituted a "Bury Murdoch" campaign. Their salesmen were given "pallbearer" awards if they managed to take advertising away from the *Post*. Pete Hamill, who had been at the Elaine's celebration party when Murdoch took over, wrote a column in the *News* likening him to the guest who throws up at dinner.

A few months later another article appeared in *Esquire*, by Chris Welles. It began with a quote from Barletta. "In Murdoch's world there are no rules. His world is amoral. I'm not going to lecture him that what he's doing is outside the bounds of agreeable behaviour. But now that he has shown how he works, we'll do it too. We're willing to play the game with him by his rules if that's what he wants." Offended, Murdoch wrote to Barletta, ostensibly to return a book. In the covering letter he said he had just read the "amazing statement" in *Esquire*. It was, he continued, a malicious falsehood. "Maybe God will forgive you but I will have more difficulty." Barletta said later: "It's a measure of the man that I don't know whether he was joking."

Murdoch was not the only person to feel wounded by the debris of rancour that continued to rain down after the strike was over. In its issue of January 8th, 1979, his *New York* magazine had as its cover story a profile of Kheel by Richard Karp. It detailed deals of what Karp called a "questionable nature" in which Kheel had been involved. *New York* printed a long reply from Kheel together with its reply to the reply. Kheel then sued for defamation, in a thirty-page complaint, alleging that Murdoch had approved the hostile article partly as revenge against Kheel for having helped settle the strike against the *Times* and *News*, ending the *Post*'s temporary monopoly. After two years the action was dropped after an agreed statement in which Kheel conceded that Murdoch had taken no part in preparing the article, while Murdoch accepted that it had been "inappropriate", although Karp did not associate himself with the statement.

The *Post* quickly lost most of the readers it had borrowed from the *Times* and the *News*. After the rival papers resumed, its circulation settled at about 650,000 – not far above its level when the strike began. And the advertising position continued unhealthy. Although Murdoch sold something like twenty per cent of the newspapers bought every day in New York, he had less than a seven-per-cent share of the advertising market. He thought this was partly to do with prejudice against him by the large department stores, persuaded by representatives of the other two papers to take a lofty, disapproving view of his defection during the strike. The same had happened to Mrs Schiff in 1962/3 but this was something new for Murdoch. Nowhere else had he heard of commercial decisions taken for essentially sentimental reasons.

The store executives did not admit to such motives. They said their reluctance to advertise in the *Post* was based on demographics. The paper did not reach the people they wanted to attract to their stores. "Our customers are sophisticated and urbane and don't want to hear about the violence and sex the *Post* touts," one advertising executive told the *Wall Street Journal* in 1980. And *Newsday*, a year later, quoted a discussion between Murdoch and a space buyer from Bloomingdales, the most chic of the New York stores, in which the buyer was supposed to have said: "But Rupert, Rupert, your readers are my shoplifters."

Murdoch was concerned at first about the criticism that most of the *Post*'s senior staff were from Britain or Australia. For a time he tried earnestly to do something about it. After the unhappy experience with Bolwell he was not going to oust Roger Wood, whose cheerful lack of the finer sensibilities makes him an ideal Murdoch editor. He thought the number two post on the news side, managing editor, should go to an American if at all possible. He tried several, none of whom lasted more than a few months, until, at a lunch at *New York* magazine, he sat next to John Van Doorn, a former editor of the "Week in Review" section that appears in the bulky Sunday edition of the *New*

Murdoch's parents, Sir
Keith Murdoch and Dame
Elizabeth (*Melbourne
Herald* and *Keystone Press*)

Murdoch and Anna Torv on
their wedding day, Sydney,
1967 (*John Fairfax and Sons
Ltd*)

In 1960, Murdoch breaks into Sydney journalism when he buys the *Daily Mirror (Keystone Press)*

On a visit to Washington in 1962, Murdoch and Zell Rabin (left), editor of the Sydney *Daily Mirror*, meet President Kennedy *(Keystone Press)*

Threatened with takeover by Robert Maxwell, the Carr family, owners of the *News of the World*, show solidarity by having a group photograph taken *(The Press Association)*

On January 2nd, 1969, Sir William Carr and Rupert Murdoch congratulate each other on Maxwell's defeat. Sir William had less to smile about a few months later *(The Press Association)*

Frost assuming the role of prosecutor on his show in 1969, when he interviewed Murdoch about the *News of the World*'s serialisation of Christine Keeler's memoirs *(London Weekend Television)*

After a row over the Keeler memoirs, Murdoch restores his image as a family man by posing with his wife Anna and fourteen-month-old daughter Elizabeth at their London home in October 1969 *(Keystone Press)*

November 1969: Rupert Murdoch with the first issue of the *Sun* under his ownership (*The Press Association*)

At a luncheon in September 1969, Murdoch is photographed with Denis Hamilton (left) and Lord Thompson of *Times* Newspapers and Sir Eric Clayson (right) of the *Birmingham Post and Mail*. Hamilton was to play a key role in Murdoch's acquisition of *The Times* eleven years later, after Thomson's death (*The Press Association*)

When Murdoch bought the *New York Post* and *New York* magazine in the space of a few weeks, the American press started taking him seriously. On January 17th, 1977, he appeared on the front cover of both *Time* and *Newsweek* (*Popperfoto*)

Below: Clay Felker, who felt betrayed by Murdoch's takeover of his magazines, *New York* and the *Village Voice* (*Associated Press*)

Below right: Larry Lamb, Murdoch's first editor of the *Sun*, wearing the insignia of his knighthood, awarded in 1980 (*Popperfoto*)

Above: Kenneth Thomson (*Central Press Photos*)

Above right: Gordon Brunton (*International Thomson Organisation*)

Murdoch with Harold Evans, editor of the *Sunday Times*, and William Rees-Mogg of *The Times*, at the announcement of his purchase of the two papers in February 1981 (*Associated Press*)

Above: Harold Evans puts on a brave face to interviewers outside *The Times* building during his fight to keep the editorship in March 1982 (*Express Newspapers*)

Above right: Charles Douglas-Home, who succeeded Evans as editor (*Popperfoto*)

Rupert Murdoch meeting Marshall Field V at a news conference, November 1st, 1983, after Murdoch's purchase of the *Chicago Sun Times* (*Popperfoto*)

York Times. Van Doorn, a respected figure among the city's journalists, had gone to *New York* early in 1978. In the conversation with Murdoch he said he would like to get back into newspapers. "Why not come down to the *Post?*" Murdoch asked. It was settled at a private lunch a week later. Van Doorn was to edit the *Post's* own weekly review section, appearing on Saturdays. And he would, he was assured, have wide powers to shape the rest of the news coverage as he saw fit.

After only a few days, as Van Doorn now recalls it, he could see that neither Murdoch nor Wood really wanted any change in the paper's essential direction. They liked the *idea* of employing American executives so long as they did not bring with them notions that would cut across Dunleavy's brand of fact-stretching journalism. It was not that the Americans were too timid or conscience-stricken to do a properly ruthless job. Sometimes it was the other way round. They had no native instinct for just how far they could go. Fleet Street has perfected a way of handling scandal and sensation that seems crude but can be subtle, and few Americans, he found, had developed sufficiently sensitive antennae to judge just where the line should be drawn. If anyone complained to Murdoch of an excess of bad taste he would often respond: "That must be one of my American editors. They try too hard." And once, standing in the news room, he told Van Doorn: "Americans don't know how to do journalism."

Friends had warned Van Doorn before he joined that it would be like this but, won over by Murdoch's persuasive enthusiasm, he had preferred to believe he would be the exception. Wood, though, ignored his ideas, changed things he had done without consulting him and progressively whittled away the space given to the Weekly Review, which was obviously continued only under sufferance. The influence of Dunleavy, who ran the news-gathering operation at key times of the day, was paramount. Murdoch and Dunleavy together were like a benevolent uncle with his nephew. If the younger man behaved outrageously, as he often did, Murdoch would humour him. "Now Steve, now Steve" he would chide playfully if Dunleavy made an especially aggressive remark to a guest at one of the lunches

Murdoch gave in his private dining-room for prominent
civic personalities. Dunleavy is tough and macho and Murdoch likes that.

After a few months Murdoch was as unhappy with Van
Doorn as the newcomer was with his own position. In
February 1979 Murdoch had lunch with the Associated
Press. Afterwards, he left their headquarters in Rocke-
feller Centre with Craig Ammerman, head of AP's New
York bureau, and they strolled along Fifth Avenue
together. He had known Ammerman since acquiring the
Post, and had been impressed with him from the start.
Ammerman was a youngster of twenty-eight when he first
went to see Murdoch in November 1977, a few days after
the *Post* deal was announced. He wanted to discuss
whether, under the new management, the paper still
wanted to subscribe to the AP service.

"The one question I hoped he wouldn't ask me was how
much they were paying for the service," Ammerman remembers. "He asked it before I got in the door and I
thought: 'Boy, this is headed for no good.' " When
Ammerman said the fee was around $12,000 a week – the
same as the other papers paid – Murdoch replied: "You
must mean a month." The price did not go down but the
two men became friends, meeting from time to time for
lunch. They drew closer during the strike, when Murdoch
would phone Ammerman, sometimes more than once a
day, to check what was happening.

Walking down Fifth Avenue, on that February afternoon, Ammerman told Murdoch he had been offered a job
as deputy editor on the Boston *Herald American* and asked
him what he thought. Murdoch said he would consider it
and within a few weeks Ammerman was on the staff of the
Post as joint managing editor. His partner, Van Doorn, was
not told why the appointment had been made, and viewed
it with foreboding.

Ammerman, despite being American, was much more
Murdoch's kind of person. One of the first projects he
masterminded was a series raking over the coals of the
Chappaquiddick scandal. It was based on the allegations of
a woman who said she had been Senator Edward Kennedy's mistress. She maintained that the party at Chappa-

quiddick in 1969, resulting in the death of a young woman, was not the first he had attended there. This was the kind of journalism Murdoch liked, especially because it was conveniently timed just before Kennedy's planned campaign for the Democratic presidential nomination.

Ammerman quickly eclipsed Van Doorn but they both left at about the same time, in mid-1980, Van Doorn to edit *Next*, a new but short-lived magazine, Ammerman to run *The Bulletin*, an afternoon paper in Philadelphia. Van Doorn received no send-off except a farewell call from Don Kummerfeld, Murdoch's chief American executive. The call was interrupted: "Rupert's on the line. I'll call you back," Kummerfeld said, but he did not. That was the last link Van Doorn had with the Murdoch empire. The pair were replaced by a New Zealander and an Englishman.

Chapter 6

TAKING TO THE AIR

> I don't think that a newspaper should own outside interests . . .
> By owning something outside journalism you lay yourself open
> for attack. And newspapers should be above that.
> – *Rupert Murdoch, November 1977.*

While trying to secure his position in New York, Murdoch was not neglecting his interests in Britain and Australia. Early in 1977 Sir Max Aitken, son of Lord Beaverbrook, decided that the Express group of papers – chiefly the *Daily Express*, *Evening Standard* and *Sunday Express* – could not survive without an injection of capital beyond his resources. The *Express* had been brought to prosperity by his father and in the immediate post-war period it and the *Daily Mirror* had been the most successful popular papers in Fleet Street. But now it was being challenged by Lord Rothermere's revived *Daily Mail*, and both were being affected by the vigorous struggle between their down-market competitors, the *Mirror* and the *Sun*. The *Standard*, while for years the more admired of London's two evening papers among Fleet Street opinion-formers, still lagged in circulation behind Rothermere's *Evening News*. Both were losing money and it was doubtful if there was any longer a sufficiently prosperous market in London for two evening papers. Only the *Sunday Express* made money consistently and it was not enough to cancel out the losses of the other two. The trouble was that, unlike most of his competitors, Lord Beaverbrook had never been much inclined to diversify outside newspapers – for instance into television or magazines. This left the group vulnerable and in 1977 Sir Max felt it was time to seek help.

Most of the familiar cast of potential purchasers – familiar from the *Observer* struggle a few months earlier – rushed into the arena. Sir James Goldsmith was an early contender, cobbling up a joint bid with Tiny Rowland's Lonrho group. Rothermere would certainly have liked to buy, but would have wanted to merge the *Standard* with the *News* right away, and probably the *Express* with the *Mail* before too long. Olga Deterding again expressed interest, as did Trafalgar House, the property company that also owned Cunard shipping and hotels.

Early in June the *Sunday Times* reported that Murdoch was now in the hunt. At a meeting with Sir Max the previous week he had offered a ten million pounds capital injection in return for a say in running the papers. "I am a friend of Sir Max's and want to stay so," he said. "I have told him that if at any stage there is a question of closing down the titles, and I can help in any way to avoid it, I would be happy to do so." If Sir Max reflected that it was in these terms Murdoch had come to "rescue" Sir William Carr nine years earlier he did not say so. Indeed, for a time this seemed the deal he favoured, and he was urged by Murdoch's friend Lord Goodman to consider it seriously, if only as a way of keeping out Goldsmith, who then seemed the front runner.

But Murdoch's bid was opposed by Jocelyn Stevens, Beaverbrook Newspapers' flamboyant chief executive. Discretion has never been a Murdoch forte and nobody was in much doubt that among the privileges he sought in return for his ten million pounds was the right to change the management team, and that Stevens did not form a part of the future he envisaged. The two had never been friendly. Stevens had master-minded an *Express* campaign against Murdoch in 1974, attacking the role of *The Sun* and the *News of the World* in unmasking Lord Lambton's sexual peccadilloes. It was in a sense a replay of the Profumo affair, though less grave. Lambton was a junior minister in the Ministry of Defence and also a friend of Stevens: he was a contributor to the *Evening Standard* when Stevens was the paper's managing director.

This was presumably why Murdoch approached Sir Max Aitken direct with his offer of help, without consulting

Stevens. He may have over-estimated the real power that Sir Max, in declining health, was able to exert. He did woo some of the trustees whose approval was needed for any sale, notably John Junor, editor of the profitable *Sunday Express*, and Lord Robens – an acquaintance that would prove important to him three years later in his bid for *The Times*, of which Robens was a national director. He also took care to burnish his contacts with print union leaders. One of the arguments Robens used in favour of Murdoch to the other trustees was that he knew how to handle the unions. Stevens retaliated by pointing out that Murdoch's papers had suffered more union disputes than those of the Express group.

Murdoch offered to buy Sir Max's twenty per cent of the Beaverbrook shares, going so far as to send him a cheque for £1,400,000 with the letter in which the offer was made. But Sir Max was never to cash the cheque, for Stevens's ability at in-fighting won the day and Trafalgar House bought the company for £13,690,000. Murdoch had sustained another defeat but not one that hurt his pride unduly. He had more important things to worry about in America and Australia. Yet he can scarcely have resisted a smirk when Stevens was dismissed by Lord Matthews, the new chairman of the Express group, in 1981.

Discussing Murdoch's bid later, Stevens said: "He's got the appetite of a snake. He'll swallow a sheep if it's passing."

There was one respect in which Murdoch did not measure up to his Sydney rivals, Fairfax and Packer, and that was television. While he controlled more newspapers than either, they both had strong TV stations in Australia's biggest markets, Sydney and Melbourne. All Murdoch owned was Channel 9 in Adelaide and the station in Wollongong, a suburb of Sydney, that he acquired in 1963 hoping – vainly as it turned out – to compete with the central Sydney stations. Apart from the (not insignificant) question of prestige, the ownership of two small stations gave him no muscle when it came to buying programmes and, by extension, deciding what Australians should watch. The bulk of programmes on Australian television are

bought from America. Since Sydney and Melbourne are
the wealthiest markets, companies with stations in both
centres generally buy all the Australian rights to suitable
American material and resell them to stations in smaller
cities. Murdoch's 1963 coup, when he bought all the best
programmes as part of his battle with Packer, had been
strictly a one time aberration.

With only three privately-owned channels in both major
cities, the chance for an outsider to break in was limited. In
1962 his bid for Channel 10 in Sydney was rejected. Since
then, the closest Murdoch had come to getting his foot in
the door was in 1972 when it looked as though Ansett, the
internal airline that owned Channel 0 (later Channel 10) in
Melbourne, might be taken over by Thomas Nationwide
Transport (TNT). If that happened Murdoch was confident
that TNT would hive off the TV interest to him: but in the
event the deal did not take place.

Sydney's third channel, also Channel 10, was owned by
United Telecasters Ltd., a public company headed by Sir
Kenneth Humphreys in which no single group had a controlling interest. Early in 1979 two of the major shareholders indicated a desire to sell their holdings, totalling
twenty-two per cent. Sir Kenneth was worried that another
existing large shareholder would buy the extra shares and
put itself in a position where it could take control.

To thwart this, he acted rather as Sir William Carr had
done. He phoned Murdoch and asked whether he would
like to bid for some of the available shares. Murdoch,
through his Wollongong station, already owned slightly less
than five per cent of United Telecasters. Humphreys' plan
was to let him buy another sixteen per cent and sell the
remaining six per cent of the available stock to the existing
largest shareholder, Amalgamated Wireless Australia
(AWA). This would have left AWA with about twenty-five
per cent and Murdoch with twenty-one per cent, allowing
neither to take full control.

This cosy arrangement was not quite what Murdoch had
in mind. He began a classic takeover move on the Sydney
exchange, seeking as many shares as possible on the open
market. When AWA put in a better bid Murdoch raised his
again and, after cutting a private deal with the owner of one

of the large blocks on offer, he was able to announce that he had 46.6 per cent – effectively a controlling interest.

To satisfy broadcasting rules he had to sell his interest in Wollongong, for nobody is allowed to hold more than five per cent in more than two television stations. He also had to have his ownership approved by the Australian Broadcasting Tribunal, where he was opposed by the Labour Party, still bitter over the performance of Murdoch's papers in the 1975 election, and by Fairfax, by now so obsessed with Murdoch that they opposed any extension of his empire.

Before the tribunal, Murdoch gave a plausible performance of high dudgeon, affecting shock and horror that his motives or record should be impugned. It is a role that, after years of practice, he plays to perfection. He said Fairfax were "trying to paint me as a crazed tycoon who cannot be trusted with a TV company". He maintained the Fairfax papers had run "a gutter campaign" of misleading and insulting articles about him, alleging that the policy of his papers was motivated by personal political ambition. He had, he said, been fighting the Fairfax monopoly since he was twenty-three. And he defended himself against charges that because he spent so much time abroad he was not really an Australian.

"Because I love this country, because my wife and children do, I bring them here as often as I can," he said. "Who else has risked everything to start a national newspaper which goes across the length and breadth of this country? Who employs more than 15,000 people with opportunities to work throughout the world? I started the *Australian* fifteen years ago as a dream. Nearly thirteen million dollars has gone into making that dream a reality."

He was asked whether he would make any changes in management if he acquired the station and he was firm in his denial. Sir Kenneth Humphreys, he vouchsafed, had performed "a magnificent job in steering the company through difficult waters". Moreover, "it would seem from the results of the company, the ratings, the service it is giving the public that it would be madness to contemplate any changes at all . . . I wish to give an assurance to the tribunal that no change is contemplated." He did not let it stop there. Channel 10, he insisted "will continue exactly as it is today". And he concluded: "There has been so much industry hearsay that I am about to march in and fire everybody, which I hope I have laid to rest today. . . It will remain totally independent . . . We will not be interfering."

Unambiguous words, yet two weeks after the tribunal decided in his favour, Channel 10's general manager, Ian Kennon, was dismissed and replaced by Brian Morris, a director of News Ltd. with a background in advertising and no experience in television. Two months later Sir Kenneth Humphreys resigned as chairman, no doubt reflecting, like many Murdoch victims before and since, that he had brought it all on himself. His successor was Murdoch's financial wizard, Mervyn Rich.

Gossips speculated that as soon as he won control of a Sydney channel, Murdoch would go for a Melbourne station to complete his network, but at the tribunal he denied it. "I do not see why I should give up a very profitable station in Adelaide for a loser in Melbourne," he said.

Three months later he could see why very clearly. Sydney–Melbourne was the proper axis for a network, not Sydney–Adelaide. Together, Australia's two largest cities account for sixty per cent of the country's advertising revenue. Of the three Melbourne stations, one was owned by the Packer organisation and effectively impregnable. The second belonged to the Herald and Weekly Times, the group Sir Keith Murdoch had built up that now controlled more than half Australia's newspapers. It was in the hands of a large number of shareholders and possibly vulnerable to a takeover bid. But the most likely target was Channel 10, owned by Ansett – the one he had made a pass at seven years earlier.

The market in Ansett shares had been volatile through most of 1979, because of the enforced liquidation of a finance company the airline group had only recently acquired. The shares had fallen in value and that made them attractive to ambitious speculators. One of the rising stars of Australian finance was Robert Holmes à Court, who, at forty-two, ran the Bell Group, a diversified conglomerate based in Perth, Western Australia, with important interests in transport and some in television. Holmes à Court, born in South Africa, is a lean, canny, soft-spoken man with a distinctly different business style from Murdoch. While Murdoch is an opportunist, Holmes à Court takes the long view. He plans ahead and is prepared to wait years for his aims to be accomplished. That is an unfamiliar technique in Australia, where the outback tradition of the huckster and the fast deal remains a powerful influence. That is why Holmes à Court has been regarded as something of a dilettante in Australian business and why for a long time he was not taken too seriously – that, and because, as Murdoch had discovered when he moved to Sydney nineteen years earlier, it is not in the nature of competitors to make life easy for the *arriviste*.

Holmes à Court began buying Ansett shares on the market and by May he had acquired about five per cent of the company, paying little more than one dollar a share on average. Thomas Nationwide transport, run by Sir Peter Abeles, had a fifteen-per-cent holding left from their abortive 1972 bid, but there was an agreement between Sir Peter and Sir Reginald Ansett that Ansett would have first option on them. But he could not afford to take up his option. Holmes à Court sought to buy the TNT shares, bringing him up to twenty per cent – a sound base for a long-term assault on the company. Abeles agreed to sell and Sir Reginald,who trusted Holmes à Court, would have given permission.

Murdoch was temporarily rich in cash after selling his bauxite holdings in Western Australia for more than fifty million dollars. (Throughout his career he had been excited by the potential of Australian minerals and had made useful profits from investments in that area.) He approached Holmes à Court and Abeles and indicated his intention of buying five per cent of the Ansett shares. When control changed hands, he said, he would like to be allowed to run the television station, or at least to enrol it in a network with his Sydney station.

At this point Ampol, the Australian oil company, made a swift market raid and mopped up twenty per cent of Ansett shares. Abeles decided to defer his deal with Holmes à Court, who instead bought on the open market and brought his holding up to fifteen per cent. By the end of October he and Abeles had fifteen per cent each, Ampol twenty per cent and Murdoch had gone beyond his intention and bought about nine per cent.

Sir Reginald Ansett, at seventy-one, had a reputation as a flamboyant, dictatorial and tough businessman. But with only one-per-cent holding in the company himself he could see the danger of being crushed in the scramble for control. Seeking a survival route, he telephoned Holmes à Court. "Are you just playing with my shares or are you genuinely interested?" he demanded gruffly. When Holmes à Court said he was serious, and that he would run the company personally if he won, Sir Reginald agreed to back him. Now an old though still vigorous man, Sir Reginald viewed business largely in terms of personal relations. He disliked Sir Peter Abeles and was keen that, whatever happened to the company, Sir Peter should be kept away from control.

Holmes à Court then phoned Murdoch and suggested that, to break the log-jam, one of the four contending parties should take control, with the agreement of the others. The necessary share transfers would be made at a mutually negotiated price. Murdoch invited Holmes à Court and Sir Peter Abeles to Cavan for the last weekend in October.

It was mainly a social weekend for it took the trio less than an hour, after the two guests arrived mid-morning on the Saturday, to conclude their business. Sitting in Murdoch's study, they agreed that it was in nobody's interest to let things drift. Holmes à Court strengthened his case by saying that if he took charge he would have the support of Sir Reginald Ansett. The other two quickly agreed to sell their shares to him and he in return undertook that if he was not able to go through with his bid he would sell back to them at the same price. Murdoch phoned Sir Reginald Ansett during the meeting to confirm that Holmes à Court was his favoured candidate. When the old tycoon concurred, Murdoch arranged a meeting between the four men in Sir Reginald's Melbourne office the following Tuesday to complete the deal.

Their business done, the three men were able to enjoy the rest of the Cavan weekend. Over a late barbecue lunch, cooked by Murdoch, they listened to a commentary on the

Cox Plate in Melbourne, in which Holmes à Court's horse Lawman came a creditable third. They inspected the ranch and the livestock. Next morning Murdoch was chef again at breakfast. His two guests left before lunch on Sunday.

At the Tuesday meeting with Sir Reginald they were joined by Ted Harris, of Ampol. Murdoch, although the smallest shareholder of the four contenders, took the initiative. He told Sir Reginald the others would sell to Holmes à Court and stressed that he, Murdoch, wanted the television station. Holmes à Court said he could probably have it but gave no firm commitment. Sir Reginald agreed, with some relief. For months he had felt beleaguered, like a dying man encircled by wolves, any of which could have turned and chewed him up. Now he had seen off three of the wolves and the one that remained seemed the least hungry and dangerous. At any event, it was not the hated Abeles or the disconcerting Murdoch. He could handle young Holmes à Court: Sir Reginald was sure of that.

With the pressure off, Sir Reginald reverted to delaying tactics. He saw no need, he said, to announce the result of the summit meeting there and then. They could draw up a considered statement and release it to the press in a few days. Murdoch, with some amusement, told him that newspapers did not work like that. They would want to know tonight. At that moment a woman from the outer office informed them that three reporters had arrived, from the *Australian*, the *Mirror* and the *Telegraph*. The announcement was made that night, and the following day Sir Reginald held a press conference, giving a glowing account of Holmes à Court's honesty and straight dealing. The engagement was confirmed, the father of the bride was delighted and there seemed no obstacle to the solemnisation of the marriage.

But losing a daughter is never easy, even to so personable a suitor as Robert Holmes à Court. In the succeeding days Sir Reginald began to have his doubts. Now the immediate threat was cleared, he wondered whether he might be able to save everything for himself. The press were saying that, at seventy-one, he had lost his touch, the old fox had been outsmarted at last, and by someone little more than half his age. This hurt. He questioned Holmes à Court why his giant company should be taken over by his comparatively puny outfit from Perth. Should it not be the other way round? And he asked himself why he couldn't do what he had always done, play one party off against the other, and so stay in charge.

In little ways, Sir Reginald's irritation became clear. There had been a well-publicised dispute not long before about his refusal to hire a qualified woman pilot. A newspaper reporter telephoned Holmes à Court's wife and sought her view on the matter. She said she and Robert had been travelling in the Soviet Union recently and had found the female pilots for Aeroflot perfectly competent. Sir Reginald was furious. He phoned Holmes à Court and said: "You tell your wife from me that those Russian women pilots have got balls."

Murdoch was getting impatient. By mid-November, thinking that Sir Reginald might succeed in delaying things indefinitely, he decided to embark on a quite different tack to attain his Melbourne television outlet.

Sir Keith Macpherson had been with the Melbourne Herald and Weekly Times group for forty-three years, since he was sixteen. He had joined as an office boy: one of his first jobs had been to clean Sir Keith Murdoch's fountain pens. He had worked his way up to be chairman and chief executive of the group; a plump, mild, comfortable man.

Normally he arrived in his office on Flinders Street – the same panelled and polished office Sir Keith Murdoch had worked in – sharp at nine. But on Tuesday, November 20th, 1979, Macpherson was about half an hour late, because he had returned only the night before from a trip out of town. On arrival he was told Rupert Murdoch had just phoned to say he was in Melbourne and would stop by at about twenty to ten, hoping to catch him in. He would be bringing with him his chief lieutenant, Ken May, chairman of News Ltd., and nobody had to tell him the way, for he used to visit his father and worked briefly there as a cadet reporter during the holidays.

Macpherson guessed it would be something more than a social call. The pleasantries were short: the two men inquired after each other's health and Macpherson asked Murdoch to what Melbourne owed the pleasure of this, one of his infrequent visits. Murdoch told him. He was going to make a bid for the Herald and Weekly Times group. There was no rancorous argument. Macpherson told Murdoch he had no hope of winning control and Murdoch politely disagreed.

"We'd want you to stay on," Murdoch said.

"Oh yes," May concurred. "We'd want you to do that" – the only words he spoke during the brief encounter.

"What?" rejoined Macpherson. "Like all those other gentlemen who have been sacked so frequently from everything you've taken over?"

"Oh, they were no good," Murdoch declared. "You would have sacked them, too."

"Well, I don't know about that," Macpherson replied. "If I'd already given an undertaking not to, I doubt that I would have."

From the *Herald* office, Murdoch and May went to the Melbourne stock exchange and formally delivered a letter setting out the terms of their bid. It amounted to $126 million for just over half the HWT shares, valuing the company at $250 million. Murdoch's News group was itself valued at only $150 million. As with Holmes à Court and Ansett, the smaller beast was seeking to gobble up the larger. Or, as Jocelyn Stevens would have put it, the snake was swallowing the sheep.

It was not just for that reason that Murdoch's bid for HWT was the epitome of cheek. He could not possibly have expected that it would go unchallenged, for if it succeeded he would control something like three-quarters of the Australian media and wield unprecedented influence. He enjoyed particularly the historical neatness of the attempt. For this was the group that his father had built up – the father who had never been confident that his son had inherited his flair for journalism and business. And Rupert had always felt in some way cheated by the HWT directors. He believed it was they – particularly Sir Keith's successor Sir John Williams – who had so manoeuvred things after his father's death that the *Courier-Mail* in Brisbane had fallen out of family ownership. If he were to succeed now in buying the company, the injury would be avenged.

As soon as his two visitors had left, Macpherson telephoned Robert Falkingham, the chief executive of Fairfax in Sydney. A horrified Falkingham summoned a hurried meeting with his colleagues on the board, who agreed that urgent action had to be taken. Again, the irony was exquisite. Nineteen years earlier it was Fairfax who had launched Murdoch into the big time by favouring him as the buyer of the *Daily Mirror*, in order that the HWT group should not get a foothold in Sydney. What Murdoch was now proposing was not just a foothold, but a giant step under which Fairfax could, they feared, be crushed.

One of the most alarming prospects for Falkingham and his colleagues was that if Murdoch bought HWT he would become a partner of Fairfax in Australian Newsprint Mills and the news agency Australian Associated Press, both controlled jointly by Fairfax and HWT. How could they trust him as a partner? After a telephone talk with Sir Warwick Fairfax, visiting London, Falkingham decided that Fairfax would have to go into the market and buy HWT shares to thwart Murdoch. The shares stood at $2.74 when Murdoch put in his offer of $4. Before long they had gone substantially above the offer price.

News of the bid was reported in Murdoch's *Australian* on a scale usually reserved for war or disaster. The front page carried a photograph of the proprietor across three columns and some eight inches deep, accompanied by an idolatrous interview by the paper's star columnist, Buzz Kennedy.

"Rupert Murdoch is a forty-eight-year-old groupie – a newspaper groupie," Kennedy twittered. "He has had a lifelong love affair with newspapers." Then he broke off to make some sort of apology for the nature of the piece:

"Sympathetic readers who have made a study of the art of walking on eggshells will appreciate that conducting last night's interview had its problems, not all of them to do with having the subject of the interview continually breaking off to make and answer phone calls, issue instructions and display an eager elation and energy which belied an enormously strenuous day – and days before."

There was a desultory attempt to give a thumbnail sketch

of Murdoch, his style of administration – "What I do is delegate, then interfere" – and his personal foibles: "I inherited a Presbyterian conscience. My family calls it stinginess." And Murdoch declared, for the benefit of people who shared the Broadcasting Tribunal's doubts about his being an authentic Australian: "Even before the idea of the Herald offer came, my wife and I decided we would make our base in Australia. The children will go to school here – although they haven't been told that yet. We will be back here, whatever comes of the Herald affair." Like many of Murdoch's publicly stated intentions, that was not to be.

The takeover bid for the Herald group lasted just two hectic days. Faced with the determination of Fairfax to deny him control, and a threatened intervention by the Trade Practices Commission, there was little Murdoch could do. Fairfax spent $52,300,000 to buy a fifteen-percent stake in the group. While they achieved their object of thwarting Murdoch it was an expensive manoeuvre, for as soon as Murdoch withdrew, the value of their holding fell by some twenty million dollars – and they were still saddled with the interest on the borrowed capital. It is a measure of their paranoia about Murdoch that they felt it was money well spent. Murdoch, although he failed to gain control, came away with a handy profit of some three million dollars on his shares and was so pleased with his cleverness that he allowed the *Australian*, next day, to describe in detail how he had managed to retreat in such good order, even if the ethics of the operation were questionable.

Murdoch knew that once the word spread that he was pulling out the share price would drop from its level then of $5.52. To mislead the market – and Fairfax in particular – he worked through two brokers. To sell his shares he used May and Mellor, a broker not previously associated with him, while his regular broker, J. B. Were, pretended to be still in the market as a buyer. Thus when the new broker put the shares on sale at $5.52 and Fairfax's broker tried to push the price down, the second Murdoch broker would express an interest at just below that price, forcing a still desperate Fairfax to pay the full sum. In the first hour of trading on

November 22nd, Murdoch unloaded the 3,500,000 shares he had acquired during the previous two days. Then he announced his withdrawal from the contest and the share price fell to $3.45. Not a man to let such a coup go by without pressing home a propaganda advantage, Murdoch called the Fairfax rescue of the Herald "two incompetent managements throwing themselves into each other's arms at the expense of their shareholders".

A week later Murdoch was back on the Ansett trail as the deal between Sir Reginald and Holmes à Court collapsed. Part of the agreement had been that, when the Bell Group bought Ansett, Bell's transport operations in Perth should in turn be sold to the airline. After stalling for a month, Sir Reginald and the Ansett board decided not to go through with that part of it and announced that decision, without first telling Holmes à Court. Hearing the news on television in his hotel room, Holmes à Court rushed angrily to Sir Reginald's office and told him the whole deal was off. Sir Reginald did not believe him. "The deal's still on," he said. "Cool down. Things will look better in the morning." Holmes à Court replied: "By morning I'll have sold my shares and I'll be back in Perth."

He returned to his hotel and phoned Murdoch, tracking him to a tennis court where he was playing with former Wimbledon champion John Newcombe. He offered him his Ansett shares on the same terms Murdoch had given him – $2.50, half down, the balance in twelve months. "How long have I got?" Murdoch asked. "The duration of this call," was the reply. At the end of the call, Holmes à Court told the press that the deal was done. It was announced on the evening television news. A flabbergasted Sir Reginald made repeated calls to Holmes à Court trying to get him to change his decision, but it was too late.

With Holmes à Court's shares, Murdoch had twenty per cent. Then he arranged to buy the Ampol shares, which gave him forty per cent, and he kept on buying in the market. Abeles had fifteen per cent, so between them they had control. Holmes à Court came away with a profit of eleven million dollars on the shares and was given a standing ovation by shareholders at his annual general meeting.

He said later: "After I withdrew I had a long philosophical discussion with Rupert about winning."

Murdoch had not quite won yet, for Sir Reginald Ansett mounted a rearguard action. He told Murdoch he would not agree to the registration of his new shares. "Good luck to you," Murdoch replied, and predicted a long battle in the courts. Then Sir Reginald appealed to the Broadcasting Tribunal to veto the deal because it would mean Murdoch had violated the law by owning more than five per cent of four TV stations – double the maximum allowable. But Murdoch had already assured the tribunal that he would sell Ansett's station in Brisbane and his own in Adelaide once he gained control, and his assurance was accepted. When Sir Reginald discovered he would get no government help in warding off Murdoch – who had, after all, made it his business to cultivate Malcolm Fraser – he capitulated. Murdoch then agreed that Thomas Nationwide Transport should increase its stake in the company and Sir Peter Abeles become joint chief executive of Ansett with Murdoch – the one outcome Sir Reginald had striven so hard to avoid.

Sir Reginald stayed on for a while as chairman but, like Sir William Carr ten years earlier, he found that this position gave him no share of power. His impotence was symbolised right away, when Murdoch decided that Sir Reginald's personal helicopter, in which he was accustomed to commute to Melbourne the thirty miles from his home in Mount Eliza, could be better used by the television station for fast-breaking news and traffic reports. In theory Sir Reginald was still entitled to use it, but in practice it was always engaged on other business. He commented: "Of recent times I don't take any notice of what anybody says. I have never had that experience with people like I am dealing with at the present time. I have always been able to make my verbal arrangements. My word's been my bond and I have expected it to be with people I am dealing with. That sort of attitude and principle in business today has gone right out the door."

Early in 1980 Sir Reginald left with a payoff of five million dollars and bought a company farm to retire to. The following year he died.

Before he could cement his control of Channel 10 in Melbourne, Murdoch had to endure another long series of hearings and once again was forced to listen to complaints by the Australian Journalists' Association, the Labour Party and others who felt that the overt political partisanship of his newspapers disqualified him from owning a TV station. The journalists' strike of 1975 was brought up again, as was the question whether or not he was a true Australian. And this time there were new charges that, since his acquisition of Ansett, Murdoch's papers had given the airline unduly favourable publicity at the expense of the government-owned competitor, Trans-Australia Airlines (TAA). The Broadcasting Tribunal at first rejected him as the proprietor of Channel 10 on grounds of public interest. Then the government obligingly amended the Broadcasting Act to circumscribe the power of the tribunal. They decreed that the only criteria as to a person's suitability to own a TV station should be financial and technical competence and moral fitness. It was hard to believe that this was not done as a specific favour to Murdoch in return for his past support. The new legislation made it inevitable that, on appeal, the tribunal's decision was reversed. Murdoch had his national television network at last – and an airline to go with it.

One unforeseen result of the Ansett purchase was to embroil Murdoch in the suspicion of a scandal involving President Jimmy Carter. In the end, a Senate inquiry and several newspaper investigations could find no evidence that either had behaved improperly: but the story sheds an intriguing light on Murdoch's astute business methods. He exposed the limitations as negotiators of the supposed financial wizards in one of the most important government agencies in Washington.

Ansett and TAA had for years operated a cosy pact that imposed clear limits on the extent of their competition. They used the same kind of aircraft and flew them on almost exactly the same schedule between the major Australian cities. This meant that they split the market fifty-fifty and both could make a reasonable profit. That kind of arrangement is anathema to someone of Murdoch's com-

petitive spirit. He was determined to enter into battle with
TAA. If he could win sixty per cent of the traffic he would
count it a success. The risk that he would end up with forty
per cent was one he was prepared to take.

In November 1979, when Murdoch acquired Ansett,
both airlines were in the process of renewing their fleet of
jet passenger planes. On December 7th TAA ordered four
wide-bodied Airbus A300B4s, made by a consortium of
European countries, and took an option on another eight.
If past practice was to be followed, Ansett would be
expected to put in a similar order, and Airbus had promised
that they could expect delivery of the first aircraft almost
simultaneously with TAA, on the same favourable financing terms.

Murdoch was disinclined to accept an Airbus order as a
fait accompli and wondered whether there was an alternative. The most advanced American competitor to the European jet was the Boeing 767, so new it was not yet in
service. Murdoch decided it was the one he wanted, provided he could get financing on at least as good terms as
those Airbus offered.

The Export-Import Bank exists to foster American ex-
ports by offering low-interest credit to overseas buyers of
American goods. In its modern headquarters, a short walk
from the White House in Washington, are often to be found
lobbyists for the larger industrial concerns, pleading the
case for generous loans to their customers. One of the most
frequent visitors was Jack Pierce, the treasurer of the
Boeing Aircraft Company, based in Seattle. The country's
largest manufacturer of aeroplanes, much of Boeing's business was done with foreign airlines. In January 1980 Pierce
started to sound out officials at the bank about how much
help they could give his company, in terms of a low-rate
loan to Ansett, if the airline should decide it wanted
Boeings.

The American consulate in Melbourne and the embassy
in Canberra had raised the prospect of an Ansett/Boeing
deal in cables to the State Department in December. They
said Ansett favoured the more economical Boeing 767 but
might be forced to go along with TAA in buying the Airbus
because of the earlier delivery dates and the generous

financing terms. A team of officials from the Export-Import Bank went to Australia at the end of January. At a meeting with Ansett officials on February 15th they were told that the airline had all but decided to buy Boeings. The late delivery dates of the 767s compared with those of the Airbuses would be offset by buying additional narrow-bodied 727 and 737 planes and using increased frequencies as a marketing weapon against TAA's newer and bigger jets. The bank team expected a formal loan application to be made while they were in Australia, but by the time they left on February 22nd Ansett had still not decided finally what combination of planes they wanted to order.

The president of the Export-Import Bank was John Moore, an affable, distinguished southern lawyer, one of the many old Georgia associates Carter appointed to federal positions when he became President. (The senior among them was Bert Lance, the banker, who had had to resign as head of the Office of Management and Budget because of questions about loans his banks had made to members of his family.) During the "transition period" before Carter took office, Moore was given the job of screening potential government appointees for any conflict of interest. He had earlier served on the Georgia mental health commission with Carter's wife Rosalynn.

The senior partner in Moore's Atlanta law firm was Phillip Alston, an even closer associate of Carter. Alston, born in 1911, was eighteen years older than Moore. "I sort of feel like I helped raise Mr Moore," he told the Senate Banking Committee during their hearings into the Ansett loan affair. He had a similar paternal relationship with Carter who, on becoming President, asked Alston to be his ambassador in Australia.

One of the most important duties of American ambassadors is to foster trade between their own country and the one to which they are accredited. That is why the embassy in Canberra had alerted the State Department in December about the possibility of a Boeing purchase by Ansett. Yet despite his friendship with Moore, Alston, according to his evidence before the committee, did not personally get involved in the transaction until late in February. At two earlier meetings (one of them quite fortuitous) with principals in the case, the subject, he said, did not come up.

On January 27th Ambassador Alston flew to America to help prepare for a forthcoming visit to Washington by Malcolm Fraser, the Australian Prime Minister. By chance, as he was leaving the VIP room at Sydney airport, he noticed Murdoch, whom he had met once or twice socially in Canberra. They waved to each other. Murdoch went to sit in the upstairs portion of the plane's first-class section. About half an hour after take-off Alston climbed the stairs to say hello and they exchanged pleasantries for less than a minute, according to the ambassador's estimate. Murdoch was on his way to Seattle to see Boeing and got off at Los Angeles. From there he would go to see Moore in Washington, but the subject of the proposed loan did not come up in this airborne talk, Alston said. And neither, he affirmed, was it discussed when he met Moore and his wife, and another of their former Georgia law partners and his wife, for dinner at the Metropolitan Club in Washington on February 4th.

Alston, then, went back to Australia apparently without having discussed the Ansett aircraft purchase with anyone. Murdoch, when he had completed his visit to Seattle, flew east, where he had two important engagements.

Since the autumn of 1979 the people running Carter's re-election campaign in New York had been anxious to arrange a meeting between Murdoch and the President. If Carter was to beat Senator Edward Kennedy in the Democratic primary in New York, it was important, they thought, that he should get the endorsement of the *New York Post*. Joel McCleary, a former White House aide, was head of Carter's New York campaign. He worked to arrange a meeting through Howard Rubenstein, who did public relations work for Murdoch. Dates had been arranged in November and December but Murdoch had cried off from both because he had to be out of the country. At the end of January a third date was agreed: February 19th.

In Seattle the people at Boeing had told Murdoch it would help him get a favourable loan from the bank if he went and put his case personally to Moore and his fellow officials. Murdoch told Pierce, the treasurer, about his date with Carter and suggested that, to get maximum value from his visit to Washington, the Eximbank meeting should be fixed for the 19th also. Pierce telephoned Moore on the 12th and made the appointment for 11.15 a.m. He pointed out that Murdoch, because of his arrangement to see the President, would not be able to join them for lunch afterwards.

Moore had an appointment outside the office on the morning of the 19th and returned a bit late to find the Ansett and Boeing party being received in the lobby by Charles Houston, vice-president of the bank's Asian division. Moore had left the memo with Murdoch's name on it on his desk in the office. He has a poor memory for names and at first could not remember who Murdoch was, but he plunged in to join the party, forced to mumble when the time came to address his guests directly. During the meeting, everyone's identity was clarified.

Murdoch felt himself in a reasonably strong position to drive a hard bargain. He had in his pocket a firm offer of financing for four Airbus planes that he was sure would be extended to the full twelve envisaged. The loan was to be in a "basket" of currencies – forty per cent French francs at an interest rate of 8.75 per cent, forty per cent German marks at 6.5 per cent and twenty per cent U.S. dollars at 9.25 per cent. This worked out at a blended rate of a shade under eight per cent. Though the Eximbank loan would all be in U.S. dollars, Murdoch insisted that the interest rate should not exceed that eight per cent.

Commercial interest rates were then running at around seventeen per cent but the bank customarily offers much better terms to overseas customers buying American products. However, the bank's recent rate for aircraft sales had seldom gone below 8.5 per cent. And when talking in terms of $657 million, the amount of the original loan request, the extra half per cent means a difference of more than three million dollars a year in repayments.

There was also the question of the differential rates between currencies. Although it was impossible to predict precisely how exchange rates would move during the term of the loan, the conventional wisdom among financiers was that in the long term the mark and franc would increase in value against the dollar. That was why interest rates on the dollar loans were higher than those for the other two currencies. On this assumption, the interest rate on a dollar loan by Eximbank to Ansett could have been higher than 7.95 per cent but still competitive with the Airbus package.

When Moore made this point at the meeting, Murdoch contested the reasoning. He used the peculiar argument that he was not worried about taking on obligations in francs and marks because he was confident of the strength of the *Australian* dollar against other currencies, due to the country's healthy gas reserves, mineral resources and other bull points. Yet the strength of the Australian currency was not in question – the argument hinged on the future performance of the *American* dollar vis-à-vis the franc and the mark. But Murdoch insisted on his point and repeated it strongly in a follow-up letter to Moore the next day, stressing also that to match the Airbus offer the repayment of the loan would have to be over twelve years, although documents showed the Airbus term for repayment was ten years.

Murdoch and Pierce were negotiating with every trick they knew. They were adamant that a decision on the loan had to be made by February 29th, just nine days after the meeting, because that was when Murdoch's option on the first four Airbus A300 aircraft would run out: if he did not confirm the order by then but decided later to go ahead with the Airbus purchase, he would get his planes later than TAA.

At 12.30 Murdoch left the bank for his lunch appointment with President Carter. The lunch, timed as it was in the middle of the loan negotiations, gave rise to the subsequent suspicions and the Banking Committee's investigation. When press reporters got wind of the meeting, they could scarcely be blamed for suspecting that Murdoch was asking Carter to intervene with the bank to ensure that he got the best possible terms for the loan – and that in return Murdoch was offering the *New York Post*'s support for Carter in the Democratic primary. Exhaustive official and unofficial inquiries eventually turned up no evidence of such a link. Three days after the lunch the *Post* announced its support for Carter but the decision had been taken some weeks earlier, at a meeting attended by Murdoch, Wood, Rothwell, Ammerman and other senior executives at the paper. Their motive was to oppose the too-liberal Kennedy rather than to make a positive gesture of support for Carter; and the decision did not imply that Carter would keep Murdoch's backing when the actual election came in November. At the White House lunch the talk was of political affairs. The loan, according to Murdoch's evidence, was not mentioned. And he told friends that he had been unimpressed with the menu: hamburgers.

Murdoch, drawing on his rich experience of negotiations of all kinds, could see he had reached the point at which he should apply the most extreme pressure. He penned his cordial but no-nonsense letter to Moore. And he telephoned Boeing in Seattle to restate what he called his minimum conditions. The loan would have to be for 7.9 per cent over twelve years. "Our deal is dead unless it's eight per cent or less," wrote Clarence Wilde, the Boeing executive who took Murdoch's call, in an internal memorandum.

At the same time, Boeing's representative in Australia was working on Alston to see if the ambassador could put pressure on the bank. Alston telephoned Moore in Washington to stress his concern that the loan should be made, in the interests of trading relations between the two countries. Both men insist they did not relate the question of the loan to Murdoch's publishing interests, his visit to the White House, or their old friend Carter's re-election prospects.

If Murdoch's deadline was to be met, the bank would have to move fast. Their procedure for approving large loans like this was that, following a preliminary request, officials would draw up a report on the loan and its background and this would be given to the bank's directors for a decision at their weekly meeting on Tuesdays. They would normally receive papers relating to the cases on the Friday before the meeting, so that they would have the weekend to look over them. Only two of the bank's four directors (not counting Moore) were available for the meeting on Tuesday, February 26th. They were Thibault de St Phalle, an expert in international finance, and Mrs Margaret Kahliff, who had been an independent businesswoman. No papers relating to the Ansett negotiations were handed to them on the previous Friday, and neither of them knew of the visit Murdoch had made to the bank earlier that week.

It was the custom for the directors to meet early – shortly after 8 a.m. – before their Tuesday meetings. Under the so-called "sunshine laws" applying to the conduct of public bodies like the Eximbank, they are not allowed to engage in substantive discussion of forthcoming cases at these preliminary get-togethers. That has to be done in a properly convened session where a record is taken. The early meetings are to discuss "housekeeping" matters relating to the conduct of the bank: if any of the directors tries to raise an issue of substance about a loan, he or she is normally slapped down by the others. At the early meeting on February 26th, Moore came close to putting himself out of bounds when he told the other two that the Ansett case they were going to discuss that morning was especially interesting: they should give it particular attention.

De St Phalle and Mrs Kahliff were puzzled; neither was aware of any Ansett case, because the documents had not been among those they took home on Friday. Both hurried back to their offices and found the relevant file on their desks. It had been placed there late the previous afternoon. They had less than half an hour to digest the outline of the case before their main meeting began.

Everything had been rushed. Dave Peacock, a loan officer at the bank, apologised for any "rough spots" in his memorandum about the loan. "We had to put it together in about twenty-four hours," he said. And he expressed reservations about the plan. The bank was being "put to the wall on a competitive deal". Referring to the haste, he added: "I think the negotiating tactics of Ansett and Boeing should make us very wary of this deal."

Moore, following his conversation with his old friend Alston, was now thoroughly committed to the loan and rounded on Peacock for being unfair, bearing in mind that Ansett had been involved in a take-over battle the previous year that had delayed the conclusion of plans for new aircraft. "I really do think it's important not to hold any hard feelings against either Boeing or Ansett," he said.

Because of the short time for preparation, discussion at

the meeting was highly confused. There were two main points of argument: the interest rate and the number of planes that should be covered by the low-interest loan. Although the terms offered by Airbus were initially only for four planes, it was assumed that they would be extended to cover the other eight that would eventually be needed. But against that, as de St Phalle pointed out forcefully, Boeing and Ansett were asking for a loan of below eight per cent to cover twenty-five planes – twelve would be the 767s that competed directly with Airbus, the others, the smaller 727s and 737s, needed to increase capacity during the period that TAA had wide-bodied planes and Ansett had not.

De St Phalle did not see why they should get the smaller planes, which did not have serious European competition, at eight per cent, but Moore was at first adamant. "I'm convinced that whether we like it or not it's an all or nothing situation," he said. "We cover this whole thing, eighty-five-per-cent cover at eight per cent, or there's just no decision."

But de St Phalle persevered. He suggested financing a lower portion of the purchase price of the smaller planes – around forty per cent – and increasing the rate on them to something like 8.5 per cent, closer to the bank's recent average for aircraft. Of course, he pointed out, Murdoch would say it was all or nothing, because that was the way he negotiated. Thinking back to that quarrelsome dinner party where they last met, de St Phalle said: "Murdoch is one of the brightest men that I have ever come across . . . Murdoch is a really shrewd negotiator and I don't blame him for doing that, but I think that we ought to exercise control."

Mrs Kahliff concurred with the judgment on Murdoch. "I think that he is very, very aggressive," she commented.

Several aspects of the deal troubled de St Phalle. He was puzzled by the last minute nature of the documentation. Murdoch had visited the bank, he now learned, the previous Tuesday, so there was no reason why the staff should not have been able to make most of the background documents available by the Friday. Nobody seemed certain about the details of the rival offer from Airbus – how many planes it covered, how long the repayment term was, and so forth. Finally there was Moore's unusual decision to go personally to see officials at the Treasury and Federal Reserve Bank, who have to approve the bank's loans. It was presumably a bid to pre-empt likely objections on the grounds of extravagance. In most cases Moore would contact these two officials by telephone or written memorandum.

By the time the board met again two days later, some of the questions had been resolved. The Airbus offer was for only four wide-bodied aircraft and there was no written commitment from them to finance any more on the same terms, although there could have been a verbal understanding. The term of the loan was ten years. All this confirmed de St Phalle's mistrust of Murdoch as a negotiator, and others at that second board meeting agreed with him. John Lange of the Treasury observed that "the decision maker in this case is playing Mexican standoff with us", a phrase meaning roughly that he is playing hard to get. And George Heidrich, deputy vice-president for Asia at the bank, said: "It seems to me that the fellow that talks about an eight-per-cent dollar rate is either financially naive or thinks we are," to which Moore replied: "The latter."

In the end, though, the result of all this impressive wizardry in negotiation was much less satisfactory for Murdoch than the deal he originally sought – a point overlooked in most of the critical and suggestive articles written afterwards. He won his eight per cent rate all right, but only on five aircraft instead of the twenty-five in the package. These were five 767s, broadly equivalent in seating capacity to the four Airbus A300s for which he had the rival financing commitment. The loan for the five was just over $200 million, less than a third of the original request. It represented eighty-five per cent of the cost of the aircraft. Loans for the 727s and 737s, amounting to some eighty-nine million dollars, were at around 8.4 per cent, covering fifty per cent and forty per cent of the purchase price only. The offer was finalised just before the February 29th deadline – which Airbus promptly extended, as most had assumed they would.

Moore had one more try at improving the deal. He

drafted a letter to Murdoch saying that future purchases of 767s up to twelve would be financed at the same favourable rate. De St Phalle saw it before it went out and had it altered to read that terms for later loans would be discussed in the light of circumstances prevailing at the time. Murdoch, despite his uncompromising earlier posture, accepted the bank's terms.

Looking back at the affair later, de St Phalle remains puzzled. "I just don't understand the transaction," he says. "I don't know how to explain this. I don't know why the board wasn't given the time to consider the transaction. I don't know why this rush was on on that particular day. I don't know why there wasn't an extension of time. I don't know why the people who reported seemed to know so little about the transaction. I don't know why they hadn't made the usual checks with the French. I don't know why Mr Moore thought it important to go personally and check with the Treasury Department or with the Federal Reserve." But he stresses that he knows nothing to suggest Moore had any political motive. "I consider Mr Moore to be an extraordinarily bright individual and a very honourable person and I just can't conceive of his doing anything in a given deal because it had political implications."

It took a little less than three weeks for the press to begin to question the deal. It began with an article in the *New York Times* on March 18th – the day after Murdoch formally announced the Boeing purchase at a Melbourne press conference. The article stressed doubts among officials at the Bank and Treasury about the low interest rate given on the 767s, and the apparent lack of financial logic in equating the rate for a dollar loan with the rate for the basket of currencies. And it raised the possibility of a link with the *New York Post*'s endorsement of Carter. Other papers soon started to run follow-up stories.

The Senate Committee on Banking, Housing and Urban Affairs is charged with overseeing the Export-Import Bank. Its chairman is Senator William Proxmire of Wisconsin, who has made a reputation as a rigorous watchdog against waste in public spending. Three days after the first *New York Times* article appeared, he wrote to Moore raising questions about the loan. He pointed out that the

New York Post's endorsement of President Carter so soon after the bank gave its preliminary approval for the deal "gives an appearance of impropriety and leaves the impression that a key government agency may have been politicised to further the President's re-election".

He wrote also to the Treasury Department and the Federal Reserve Bank. The Treasury, in reply, sent a copy of an internal memorandum criticising the loan as one which "fritters away bank resources" by offering overgenerous terms. And the equation of interest on a dollar loan with that on a mixed-currency loan was described as "interest rate illusion at its most galling".

After considering these replies, the committee held hearings on the question on May 12th and 13th, in their hearing room on the fifth floor of the Dirksen Building next to the Capitol. It is a modern, fairly anonymous building, used mainly as offices for senators. The hearing room seats about eighty people. On the afternoon of the 13th, when Murdoch was due to give evidence, there were almost double that number of spectators, many of them reporters. They stood leaning against the walls. The press table was jammed full and television cameras were everywhere. Members of the committee sat round a horseshoe-shaped table and the witnesses faced them.

They had no power to make Murdoch attend but he agreed to do so. He was the last witness, accompanied by Donald Kummerfeld, his most important American executive, and Howard Squadron, his New York lawyer. Murdoch's evidence was fluent, given in a kind of aggrieved tone suggesting that he was always being maligned unfairly, but it was something he had learned to live with.

"No matter what your approach is to interest and cost computation, the Exim loan proposal cannot be regarded as more favourable than the Airbus loan offer. Even after the Exim commitment was received, it was a very close question for Ansett . . . Nobody at Ansett, myself included, ever regarded the Exim loan proposal as containing unusually favourable terms. . . The Exim loan application was not made until after the last luncheon appointment (February 19th) had already been scheduled. Neither at the luncheon nor at any other time – with the President or anybody else connected with the White House or the President's campaign – did I or anybody else representing Ansett discuss the purchase of Boeing aircraft or the Exim loan." And he ended his prepared statement with a pious homily: "I publish newspapers and have been subject to misleading publicity in the past so I am personally able to keep this situation in perspective. It would be most unfortunate if other potential foreign purchasers from American companies that compete with aggressive and successful foreign producers like Airbus were to receive a signal that American financing is unavailable or unnecessarily difficult to obtain."

Under questioning, Murdoch began truculently. When he was read a passage critical of him from an article by William Safire in the *New York Times* he responded: "He works for other people who have other barrels to roll." But he did admit to an error of judgment in going to meet Moore at the bank on the day he went for lunch at the White House. "I'm sorry I agreed to do that . . . I'm sorry we had this meeting with Eximbank and it could have been misinterpreted in this way. We have always been extremely careful to keep our duties as publishers quite separate from any other business interest, although we all behaved in the most responsible way as businessmen and all behaviour involves a public duty."

Senator Donald Riegle of Michigan was bemused by all this self-righteousness. "Everyone comes in and says 'not me' . . . Maybe what we have here is a series of innocent parties who were involved in a situation that certainly has a disturbing appearance." Riegle did manage to catch Murdoch out on a claim that his attacks on Senator Edward Kennedy had been made before he bought Ansett. The Senator brandished a March edition with the headline DESPERATE TED STORMS NEW YORK and in January TED KENNEDY'S SECRET PARTIES.

"The *Post* really worked Senator Kennedy over," Riegle said. "This may be the norm in other places or in other countries. It's certainly not the norm here . . . If somebody did want to get a good reception here in Washington from the administration, it just might occur to somebody that this might be one way to do it."

Murdoch said: "I see my papers. I don't write them."

Senator Riegle went on: "If you had been running the equivalent pieces on President Carter, you wouldn't have been invited to lunch. I think that's one way not to get invited to lunch."

Murdoch picked that up with characteristic bravado. "On the contrary, sir, we ran in another newspaper with five times the circulation of that, an extremely embarrassing article about President Carter's family on page one."

"Which paper would that have occurred in?"

"The *Star*, which has a circulation of 3.5 million. That was about President Carter . . ."

"I am not a regular reader. I have heard of it."

"Well, you're missing something."

"I may be glad I am missing it. I am not sure."

The session ended with pointed questions from Senator Proxmire. Murdoch replied that Ansett and the loan were not mentioned in the lunchtime discussion. It was about political issues including the Iran hostages and New York City's finances. "Nobody even knew that I had an investment in an airline, no knowledge at all . . . I just told President Carter that we expected to be endorsing him in the primary, although we hadn't made up our mind about the general election, which he didn't seem very pleased with."

It was clear that Murdoch had made a good impression on the committee and Senator Proxmire was patronising enough to say so:

"You are a remarkable man, Mr Murdoch. We have had a lot of witnesses before this committee but I was especially impressed with what a quick study you are. You seem to know a whale of a lot about an industry which you've just gotten into. You are very refreshing, intelligent and an effective witness, and responsive."

"Thank you, sir."

"You are also able to win your way with the Export-Import Bank."

Nine days after the hearing, Proxmire wrote to Moore to inform him of the committee's conclusions. The letter criticised bank officials for being "sloppy" because of their "failure to question the factual assertions and bargaining tactics of Mr Rupert Murdoch of Ansett Airlines and Mr Jack Pierce of the Boeing Company". It said the loan offer was too generous, resulting in a waste of public money. It added that the bank seemed to devote too great a proportion of its resources to loans for aircraft purchases and concluded: "Bank lending at interest rates several percentage points below the US Government's cost of borrowing constitutes an extraordinary subsidy and, if continued, could erode the financial soundness of the bank."

Proxmire's letter did not mention the allegations of collusion between Murdoch and President Carter, and the hearings had uncovered no solid evidence to substantiate the charges. In the wake of Watergate, questing reporters seek conspiracy everywhere and some who examined the affair remain convinced that the full story has not been uncovered. Yet the theory seems palpably improbable. It was never conceivable that the *New York Post*, vehemently critical of Senator Kennedy's advocacy of improved welfare services and his liberal philosophy, would support the senator in the primary, and Carter's staff were aware of this. So a promise to back Carter was scarcely credible as a bargaining chip. A pledge to support him in the election proper in November would have been of real value but in the event the *Post* plumped for Reagan. An alternative theory is that the political implications of lending federal money to an influential newspaper proprietor occurred independently to Carter's old Georgia chums, Alston and Moore, with no prompting from the White House. Yet they deny it and there is no evidence to suggest they are not telling the truth.

The incident is significant chiefly for the reason Proxmire suggested as he thanked Murdoch for his appearance as a witness, and later in his letter to Moore. It shows Murdoch as a ruthless and single-minded negotiator, firm and even self-righteous in going after the best possible deal and not too squeamish to bend the facts a bit to attain it: yet flexible enough to settle quickly for less when he sees he is not going to get all he wants. For the clinching fact is that the loan he was finally granted was less than a third of the amount originally envisaged and only part of it was at the eight-per-cent rate. If Carter had intervened as was suggested, he would surely have done a bit better for Murdoch.

Chapter 7

SHOWDOWN AT GRAY'S INN ROAD

To buy *The Times* would be a highly irresponsible thing to do for your shareholders.
– *Rupert Murdoch, November 1979.*

A man who has known Murdoch longer than most is Richard Searby, a Melbourne lawyer who was at school and university with him and has been an important business adviser for years. He is now chairman of the News Corporation Ltd. and Deputy Chairman of Times Newspapers. In Simon Regan's book on Murdoch, Searby was quoted as being responsible for possibly the most useful – if scarcely profound – characterisation of him: "Fundamentally, Rupert's a fidget." In a letter to *The Times* in 1983 Searby denied ever having said it, but in any case it does support an impression others have of him. Robert Holmes à Court put it a bit differently: "Rupert loves the macro-deal." And when one macro-deal is in the bag, he cannot wait to get started on the next.

By the middle of 1980 his Sydney-Melbourne television network was formed and he had bought the expensive new jets for his airline. What else was there to do? For sure, he could always slip down to the stone and write a headline or two, fire one of his editors or deal with any of the hundreds of things a tycoon can involve himself in. But where was the next really big challenge to come from?

Throughout his career, Murdoch had repeatedly been asked whether he would like to own *The Times* of London. Often the question would be put almost satirically, for *The Times*, though with an insignificant circulation and scarcely ever profitable, was still Britain's most famous paper, a symbol of access to the upper echelons of power. It represented everything in Britain he disliked – subservience to authority based on tradition rather than on merit, a toffee-nosed morality and a general air of tedium. Even when it did resort to light relief – in its letters page and sometimes its Diary column – it was of a whimsical variety that Murdoch found unappealing. His answers to the oft-put question would generally be discouraging.

In an Australian television interview in 1971 he was asked about speculation that he was interested in *The Times* of London and that he planned to own the *New York Times* within ten years. He replied: "I think you can certainly discount the latter. As for the former, you can discount that, too. Without any disrespect, I think Lord Thomson might be persuaded to make a gift of the London *Times*. We have other ideas there." More recently, in November 1979, he had said: "To buy *The Times* would be a highly irresponsible thing to do for your shareholders."

Indeed it would have been, for that was the point at which *The Times* and the *Sunday Times* were just struggling back to life after a debilitating year of non-publication, during which their survival was many times called into question. Not many papers would have appeared again after so long a break. That they did was in large measure due to the unique position *The Times* holds in British life. Even people who do not read it regularly find it hard to imagine doing without it over the long term.

The dispute that caused the suspension was partly over new printing technology – an issue that has plagued the paper throughout its 200-year history. When John Walter founded it as the *Daily Universal Register* in 1785, he did so to advertise a new printing process called logographics in which type was bunched into logograms of several letters instead of being set letter by letter. It proved no cheaper or quicker than the conventional single-letter setting and by the time the name of the paper had been changed to *The Times*, in 1788, the process had been abandoned. Walter became more interested in what went into his newspaper than in how it was produced, and on March 25th, 1788, he published a long, self-important manifesto of its ideals and virtues, starting by criticising its rivals who "too frequently present details of events that never took place and prostitute the language of eulogium to persons and things unworthy of public favour". *The Times*, on the other hand, employed "correspondents of the first literary abilities which this country can boast . . . and the repetition of whose names, were we at liberty to publish them, would, on the first mention, insure to this paper a sale infinitely more extensive than that of any contemporary publication." Parliamentary debates would be reported impartially, "our reporters being of the first class, equally incapable of perverting the language of debate to serve the purposes of faction, or to support the popularity of administration". Arrangements had been made to get the earliest foreign news as well; and finally "to indecent language or double entendre, no place shall be given in *The Times*, nor shall it contain any passage capable of insulting the eye, or ear, or modesty, or suffusing the cheeks of innocence with a blush".

Despite that hype, as it would nowadays be called, the paper lived up to some of its promises. It had the best and earliest reports of the French Revolution in 1789 – the year Walter began serving a sixteen-month jail sentence for libelling a handful of royal dukes. The paper soon reached a healthy circulation of some 5,000.

It was under Walter's son, John Walter II, that *The Times* first rose to a position of great influence. By 1803, at the age of only twenty-seven, the younger Walter was both editor and manager of the paper. His refusal to enter into corrupt deals with postal officials to receive journals from abroad forced him to create his own foreign news service – the first London paper to have one. Amongst early scoops were the death of Nelson in 1805, and the capture of Flushing in 1809, of which *The Times* had news before the government. The nickname "The Thunderer" dates from this period, provoked by the outspoken editorials of Edward Sterling and John Stoddart, who edited the paper briefly before he fell out with Walter and was replaced by the redoubtable Thomas Barnes, editor for twenty-four years until 1841.

The paper's second attempt at technological innovation

was more successful. A steam press was introduced in 1814, after being installed in great secrecy to overcome opposition from the printers.

The pressmen were astounded when Walter walked into the press room and told them: "Gentlemen, *The Times* is already printed – by steam." Thirteen years later two staff engineers invented a better press that printed papers at a rate of 5,000 an hour, four times as fast as that first steam model.

Barnes died in office and was succeeded by another long-serving editor, John Delane, only twenty-three when he assumed the chair. During his thirty-six years as editor the paper gained an international reputation and its circulation climbed steadily. By 1855 it was selling 60,000 copies, nearly three times the total sale of all five of its rivals in London, until the repeal of the duty on paper meant cheaper papers and higher circulations for all. In the Crimean War, sales went up to 70,000, largely because of the vividly searing despatches of William Howard Russell, who some regard as the first-ever war correspondent. When Russell went to cover the American Civil War in 1861, President Lincoln told him: "*The Times* is the most powerful thing in the world, except, perhaps, the Mississippi." And he regretted that it was using its power to back the southern states, reflecting the opinion of most of its readers.

Towards the end of the nineteenth century the paper's fortune began to wane. Increasing literacy was causing the readership of all newspapers to grow tremendously. New titles, using more modern printing methods than *The Times* and catering to a less élite audience, were mopping up the new readers. The paper ailed and in 1907 the courts, at the request of some of the smaller partners in ownership, ordered that it should be sold.

This opened the door to the first of the disreputable proprietors of *The Times*, Lord Northcliffe. I do not use the word in any personal denigratory sense but to convey that Northcliffe – like Roy Thomson and Rupert Murdoch later – had made his fortune in newspapers of a racier, more popular nature. There would be nothing very harmful in that were it not that *The Times*, as a result of its excellence in the middle years of the nineteenth century, had come to be regarded as a national institution. Northcliffe, who as Alfred Harmsworth had created the immensely successful *Daily Mail*, understood the hostility that would be provoked if he made an overt bid, so he did a secret deal with Moberly Bell, the paper's manager, to buy a controlling interest for £320,000. And he agreed, as Thomson and Murdoch would have to do in time, to leave the editorial policy of the paper strictly in the hands of the editor.

When Northcliffe bought it, *The Times* sold about 30,000 copies a day at 3d. By 1914 he had taken the price down to a penny and the circulation was up to 150,000. During the First World War it jumped again to 278,000. But it was not in Northcliffe's nature to leave the editorial side to its own devices and his pledge to do so soon fell by the wayside. He sat in at editorial conferences and the paper conducted for him his campaigns against or on behalf of the leading politicians of the day. And he became angry when *The Times* followed a policy that conflicted with the *Daily Mail*.

Northcliffe had appointed Geoffrey Dawson as editor when he took over but his increasingly dictatorial attitude led to clashes and to Dawson's departure in 1919. By now the press baron's erratic behaviour was weakening the paper and lowering the morale of the staff. On a notorious visit to the Continent shortly before he died, he became convinced the Germans were trying to kill him by poisoning his ice-cream. His last important contribution to the paper was his introduction in 1922 – the year of his death – of a daily page of photographs. Traditionalists on the staff and among the readers deplored this development, seeing it as out of character with the paper, which had in the past gone largely unillustrated. There were numerous letters of protest. But the picture page soon became a popular feature and when it was dropped in 1966 the complaints were equally vociferous.

The Times was not making much money when Northcliffe died. Circulation had fallen to a little over 100,000. It had also lost its reputation for judicious even-handedness. All the same, there was no shortage of potential purchasers when the paper was put up for sale. One of them was

Northcliffe's brother Lord Rothermere, proprietor of the *Daily Mirror*, but the establishment were determined that this time it should not fall into such hands. John Jacob Astor, from one of Britain's and America's wealthiest families, joined forces with John Walter IV, a descendant of the founder, to buy the paper for £1,350,000 – a high price given its lack of commercial success. Dawson was reappointed editor.

To prevent, as they hoped, any further unsuitable transfer of power, Walter and Astor established an ex-officio committee of five worthies to ensure that any future change of ownership would be to someone within the paper's tradition. They were the Warden of All Souls, the Governor of the Bank of England, the Lord Chief Justice, the President of the Royal Society and the President of the Institute of Chartered Accountants. The innovation strengthened the concept of *The Times* as a national institution that should rise above squalid commercial considerations. One reason it has never for long proved able to increase its circulation to much above 300,000 may be the unstated implication that readers who are not from the privileged class are in some way interlopers – voyeurs, in a sense, of rites in which they are not allowed to take part and do not fully understand. The high-minded letters to the editor, the opaque announcements of the new term arrangements at exclusive but insignificant fee-paying schools – what is it all supposed to mean? Is it some kind of elaborate joke? The 1958 slogan that "Top People take *The Times*" seemed to suggest that unless you were a top person by *The Times*'s own reckoning, you were not wanted as a reader.

Things have not changed much. Even today, committees of great men are set up to safeguard the nebulous concept of "the national interest" in the administration of the paper. Its writers still congratulate themselves on the quality and probity of their detailed reports of parliamentary debates and intricate law cases, the weight and importance of the leading articles, the elegance and occasional waspishness of the obituaries, the appeal of the crossword and even of the personal advertisement columns, that remained on the front page until 1966, far beyond when reason and modern practice suggested they should have been banished elsewhere. No attempt was made early enough to explore the market and see whether these virtues might not be exploited to appeal to a wider audience. The writers enjoyed (and still enjoy) the feeling that they were communicating with an élite, "important" readership; but sadly that readership was unable to sustain the paper economically. Specifically, it was not a large enough market to attract big national advertisers.

Dawson's approach to his second editorship was summed up in a memorandum he wrote in 1925: "What *The Times* wanted first and foremost was a period of steadiness, even stodginess, before it could become an active force again . . . The process of startling the public had been carried too far." To begin with this toning-down was successful. Circulation rose to around 180,000 and throughout the 1920s annual profits increased, until the Depression started another slide. During the General Strike of 1926 *The Times* was the only paper to continue printing – sharing the market with Winston Churchill's government publication the *British Gazette*. Management staff and volunteers manned the presses and polite pickets touched their caps to Astor as he crossed their lines.

In 1932 the appearance of the paper was modernised to bring it at least to the fringes of the twentieth century and a new typeface – Times Roman – was devised for it by Stanley Morison. The journal's importance in the national life was confirmed four years later when Dawson was consulted frequently by Stanley Baldwin, the Prime Minister, during the Abdication crisis. But it suffered a grave blow to its reputation when Dawson advocated the appeasement of Hitler in the months before the Second World War.

Financially, the war was good for *The Times* as for other papers. Newsprint rationing reduced costs and cut competition, while demand for news was high. It ended the war with a comfortable circulation of around 200,000, but afterwards, when competition resumed, *The Times*'s share of the market dwindled while that of the other serious papers increased.

Almost since its foundation *The Times* had been a strictly hierarchical newspaper, with its editor usually chosen from amongst those senior members of the staff who had been

there for years. To become a *Times* man, it was felt, was
something that took patience. The paper's ambience could
be assimilated only gradually. It was not like other papers.
It encouraged eccentricity and individualism, but shunned
anything remotely flashy. An old-fashioned clubby atmosphere was cultivated deliberately: until a new building was
completed in 1962, the editorial offices at the old Printing
House Square were heated by open fires.

In 1952 an important break was made with tradition
when an outsider was appointed editor. True, Sir William
Haley, then 51, had begun his career with a short spell as a
telephonist on *The Times*, but he had made his name in
journalism in Manchester and then succeeded Lord Reith
as Director-General of the BBC. Haley was eminently
clubbable and soon the old guard at *The Times* forgave him
for not being strictly one of them. He brought energy to the
paper and reinforced its exalted image of itself but did not
do much to increase its circulation. In particular *The Times*
in Haley's early years could never bring itself to be unduly
interested in business. Years ago it had introduced a list of
stock prices but there was always the feeling that matters of
commerce were somehow beneath its attention. By that
neglect it forfeited some lucrative advertising.

In 1957 *The Times* showed a trading loss for the first time
for many years. The directors, worried with justification
about the long-term viability of their rather curious product, commissioned a firm of chartered accountants, Cooper Bros., to make a report on the paper's prospects. It made
worrying reading, and although over the next ten years
most of its recommendations were put into effect, it was
received with marked hostility by the old guard.

It recommended that the paper should try to double its
circulation to 400,000 within five years and to 600,000 five
years after that. This was heresy to those – including the
powerful manager Francis Mathew – who thought the paper's "natural" attainable readership was invariably no more
than 300,000. The report advocated more business news,
more accessible writing and a general enlivening of the
paper, including placing news instead of advertisements on
the front page. Mathew scorned such ideas as trying to take
The Times down to the level of the *Daily Telegraph*.

Horrified senior staff sent a thirty-nine-page anonymous memorandum to the paper's proprietors, denouncing the Cooper Report in extravagant terms. "Great Britain cannot function without a strong, educated, efficient, informed governing class," they wrote. "*The Times* is the organ of that class . . . The existence of a competent governing class is rightly said to be absolutely dependent upon *The Times* because no other newspaper attempts to rival it in self-respect, impartiality, independence, range of significant news, capacity to reason upon the matter printed . . . The Chief Proprietors of *The Times* are not engaged in the enterprise of publishing a newspaper interesting to the 'reading public'; they have never acknowledged among their duties that of providing a 'livelier' newspaper." The memorandum went on to speak of the folly of trying to compete directly with the *Daily Telegraph* and urged that what was really needed was an increase in morale among the senior staff, to enable them to ward off such ill-informed proposals from those who did not understand the paper's nature.

Mathew thoroughly approved of the philosophy as stated in the memorandum. He added his own contribution in June 1958, pointing out that to increase circulation would mean lowering standards to capture the interest of the Reading Public – a phrase that had clearly become a symbol in Printing House Square of all that was sinister in proposals to make the paper more accessible. Such statements seem laughably élitist today, and possibly did even then.

A sub-committee of directors was set up to discuss the commercial implications of the Cooper Report. In February 1959 Sir William Haley appeared before them, showing himself much less rigorous in his view of *The Times*'s future than Mathew or the loquacious, anonymous critics. While the paper must provide a useful record of affairs for those who run the country, it must also be balanced and entertaining, appealing to intelligent readers of all classes. But any change must be gradual.

In the event, it was gradual in the extreme. Because of staff hostility, scarcely any of the Cooper proposals were put into effect immediately. The exception was the recom-

mendation to expand business coverage. In the immediate
aftermath of the report, William Clarke was appointed City
Editor. He quadrupled the City staff and introduced many
new business features, and financial advertising increased
as a result. Had the other recommended changes been
made in the late 50s or early 60s, the restless years that led
to the election of Harold Wilson's first Labour government,
it is possible that *The Times* would better have succeeded in
establishing itself in an expanded market. The *Manchester
Guardian* had put news on its front page in 1952 and taken
the "Manchester" out of its name in 1960. By 1962 it had
doubled its circulation to 250,000, temporarily overtaking
The Times. The *Sunday Times*. The *Observer*, the *Financial
Times* and the *Daily Telegraph* had all grown impressively
through the 1950s. The "Top People" publicity campaign
that began in 1958 was much talked about but in marketing
terms did no more than confirm the paper's appeal to its
existing readership.

Haley could see all this and tried piecemeal remedies.
Foreign correspondents, trained in the production of long,
weighty political dispatches, received memorandums
saying that the editor wanted more light, off-beat, descrip-
tive material in the paper – the kind of thing the *Guardian*
was doing so successfully. In October 1965 a landmark was
reached when Haley broke the tradition of centuries and
ruled that the first person singular should be used in
dispatches instead of "your correspondent", though he did
add that it should be done only sparingly.

By the mid-1960s it became clear that something more
decisive would have to be attempted if *The Times* was not to
wither and die along with the dwindling class to which it was
addressing itself. Haley and the management devised a
series of editorial changes uncharacteristically dubbed
"Operation Breakthrough" – a bit of spy-thriller jargon
that may have been supposed to indicate a genuine departure from tradition. The most visible element was the card
they had been thinking of playing for years: putting news on
the front page. It was something they needed to be sure
about, for its only certain result would be a severe reduction in the lucrative personal advertisements, sold at a high
rate because of their prominent position in the paper.

Other elements of the plan were the introduction of a column of high-minded gossip called "As It Happens", and a daily women's page. It was bad luck – but symptomatic of the paper's lower reputation for reliability – that the first lead story on the front page on the day the change was made, May 3rd, 1966, was untrue. It stated that the head-quarters of the North Atlantic Treaty Organisation were to move to London – a scoop, certainly, but wrong.

In terms of circulation, the changes were a success. An extra 10,000 readers were added almost immediately and the graph continued to rise. But the innovations cost money and it had become increasingly apparent that the Astor family would not much longer be able to subsidise the paper from their own resources. An injection of capital was badly needed and a search for investors was begun.

Many possibilities of a merger were discussed. Potential partners included the *Guardian*, the *Observer* and the *Financial Times*. If the *Financial Times* plan had gone through, the two papers would have merged, combining the news coverage of *The Times* with a hefty business section, but the two groups could not agree a financial basis for what would probably have turned out a highly profitable enterprise.

Roy Thomson was Britain's newest press tycoon. The son of a Toronto barber, he had tried his hand at a number of ventures, including ranching and selling motor supplies, before falling by accident into the communications business. In 1928, when he was already thirty-four and had failed twice in commerce, he moved to North Bay in northern Ontario to sell radios and other modern goods. The trouble was that there was no radio station in the vicinity, so his sets were useless. His remedy was to start a station himself, then a second one in Timmins farther north.

It was there, at the age of forty, that Thomson bought his first newspaper, *The Press*. It thrived and in the 1930s and 1940s he steadily acquired more Canadian papers and radio stations. In 1952, after failing in a bid to enter politics, he bought a paper in Florida. The following year he founded his British empire by purchasing the *Scotsman* in Edin-burgh, and a few years later took a controlling stake in

Scottish Television, making his celebrated remark that a
commercial TV station was a licence to print money. Later,
through his Scottish interests, he was able to acquire a
valuable investment in North Sea Oil.

His largest British press involvement came in 1959 when
he bought the Kemsley group of papers, including the
Sunday Times, then unconnected with *The Times*. He made
his first pass at *The Times* in 1963, when he made an offer
for the ten-per-cent shareholding of the Walter family.
Gavin Astor bought the shares instead, to bolster his
family's control. Two years later, hearing rumours that the
paper was now in serious need of funds, Thomson asked
Denis Hamilton, editor of the *Sunday Times*, to sniff
around. Hamilton first approached Astor in February 1965,
with no result. In September 1966, just after the collapse of
the *Financial Times* deal, Hamilton lunched with executives of *The Times* to sound out possibilities. The proposition did not at first seem attractive, and not just because, in
Thomson's own words, he was a "rough-neck Canadian".
Less than fifty years earlier the paper had only with difficulty extricated itself from the grasp of a newspaper magnate,
and although Thomson's *Sunday Times* was a different
proposition from Northcliffe's *Mail*, it did not seem an ideal
solution. Yet balanced against that were the obvious economies that could be made by a closer link between *The
Times* and the *Sunday Times*, the latter making a profit of
over £1m a year.

The deal had to pass through several hoops before it was
approved. Recognising that to own a newspaper in a democracy is a conduit to great power and influence, the British
have instituted elaborate safeguards and procedures designed to prevent them falling into unsuitable hands. It is
surprising how often they prove ineffective.

To win the consent of the Monopolies Commission,
Thomson had to agree to play no role in running the paper.
Sir William Haley would be chairman for three years and
would be succeeded by Thomson's son Kenneth – who,
being separated by a generation from his father's humble
origins, was found more acceptable. And the old 1922 plan
of roping in representatives of the great and the good to
safeguard the national interest was revised. Four "national

directors" were appointed to the board – two each nominated by the main political parties.

Despite such seeming indignities, Thomson was as
pleased as punch about his acquisition. "This deal was the
greatest thing I have ever done," he wrote in his book *After
I Was Sixty*. "It was the summit of a lifetime's work. I had
had to agree to keep out of the running of the paper: at least
my son would be there sharing fully in the management."
And he pledged his and his successors' private fortunes to
continuing *The Times* and the *Sunday Times* "as quality
papers edited in the national interest". He affirmed: "This
undertaking will continue for twenty-one years and will be
binding on our successors and assigns." (It did not and was
not.) And he added in his book: "I was greatly moved that
my son never questioned my decision and wholeheartedly
agreed with me in passing away all those millions to save an
ideal."

Hamilton was appointed editor-in-chief of the newly
merged papers. As editor of *The Times* he chose William
Rees-Mogg, thirty-eight years old, deputy editor of the
Sunday Times, whose father came from a line of country
gentry and whose mother was an American actress. A frank
profile of him appeared in the two papers' first joint house
magazine at the beginning of 1967. "The Rees-Moggs," it
read, "never gave the country men who attained high office
but they provided the Church, services and medicine with a
plenitude of competence." Educated at Charterhouse and
Balliol, he was described as "a little pompous and somewhat pugnacious" at Oxford, where he had been elected
President of the Union in 1951. Tall and with a high voice,
he proved almost a caricature of a *Times* editor. His first
executive act was to send the cricket correspondent, John
Woodcock, to report what was left of England's tour of
South Africa.

Harold Evans, the new editor of the *Sunday Times*, was a
very different man. Small, wiry and dynamic, he had been
editor of the *Northern Echo* in Darlington when Hamilton
brought him to London as his deputy on the *Sunday Times*,
though he had come to the attention of Fleet Street partly
by some impressive appearances on Granada TV's *What
the Papers Say*. The son of an engine driver, he had

graduated in Politics and Economics at Durham University.

That issue of the house journal was a remarkable document in which, with hindsight, it is possible to detect the seeds of the misfortunes that were to befall the Thomson Organisation in their bid to make *The Times* profitable. Its front cover was in a garish shade of yellow and amounted to a crude, botched piece of graphics. A hollow star filled the top half of the page and, through its points, peered a goofy-looking Lord Thomson, the new proprietor, wearing his inordinately thick spectacles. Beneath this, in large, tabloid-size type, was the single word "WHAAM". It was a silly piece of bravado, devoid of meaning. All it succeeded in doing was to confirm the worst fears of dedicated old *Times* men about what was going to become of their paper under the new ownership. Was it going to be all razzmatazz, empty symbols, undignified attempts at "promotions", rather than a reaffirmation of the paper's firmest principles, its commitment to sobriety and reason? Was that the kind of thing that the dreaded Reading Public were supposed to appreciate?

Things certainly began with a WHAAM. With the cricket man safely despatched to Africa, the new editor plunged himself into the role – a rather unlikely role for those who knew him – of the thrusting moderniser, bringing the paper smack (WHAAM) into the swinging sixties without, as he saw it, compromising its essential traditions. One nonessential tradition he quickly abandoned was that writers should generally be anonymous. Nowadays, he saw, it would simply be impossible to attract leading writers to the paper if they were not allowed to announce their names. There had been isolated bylines before but now they were to become routine, though far from flamboyant. On January 16th, 1967, the first of them coyly appeared, with the main feature article signed "Richard Harris (a student of Asia)".

A more radical change was the addition of a Business News section as a self-contained part of the paper, folded separately. Launched at a dinner at the Savoy where Harold Macmillan, the former Prime Minister, was the principal guest, this was an attempt to emulate the earlier

Thomson changes at the *Sunday Times*, which had been a great commercial success. Another idea from the Sunday paper was the creation of the News Team, something like the *Sunday Times* Insight team, which would undertake investigations as well as acting as a "first strike" unit when big stories broke, a flying news squad. It operated for a time on a lavish budget, chartering aircraft to fly reporters and photographers to disaster sites in Britain and Europe and sending squads of people abroad on unspecific assignments – like jaunts to Africa for an expensive series called "The Black Man in Search of Power".

The News Team was run by Michael Cudlipp, Hugh's nephew, one of the few young executives Rees-Mogg brought with him from the *Sunday Times*. But it was another of Cudlipp's enterprises that caused probably the deepest anguish to stalwart traditionalists, readers as well as staff. Two reporters working on his instigation mounted an investigation into police bribery, recording on tape a transaction in which a suspect, who was the paper's main informant, gave money to policemen. As a piece of detective work it was perhaps sloppily done but the story was printed and, after much acrimony, the policemen were found guilty. Many felt deeply that *The Times* had exceeded the bounds of propriety. It was all very well for its brash Sunday sister to go in for such gung-ho investigations but the role of *The Times* should be to record and reflect upon the news rather than create it. There was an additional sense that in criticising the police and using informers the paper was assailing authority where it ought to be supporting it.

There were other changes that went right against the grain. Headlines were made larger and so was the body type, meaning that wordy writers had their work cut back. They received another shock when a circular came round urging them to write shorter sentences. The leader writers, used to thrashing out a common line in solemn conclave, were horrified when the editor would impose his own opinions, sometimes ignoring them entirely. Why, he even wrote a long leader about drugs and the Rolling Stones – not a *Times* subject at all. And Cudlipp brought with him some of the bustle for its own sake that is a feature of the sort of popular journalism people on *The Times* had long felt to be beneath them. He even began hiring staff from newspapers such as the *People* and the *Sun*, which the old guard thought of as being more in the way of entertainment than information. The people manning the desks at night were appalled at Cudlipp's concept of making radical changes to the paper in the small hours. Traditionally, *Times* correspondents had not been obliged to keep on top of a breaking story and file every new fact as it occurred, until the last edition had gone to press. What was mainly required of them was judicious interpretation of the news and its meaning. If something else happened after a correspondent had filed his report, short news agency despatches could always be tacked on to the end of his message, carefully distinguished from it. This was not good enough for the new, thrusting *Times*. Cudlipp, whose first job on the paper was night editor, wanted all his correspondents to keep up with the news. In New York Eric Britter, who had been there as long as the United Nations and whose main job was to chronicle the affairs of the world body, would increasingly find his dinner interrupted by telephone calls from London demanding news files about floods, plane crashes, bridge collapses and other sensational but in the long term insignificant events, often happening thousands of miles away on the west coast of America. In vain he would argue that the agency reports from the spot were likely to be more complete than anything he could rustle up. Unwilling to adjust the work habits of a lifetime, Britter retired earlier than he had intended and went to live in the West Indies.

Yet although not universally approved, the changes were having a healthy effect on circulation. It was up to 325,000 by the summer of 1967, an increase of some 50,000 in six months. "By 1970 we shall be selling 500,000 copies a day," declared an enthusiastic unsigned article in the house journal. By the end of 1967 the figure was 364,193 and there were signs that Rees-Mogg's head was being turned. In a radio interview in March 1968 he exulted: "I would hope that we would get an average sales increase over ten years of 50,000 a year and that therefore in ten years' time we'd be selling about 900,000. But that's a very, very long term guess." When the interviewer raised the question of the paper's apparent loss of authority – a complaint increasingly heard – Rees-Mogg brushed it aside.

One potential advantage of the merger that was never fully realised was a co-ordination of services between *The Times* and the *Sunday Times*. In the early days, the phrase "seven-day newspaper" was heard, but that was quickly dropped when it became apparent that the staff of each paper viewed the other with deep suspicion and preferred to go their own way. Foreign coverage was one obvious area where co-operation could save money, but personal relations between the two foreign departments were never of the best: the *Times* people regarded *Sunday Times* correspondents as sensation-seeking lightweights while the view of the *Sunday Times* was that the staff of *The Times* were idle pedants scarcely entitled to be called journalists at all. The fact that Frank Giles, in charge of the foreign side of the *Sunday Times*, had once been a *Times* correspondent seemed to hinder rather than help. One or two joint correspondents were appointed and in New York the two offices merged successfully – the tolerant *Times* staff there even accepted philosophically the presence of a large *Sunday Times* Insight team noisily and untidily producing a first-rate book on the 1968 presidential election. But only a few hundred miles away in Washington, Henry Brandon of the *Sunday Times* and Louis Heren of *The Times*, both prima donnas in their own way, scarcely spoke.

These were seen only as minor setbacks, though, in the first few heady years of Thomson ownership of *The Times*. By late 1969 circulation had reached 450,000 but it fell after a penny price increase and profitability was still a distant prospect. The Thomson management were prepared to accept losses in their first few years of ownership but had not regarded their purchase of the papers as an open-ended commitment to a limitless subsidy. The new readers, they discovered, were costing them money, because they had been acquired largely through an expensive and gimmicky advertising campaign. Traditionalists found the ads vulgar and recall one with special horror. The real-life theft of some silver plate from the butler's pantry at Printing House Square was used as the theme of a jokey advertisement for

the law reports in *The Times*. Readers attracted by this
hearty approach were the smart, colour-supplement generation, whose attention could be grasped in spasms by
ephemeral fads: often people who had made quick killings
in the heady, entrepreneurial early 1960s. But the *Daily
Telegraph* sold a million and a quarter copies to just this
group of people, and even a *Times* selling half a million was
not a viable competitor for advertisers wanting to sell their
high-priced sports cars and Scandinavian kitchen furniture.
Moreover, to appeal to this broader group *The Times* was
fast alienating its traditional readers, whose interests were
altogether more sober. It was a fundamental commercial
miscalculation.

A pull-back by management was inevitable and when
Denis Hamilton wrote to the staff sounding the financial
alarm, the old guard at *The Times*, who had never really
reconciled themselves to Cudlipp and the innovations he
personified, thought it time to win back some lost ground.
A group of thirty senior journalists met at the White Swan,
a pub in Farringdon Street, and drafted a list of grievances
concerning the editorial direction of the paper. That elusive
"authority" took first place among the qualities they perceived to have been diluted. Independence, accuracy, dis-
crimination and seriousness were the others. The
mutineers drew up a document, among whose signatories
the most senior was Teddy Hodgkin, the foreign editor.
Others included Charles Douglas-Home, Brian MacArthur, Hugh Stephenson, Patrick Brogan and Geoffrey
Smith, young journalists who were all to be involved in a
more public melodrama twelve years later. *Times* editors
are never serious enough for their staff – the men Lord
Northcliffe used to call the "Black Friars of Printing House
Square". The White Swan letter was not quite so extreme a
statement of old *Times* principles as the anonymous
reaction to the Cooper Report, but it was written in the
same spirit. Rees-Mogg met the dissidents and reacted
petulantly but did agree to consult the staff more about
future changes, though the consultation process was never
effective.

Even if Rees-Mogg seemed to have brushed aside the
strictures of the White Swan group, they weighed on his

mind. Later that year substantial changes were made to the layout and character of the paper that answered many of the old guard's complaints. Headlines and bylines were made smaller, the News Team disbanded. Although it was never announced in unambiguous terms to the staff, the drive for higher circulation through popularisation had been abandoned as too expensive in relation to the likely financial benefit. The old guard were exultant. As part of the new consultation process a staff bulletin was circulated at intervals and individuals were invited to contribute. Peter Evans, the Home Affairs Correspondent, wrote a short comment that reflected the relief of the old-timers. "For a while *The Times* lost its way," he reflected. "Its strong identity was diluted. That identity is not something that can easily be replaced. It is organic, and springs from a natural and easy relationship between people on its staff . . . Some things can be left unsaid, because there is no need to say them. That understanding is communicated to the reader instinctively. He knows where he is." The paper had switched back into its role as a low-circulation journal for the knowing élite, a "paper of record". And in another move that was to have a profound long-term effect, Marmaduke "Duke" Hussey, an executive with a possibly undeserved reputation for ruthlessness, was recruited from the *Daily Mail* group to become managing-director of Times Newspapers.

Rees-Mogg, feeling the need of an old-style *Times* man to support him while the U-turn was being made, phoned Louis Heren, the veteran Washington correspondent. Heren had joined the paper as a messenger before the Second World War and had distinguished himself as a war correspondent in Korea. Rees-Mogg had been impressed with him on his first visit to Washington as editor in 1967, when he was taken to see President Johnson. The expansive President praised Heren to the skies, and as he did so delivered a sly wink to the delighted correspondent. Now, three years later, Rees-Mogg invited this presidential intimate back to London to become joint deputy editor with Michael Cudlipp. Heren, who had scarcely worked in the London office during his career, was a little apprehensive. Before leaving for London on the QE2 he spent an evening in New York, where I was *The Times* correspondent, and I invited him and his family to dinner. He knew that Cudlipp had hired me and wondered about him. "What's he like?" he asked me. "Is he the sort of person likely to stab me in the back?" I reassured him as best I could.

Once the decision was taken to abandon the drive for higher circulation, Cudlipp's authority was diminished. By the summer of 1971 *The Times* had lost a quarter of its readers, with circulation down to 340,000. By the time Cudlipp left, two years after that, there was hardly a trace of the Thomson WHAAM left. Even Business News, the most vaunted of the changes, had been incorporated into the main paper instead of being produced as a separate insert.

One of the early Thomson decisions that was not revoked was to move *The Times* into a new building next to the *Sunday Times* in Gray's Inn Road, where both papers would be printed on the same presses. When the plan was announced, soon after the takeover, it was many years in the future and opposition to it was slow to build. It was not until the early seventies, when the squat, slightly Moorish building – looking more like a holiday hotel in Ibiza than a newspaper office – began to take shape that alarm really set in. *The Times* had been printed on its site hard by Blackfriars Bridge ever since its inception. Must it really move? More practically, there were fears, later borne out, that the merging of the two printing staffs would cause industrial unrest: each would want to share the perks of the other, without giving up any of its own privileges. Printers on *The Times*, although in the same unions as the rest of Fleet Street, had been perceived as less militant and more reasonable than those on other papers. And Sunday papers were traditionally hardest hit by the labour-intensive "Spanish customs" of hiring more people than were actually needed to carry out a task. Yet Thomson's would not reverse the decision and the move was made in the summer of 1975.

It was botched, and one whole day's run of *The Times* was lost. Few of the anticipated economies came to pass. Even the libraries of *The Times* and the *Sunday Times* remained separate, because the library staffs were against a merger and so were the *Sunday Times* journalists, who feared they would no longer be able to keep cuttings folders for several days, as was their custom. Confidence in the efficacy of the management was further reduced when it was revealed that the valuable Henry Moore sundial, made specially for *The Times* only a few years earlier, had been included inadvertently in the sale of the old Printing House Square and thus could not be moved north with the paper. Instead, a tiny replica was made for the lobby of the new building.

There is in Britain a political animal known as a "saloon-bar Tory". He sits in the most comfortable bar of his local pub, sipping gin and tonic, bemoaning the state of the nation and saying how much better everything would be if only managements and everyone else would stand up to the dreadful unions. From time to time such confrontatory tactics actually work and this encourages the pub philosophers, who fail to discern that managements lose such contests more often than they win them and victory is generally achieved only after meticulous preparation of the ground. It was the misfortune of Times Newspapers Ltd. and its parent Thomson Organisation to be afflicted in the 1970s with saloon-bar management.

"Duke" Hussey is a genial aristocrat, a bear-like man with an artificial leg replacing one lost in the Second World War. His wife, Lady Susan Hussey, has for years been a lady-in-waiting to the Queen. Affable and approachable, with long experience in newspapers, he seemed at first an ideal managing director for Times Newspapers. Paul Johnson, the right-wing columnist, once called him "one of the most engaging characters in Fleet Street", and so he is. His weakness is that he is a compulsive memo writer. The kind of venom others vent in saloon bars, he commits to paper and circulates among his staff.

Not long after he joined Times Newspapers in 1970, Hussey began writing a series of gloomy notes telling the workers what a deplorable condition the finances and labour relations of the two papers were in. He would strike the same tone at meetings of the editorial consultative committee set up as a result of the "White Swan" *démarche*.

On April 10th, 1978, he wrote to report the loss of two million pounds in revenue because of industrial action. Already that year twenty-one issues of *The Times* and nine of the *Sunday Times* had failed to complete their print run because of industrial disruption. Management had to restore their right to manage. Some executives, said Hussey, were spending ninety per cent of their time dealing with disputes as they arose, giving them no time for what they liked to think was their real function, developing a long-term commercial strategy for the papers. Something had to be done. It had to stop. Meetings would be held over the next few days. Decisions of weight would be reached and communicated to the staff.

There is no reason to doubt that Hussey was accurately conveying the frustration of the management in London and Toronto over their growing problems with the newspapers. The old Lord Thomson had died in 1976 and his son Kenneth was much less tolerant of Fleet Street's peculiarities. He spent most of his time in Toronto and preferred to leave the running of things in London to Hussey and Gordon Brunton, chief executive of the Thomson organisation in Britain. In 1978 the headquarters of the Thomson group was moved from London to Toronto. Though prepared to continue his father's commitment to the papers, the new Lord Thomson did not want it to be a permanent drain on his organisation's resources, however extensive these had lately become as a result of investment in North Sea oil.

In fact *The Times* had made a modest profit in 1977, although circulation had by mid-1978 sunk to below 300,000, largely because of a fifty-per-cent price rise, from ten pence to fifteen pence since 1976. It was partly this indication that they could make money from their papers if only they could solve their production difficulties that persuaded the Thomson directors to go for what Eric Jacobs, then the Industrial Correspondent of the *Sunday Times*, called the "big bang" solution. In essence, they were warning the unions that unless they could reach agreements for the uninterrupted production of the two papers and the three *Times* supplements, and for the smooth introduction of labour-saving technological advances, management would suspend production of the newspapers until such agreements were reached. Nowhere in Fleet Street had the new technology been introduced, although it was common in the United States and elsewhere. It was partly apprehension about their long-term job prospects in the face of this modern wizardry that had provoked the print unions into the disruption Hussey was complaining about.

Although Hussey carried out the "big bang" strategy with determination once it was agreed by the board, he had doubts about it. The board of Times Newspapers was subservient to the London board of the Thomson organisation, which Brunton, with his close links to Toronto, ran in a distinctively personal style.

Brunton is a large, persuasive man, proud of having been brought up in London's East End and then risen to be one of Britain's most important industrialists. (A colleague said of him: "He's always saying that one day we must go together to the eel and pie shops he used to know in Hackney. But when I do have dinner with him it always seems to be at Claridge's.") Certainly he was not going to let the travails of Times Newspapers imperil his position. He had told Hussey and his directors that something had to be done to stop the haemorrhaging and sent them away to think about it. Such were the terms of Brunton's instruction that Hussey, if he was to retain his hard-won reputation for toughness, had to respond. Thus although Brunton, a formidably dominant man, had been the inspiration for the strategy, he was, to use a term popular at the Nixon White House, able to retain "deniability" when it came to apportioning the blame for its failure a year later. Hussey became the fall guy – and had possibly been marked out for that role from the start. He had not made it any easier for himself to resist the hard option by his recent appointment of Dugal Nisbet-Smith, a tough-talking New Zealander, to fill the substantial gap that had been left in January by the death of Harvey Thompson, the popular general manager. Nisbet-Smith had come from the *Mirror* group with a similar ruthless reputation to the one Hussey had enjoyed at the *Mail*.

On April 13th, 1978, Hussey, Nisbet-Smith and other

directors met leaders of the print unions in Birmingham and outlined to them the ultimatum they were about to issue. It came in a memorandum to staff, signed by Hussey, announcing that a series of new agreements on working conditions, staffing, restricting unofficial strikes and introducing modern technology would be presented to all fifty-six chapels operating at Gray's Inn Road. If agreement on all points was not reached with all chapels by November 30th, 1978, publication of *The Times*, the *Sunday Times* and the supplements would be suspended.

It would be, in saloon-bar terms, a short, sharp shock. Many on the board were convinced that such tactics would quickly bring the unions "to their senses". Authority would be reasserted. Others, though, had their doubts, and there was no sign of any backing-down in the unions' response to the threat. Accusations flew. The *Times* management, inexplicably, had no detailed proposals to present to the unions until the end of the summer. It seemed that the management was for a time overawed by its own threat, representing as it did such a break with traditional labour relations; the act of steeling themselves for the confrontation had quite exhausted their stock of initiatives. Yet while the unions were justified in criticising the long delay, it is doubtful whether the crisis would have been averted by a quicker presentation of the proposals. In the event, when the suspension had lasted nearly a year and the prospect of permanent closure loomed, it was the management that would have to give way in face of its own bludgeoning tactics. An earlier start to negotiations would scarcely have reduced the time this convoluted tragedy took to work itself out. Writing about it in the *Political Quarterly* three years later, Godfrey Hodgson used P. G. Wodehouse's cricketing metaphor of a slow bowler trying to bowl fast because his slow stuff is being caned by the opposition – than which, Wodehouse wrote, there is no sadder sight.

The most curious aspect of the ultimatum, persuading many that it was actually a little puff rather than a big bang, was the decision that members of those unions who had reached agreement on new contract terms before the deadline would remain on full salary during the proposed suspension. This was done chiefly to protect the position of the journalists. Rees-Mogg, Hamilton and Evans had convinced the board that the papers would be destroyed utterly if the team of journalists was disbanded. The best of them would be offered lucrative new jobs by other papers once their salaries were stopped. It was costly evidence of the management's intention to resume publication eventually. Its psychological effect was to convince their opponents in the print unions that they were not in earnest, that it was all simply a tactic that could be combated by closing ranks and holding firm. In most strikes, the most powerful weapon in the management's hand is the financial one. There is always a limit to the length of time the aggrieved workers can survive on their own resources. In this case, the Thomson board were deliberately penalising themselves by building into the suspension an equal financial pressure on their side. And any threat to follow the suspension with a total shutdown was made less credible by the millions of pounds they were spending on keeping their loyal staff, as an investment in the future.

It made little sense, and it was one of the reasons why not many people believed that the papers would indeed be suspended on November 30th. The cynical thought the management would find themselves in serious negotiation with the unions on that date and would be able to postpone the showdown without losing face. If they had this tactic in mind, however, it was effectively ruled out by the National Graphical Association, one of the most important print unions, who refused to talk unless the threat of suspension was lifted. Even when *The Times* did not appear on December 1st, or the *Sunday Times* on December 3rd, most people assumed the stoppage would be short. One man who read the signs correctly at this stage and throughout the future course of the conflict was Charles Douglas-Home, the deputy editor in charge of the foreign side, who sent a gloomy letter to overseas correspondents accurately forecasting that the suspension would be a long one, and urging them to use the time profitably though inexpensively. Short and sharp it decidedly was not.

"This is a sad moment," wrote Hussey, in yet another memo, "for everyone who shares our belief that all our newspapers and staff can enjoy together a prosperous future. It would have been sadder still if we had been forced to announce the permanent closure of the newspapers which would have been the inevitable result had the damage inflicted on them by unofficial stoppages gone on." In the same document he announced that dismissal notices to staff who had not reached agreement with the company on new working conditions, which were to have been issued on the day of the suspension, would be delayed by two weeks to allow time for a quick settlement. No such settlement was forthcoming, but those threatened with dismissal did not include the journalists who, after several days of melodramatics and an impassioned letter to each of them from Rees-Mogg, cobbled together a deal on new contract terms just hours before the deadline, assuring their continued employment at full pay however long the suspension lasted.

The following week Lord Thomson came to London and issued a statement. "I have no intention of intervening in any way in the negotiations," he said. "I am, of course, very sad that these two great newspapers are suspended, but it seems to be the only way to ensure their long term survival . . . I just hope that common sense will prevail and that the newspapers will be back on the streets very soon."

Common sense seemed a long way from the centre of the stage. Rees-Mogg would give regular briefings to senior staff about the progress of such negotiations as were under way and he became more hectoring and apocalyptic the longer the dispute continued. Swinging dolefully back and forth in his office rocking chair, he spoke of "immensely powerful forces" working against a settlement and warned his listeners that it was not confined to *The Times*. Nobody, he said, should imagine they could avoid "the storm of the world" by joining another national newspaper. "The rest of Fleet Street has just as serious battles to be fought." Politicians and others weighed in with contributions to the dispute that may not have been designed to solve it: Tony Benn, the left-wing Labour MP, suggested the paper should be taken over by the BBC, though its director-general, Sir Ian Trethowan, was not keen.

Things moved slowly until a breakthrough in the negotiations in March inspired confidence that publication could resume in April. This would have meant a gap of five months and even that was much longer than anyone had bargained for. But talks broke down again and the management decided on more blatantly adventurist tactics. They would publish a weekly edition, printed in Germany, for foreign circulation only. The reason they gave was that it would keep the titles alive and give the journalists something to do: but most saw it as a gesture – the last gesture, as it turned out – of defiance against the print unions, who by now had achieved a fearsome demonological status in the minds of the management and their supporters. Preparations for the weekly *Times* were made in the utmost secrecy. Executives flew to Frankfurt with their faces buried in copies of the *Daily Telegraph*, to avoid possible recognition by globe-trotting acquaintances. The setting and printing of the paper were being done in separate plants in the Frankfurt area. Secrecy was not maintained for long and the British unions persuaded their German colleagues to picket the plant. There was violence and only a few copies were printed. The episode made everyone even worse-tempered than before and the management decided to end the venture, although some – including Rees-Mogg and his senior lieutenants at *The Times* – were anxious, once started, to carry on with it.

Rees-Mogg was entranced by the modern production methods used at Frankfurt and enthused about them in an article in the *Daily Telegraph* in June. The women typesetters in Frankfurt had been more than three times as fast as Linotype operators in London, he recorded, and they were not even working in their own language. "The Germans embrace efficiency; the British fight to reject it," he wrote glumly. "It is, for us, a high road to disaster."

Just after the Frankfurt fiasco, clear lines came to be drawn between the hard-line, stick-it-to-the-end faction and more moderate board members. Hussey felt that he was now so committed that he had no alternative to maintaining his hard line, and he had strong intellectual support from Rees-Mogg and the two other senior journalists on *The Times*, Louis Heren and Charles Douglas-Home. Yet by early summer powerful pressure was building up for a compromise. Thomson and Brunton could see that events were moving remorselessly towards a final closure of Times

Newspapers – an outcome that had been far from their minds when the adventure began a year earlier. Their support for the hard line began to waver. Brunton had throughout the crisis wondered whether Hussey and Nisbet-Smith had clarified their war aims in their own minds. Just before the closure he sent Hussey a memo asking whether the introduction of the new technology was one of the prerequisites for a settlement and he received no cut-and-dried reply. Now, by the summer, he feared that the pair might simply be in the battle for its own sake. His doubts were shared by Harold Evans and Sir Denis Hamilton, who felt there should be a more flexible attitude to negotiation. On the union side, there was pressure for any fresh negotiations to be at the level of Thomson and Brunton, rather than the board of Times Newspapers.

In May, Thomson was still sticking by Hussey. When I telephoned him in Toronto, he went on about the malaise affecting Britain and how the battle must be fought to the end for everyone's sake – identical to the line taken by Rees-Mogg in his *Telegraph* piece. When I asked him why he did not sell the papers if he felt unable to solve their problems I found his response interesting. Selling, he said, was "low on our list of options." This was a distinct variation from the previous house line that it was not on the list at all.

The following month Thomson came to London and reinforced that hint by a distinctly ambivalent attitude to selling the titles when he was asked about it at the companies' annual meeting. At the same time he set about trying to avert the possibility by reversing his pledge of six months ago and getting involved in the negotiations himself for the first time. It was only a token appearance but it was crucial because it symbolised the end of the Thomson organisation's backing for the Hussey hard line. From now on it was moderates like Hamilton and Evans who would make the running. After many more delays, misunderstandings and alarms, the negotiations reached a laborious conclusion and publication of the papers was resumed in mid-November 1979, fifty weeks after the administration of the short, sharp shock. Both sides, as is customary on such occasions, claimed victory, but although the management

had achieved some real concessions on manning and work
practices they could nowhere near justify the thirty-nine
million pounds of Thomson money that Hussey had spent
on leading his troops to the firing line and then negotiating
the retreat. And many of the agreements on which the
return to work was based – notably the one that committed
the unions to completing negotiations within a year on the
introduction of new technology – were never to be fulfilled.

In the saloon bars, they spluttered, enraged, into their
gin, saying that if only management had toughed it out a bit
longer they could have brought the unions to their knees. If
only . . . And less than a mile south of the Gray's Inn Road
headquarters of Times Newspapers, at his offices in the *Sun*
building in Bouverie Street, Rupert Murdoch watched it all
with eyebrows raised quizzically, wondering how any newspaper executive could allow this to happen – and wondering, as always, whether there might in the long run be
anything in it for him.

Chapter 8

THOMSON'S LAST STRAW

> [*The Times*] is not something that I really want, but if Rupert
> wants it and it makes him happy I'm sure we'll sort it out.
> – *Anna Murdoch, February 1981.*

During the exciting weeks leading to the resumption of *The Times* in November 1979, its reporters and correspondents were told that the aim was to make it seem as though the paper had never been away. All should be as it was when they had stopped work fifty weeks earlier. The idea was to convince themselves and readers that 1979 was a bad dream, a year that, due to circumstances quite beyond their control, had not taken place.

So far as readers were concerned, that strategy appeared to work. Circulation of the *Sunday Times* quickly regained its former level of 1,500,000 and *The Times* actually increased by a substantial 40,000 to over 320,000 – benefiting in those first weeks from the publicity generated by the closure. It had been, if you wanted to be cynical about it, quite an effective marketing ploy, a means of getting your paper widely mentioned in the rival prints and on television day after day – effective, that is, until you calculated that each new reader had cost the Thomson Organisation about £1,000 to buy.

The snag was that not only journalists and readers regarded 1979 as The Year That Never Was: the print unions did as well. It was soon clear that they saw the return-to-work agreements not as final and immutable but simply as a basis for further apparently endless negotiation. The disputes that were supposed to have been ruled out by the agreements continued much as before, compounded by genuine mechanical problems attributed to the presses having lain idle. Three months after the resumption there had still been no agreement with NATSOPA about hiring needed new clerical staff, particularly the women who take classified advertisements over the phone. *The Times* was losing about a third of the classified advertising it would normally have expected – only 734 columns were sold in January 1980 compared with 1,164 in January 1978.

The management had gone into republication full of hope and with a spanking new philosophy of industrial relations. They had told themselves – or rather they had been told repeatedly by their critics during 1979 – that where they had chiefly been at fault over the last dozen years had been in their lack of communication with people on the shop floor. Now they decided they had to create "a new set of relationships". Those executives who in 1978 had complained that they spent ninety per cent of their time dealing with disputes as they arose, now devoted their energies to producing a constant stream of memoranda and facts sheets, and organising meetings where they would convey their insights to the workers.

What was needed, they decided, was a proper conference where leaders of both sides could get together to talk away their differences. A whole weekend was set aside for this and an hotel reserved near Gatwick airport – a curious choice of venue since nobody was planning to travel to and from it by air. As a preliminary, Sir Denis Hamilton addressed a meeting of chapel leaders at Gray's Inn Road in March. Almost alone among senior Thomson executives, Hamilton had the ability to sound dire warnings without hectoring, without seeming to wield the big stick, without threatening the workers with terminal consequences if they would not come to heel. His fondness for the military metaphor paradoxically gave the impression that his intentions were largely peaceable, for it lent his utterances an air of cosy nostalgia. "No one wants to go back to the trenches," he declared. "It is the spirit of the tow rope, of pulling each other out of temporary problems, which should be our way of life."

But, as he reported, the tow rope was breaking, or being

deliberately cut, too often. "I have to tell you that I feel some sense of letdown," Hamilton confessed. In the seventeen weeks since the resumption of publication, the *Sunday Times* had completed its full print run only ten times. "It is a disaster," he said bleakly, but later, in the proper tradition of the commander rallying his troops, he affirmed: "We are not exhausted." Not quite, he might have added in qualification.

The Gatwick conference was the occasion for much talk about improving internal communications. To show their sincerity, the management engaged as its chairman Lord McCarthy, a lawyer with experience in labour relations and with a reputation for paying scrupulous regard to the views of the workers. It was agreed to establish a regular internal newspaper to tell staff about developments in the company, and to hold consultative meetings between management and labour representatives. Everyone went home believing the weekend to have been a tremendous success.

In June there was a reorganisation of the executive structure of the newspapers, again with the aim of improving lines of communication. In terms of personalities, its most important effect was to take both Hussey and Hamilton away from the day-to-day running of the papers into a company called Times Newspapers Holdings, with the inexact brief "to protect the independence and the long-term future of the newspapers and to agree on broad strategy". James Evans, once the legal adviser to the *Sunday Times*, was made chairman of the new operating company, Times Newspapers Ltd., while Harold Evans and William Rees-Mogg became directors. Dugal Nisbet-Smith was appointed managing director. As Hamilton explained it, Hussey "needs a rest from the intolerable pressures of day-to-day management" and instead would act as a kind of fact-finder-cum-ambassador, travelling round the world representing the company and reporting back to London on developments in the industry.

As far as the operation of the papers was concerned, these were largely cosmetic changes. The essential problems remained and grew worse. *The Times*'s circulation in June dipped below 300,000 for the first time since the resumption, partly because production delays had led to missed trains on most nights during the month, meaning that papers outside London were delivered late. The National Graphical Association, representing the compositors, would not discuss the possibility of new machinery being operated by members of other unions, although the management believed they had promised to do so as part of the back-to-work settlement. Rees-Mogg, briefing assistant editors, said that while he and his fellow directors had not expected the unions to honour all agreements, they were surprised and distressed to discover that hardly any were being complied with.

By the middle of the year it became clear that the deficit of the two papers in 1980 would amount to something like thirteen million pounds. Rees-Mogg told colleagues that Lord Thomson's morale was at rock bottom. The management were still divided between hawks and doves. Some took the Hamilton line that despite disappointments it was necessary to improve relations with the unions. The Nisbet-Smith faction felt the lesson since the resumption was that the conflict between the company and the unions was essentially a power struggle and that the company's defeat last year had put it at an irreversible strategic disadvantage. Since everyone agreed that another suspension was out of the question, the logical conclusion from the latter attitude was that the game was up: they might as well call a complete halt. That view gained strength during the summer as the situation failed to improve. Then, in early August, came the blow that was to prove fatal: the company's statisticians did their sums and produced projections for 1981 that made it clear that the loss would be at least as heavy that year as in 1980.

When those figures became available James Evans, the new chairman, was on holiday at his Welsh cottage. As many directors as could be mustered – nearly the whole board but excluding the two editors – were summoned to an emergency board meeting at the Bontddu Hall hotel in nearby Dolgellau. Dire pessimism was the prevailing mood. What would Gordon Brunton say when he learned the new figures? Times Newspapers was the only unprofitable bit of the international Thomson empire he ran from London, and its continued dismal performance did nothing to improve his standing with Lord Thomson and his aides in Canada. Was the series of threats, bluster and cajoling now reaching its logical conclusion? Was this really the last straw?

It might well have been, were it not that another last straw was about to be dropped on to their backs. Wage negotiations had been in progress during the summer with the National Union of Journalists. It was recognised that the settlement would have to be a large one, since in the last few years the journalists' pay had fallen far behind the inflation rate. There seemed, at first, nothing unusual or menacing about the bargaining. The management offered an increase of eighteen per cent and saw that as generous, bearing in mind the tremendous losses. The journalists sought twenty-one per cent and the case went to an arbitrator, who largely supported the journalists and awarded twenty per cent. The management might have accepted that had they not just received the shock of the 1981 projections, which the journalists knew nothing about. But the arbitration award had not been binding and the board rejected it. *Times* journalists went on strike on August 22nd, the Friday before the Bank Holiday weekend.

It was only a five-day strike but its effect was far-reaching. Lord Thomson, in his bleak mood, had said that the only consideration persuading him to keep the papers going was the loyalty of the staff, especially the journalists. So as not to jeopardise this he had – effectively from his own pocket, as he saw it – kept paying them for the year they had produced nothing. Now they had repaid that generosity by stopping the paper again in a dispute over a mere two per cent on an already high pay offer. Was there really any point in battling on?

Hamilton, the journalists' champion in boardroom discussions, was at his holiday house in Tuscany when he heard they were about to strike. Nearly everyone in authority was away. James Evans was still in Wales. Rees-Mogg was in California and at first resisted the suggestion of his deputy, Louis Heren, that he should return at once. "Only you can stop it," Heren told him on the Wednesday before the strike. "And anyway you are the editor." Rees-Mogg replied that he did not want to be caught in mid-air, incommunicado during the twelve-hour flight, when his advice might be needed about something crucial. Only when the strike had begun did he go home, arriving on Sunday.

Hamilton had returned a day earlier and invited Heren to dinner at his London flat. Old campaigners both, they were greatly upset, even maudlin, and found a useful scapegoat in Rees-Mogg, whom they criticised for not returning to the office the previous week. But in the main they felt betrayed by the journalists – *their* journalists, as both thought they had a right to regard them. It might have been high-handed of the management to reject the arbitrator's award but all the same there was such a thing as loyalty: or at least there used to be, when Heren and Hamilton were young newspapermen. Things were not the same now and it was no use pretending they were.

On Sunday and again on Bank Holiday Monday, those members of the Thomson board who could be summoned back from holiday met at Brunton's house in Godalming, Surrey, so as to be out of the limelight. Brunton was in touch by telephone with Thomson in Canada. He told him that in the view of the directors the papers should be sold forthwith. Thomson had been moving towards such a decision since the spring but it was none the less traumatic for him. He believed he still had a heavy responsibility to his father's aspirations for *The Times*. He was swayed by John Tory, the hard-headed chief executive of his Toronto organisation, who told him that the paper was draining his resources at a rate beyond that which he could afford. Reluctantly, he agreed that it should be sold.

A distraught Hamilton felt he no longer had any ground for quarrelling with the decision. "Look at your journalists now," some of the other directors told him derisively. At these two meetings in Surrey the decision to try to sell Times Newspapers was taken in principle. On Wednesday, at a Thomson board meeting that lasted seven hours, there were those who wanted to pull the plug right away. It was decided, however, to do it in an orderly fashion and not to announce it until procedures for the sale had been worked out. They did not want to make it seem like a petulant reaction to the strike. And they agreed that, at this stage,

William Rees-Mogg and Harold Evans should not be told.

So when Rees-Mogg briefed his assistant editors that week, he believed there was still a chance to rescue something from the wreckage. His tone was even more hectoring than it had been during the suspension. For years, he said, the Thomson family had supported *The Times* because, in the jungle of Fleet Street, they felt they could rely on its journalists if nothing else. "The Thomson family link with the paper has now been damaged twice," he said, speaking truer than he knew. "First by the failure of the print unions to honour their agreements last year and secondly by the journalists." While he had never thought during the suspension that the limit had been reached, they were nearly there now. And if the papers did close, journalists on strike would be entitled to no notice or redundancy payments, although those who declared themselves willing to work would receive those benefits. There were in fact some forty journalists on the paper not in the National Union of Journalists – some belonged to the Institute of Journalists, a docile group of which Rees-Mogg himself was a member. They and executives could have brought *The Times* out during the strike and Heren was keen for them to try, but James Evans ruled it out because of probable repercussions at the *Sunday Times* and among the print unions.

In the issue of Saturday, August 30th, the day after the resumption, Rees-Mogg wrote one of his sternest editorials, attacking the strikers without restraint. It was all, he wrote, a question of loyalty. Journalists could not be loyal equally to the NUJ and to *The Times*, even if they thought they could. And if they were not loyal to *The Times*, why should they expect the proprietor to be? "It must be obvious that what they chose to do has equally threatened their own jobs and the future life of *The Times*. That is their responsibility."

It took Brunton and his colleagues two months to work out the mechanics of the sale and announce it formally, but rumours were circulating in Fleet Street strong enough for Charles Douglas-Home to circularise foreign correspondents late in September, saying he thought it likely the search for a new owner had begun, although nobody in authority would yet confirm it. The national directors were told on September 25th. Murdoch had already been given his scarcely veiled tip by Thomson in the Concorde lounge at New York, and Concorde was to be the setting for the next stage in his gradual persuasion of himself that he should become the proprietor of *The Times*. Flying to Bahrein in October for a meeting of Reuters directors, he sat for a while next to Sir Denis Hamilton, who had been in charge of travel arrangements for the meeting and had deliberately put himself and the Australian on the same flight, though he claims no ulterior motive. "I had to be pretty Delphic in everything I said," Hamilton told the *Sunday Times* later. All the same, from that and his brief meeting with Thomson a month earlier, Murdoch now had no serious doubt that Times Newspapers would be for sale before long. And he still saw no reason to alter the conclusion he had reached earlier: that while the *Sunday Times* would make a profitable addition to his newspaper collection, *The Times* was chronically unviable, despite the obvious prestige to be gained from owning it.

On October 22nd Brunton announced that Times Newspapers was for sale. "The major reason behind this decision is the continuing troubled history of industrial relations," he said. "The newspapers have continued to be subjected to industrial disruption and various forms of non-cooperation from sections of the workforce and it has not been possible to operate the new technology even on the most limited basis." The company was likely to incur a pre-tax loss of fifteen million pounds during the current year and to borrow twenty-two million pounds from Thomson British Holdings. Since Thomson's had bought *The Times* in 1967, they had advanced Times Newspapers more than seventy million pounds, and to allow the present situation to continue would threaten the whole Thomson organisation. So if a suitable buyer was not found by March 1981 the papers would close, although Thomson British Holdings undertook to fund their operations until then and to arrange an orderly transfer or closure.

Brunton's statement stressed that the sale would be conducted with the highest degree of responsibility and probity. Hamilton, Harold Evans, Rees-Mogg and the national directors would advise on a set of criteria for proposed purchasers. "These will include the interests of employees, readers and advertisers, the national interest as well as commercial and financial criteria." The aim was to secure the future of the titles as "editorially independent newspapers of high quality". And Brunton concluded: "We believe that it is very much in the public interest that matters affecting the future of great national newspapers should be conducted in an open and responsible way."

A statement from Lord Thomson was tacked on to the end of Brunton's. He said the decision to sell had been reached with great regret. "My father and I have repeatedly made it clear that our continued support for Times Newspapers was conditional on the overall cooperation of the newspapers' employees and I have sadly concluded that this cooperation will not be forthcoming under our ownership. It grieves me greatly that in spite of the millions of pounds which have been provided to Times Newspapers over the years to enable these newspapers to survive and in spite of the efforts of many loyal employees . . . we have been unable to secure the cooperation of the workforce on a reliable and consistent basis."

Nobody could deny that Thomson and his father had been long-suffering almost to a fault. Yet there were those who wondered how a more capable proprietor – Murdoch for instance – would have reacted to the same difficulties. For sure, he would not have thrown in the towel at that stage. Faced with the inability of his executives to solve the problem, the first response would have been to change those executives – and if the next lot failed too he would change those, and so on until he got it right. On October 22nd, 1980, there were few who truly believed that events were moving in a direction where such idle speculation about Murdoch's methods could be directly tested.

Next morning the *Financial Times* ran through the list of possible buyers. The only one to express an interest at that stage was the inevitable Robert Maxwell. Tiny Rowland, chief executive of Lonrho, who controlled the *Glasgow Herald* and was later to buy the *Observer* from Atlantic Richfield, said: "No interest will be expressed and that should not be surprising. They are loss-makers." Rupert

Murdoch said a bid from him was unlikely. "We've got our hands pretty full," he mused. "I doubt whether there will be any buyers." And he added a glimpse of the obvious when he stated that, from an industrial relations viewpoint, Times Newspapers was a "snake pit".

In his statement, Brunton appeared to leave open the question whether the papers would be sold as one company or separately. In fact he had already made up his mind to sell them as a unit if he could, and in the two months between the decision to sell and the announcement he and his colleagues had been devising a procedure for the sale that would offer the best chance of such an outcome. Brunton knew he had to proceed with great caution to fulfil two paramount considerations. The first was that Thomson's wanted to escape from the commitment as cheaply as possible, and if the company was broken into components they would be liable for massive redundancy payments. And although Brunton realised that he could not hope to recoup all the losses of the last few years, he wanted some cash in exchange for the titles. Second, and as important, was the concern to be seen to be acting responsibly. After selling Times Newspapers, Thomson's would still have important interests in Britain, some of them – notably North Sea oil – relying to an extent on government goodwill. At the end of it, Brunton wanted to be able to maintain convincingly that he had done what was best for the public interest by vesting the future of the papers in the hands of an acceptable owner who could be expected to make them succeed.

When he came to make a list of those who might want to buy the newspapers and who fulfilled those criteria he could find only a handful. At the top of his list were Rupert Murdoch and Lord Rothermere of Associated Newspapers. Having reached the conclusion that these were the most desirable purchasers, Brunton then had to frame conditions for the sale that would attract them. He decided to institute a strict timetable for every stage in the purchase. To begin with, Warburg's, Thomson's bankers, would prepare a prospectus on the commercial condition of Times Newspapers. Anyone with a plausible interest in making a bid would be given a copy on condition they signed a pledge of confidentiality. This was a useful primary filter, for Thomson's could simply decline to give a prospectus to bidders they thought manifestly unsuitable from the outset.

The prospectus appeared in November. It was a remarkably optimistic document. Thomson's private projections for 1981, before the sale had been decided upon, were that losses would be at least as great as in 1980 – £13 million. In the document, though, they had been whittled down to £4,295,000. This was because the Warburg projections were based on a new buyer being able to negotiate the manning cuts that Thomson's had failed to achieve during the suspension. It postulated the departure of 576 full-time staff members by 1983 – but it did not take into account redundancy payments due to those leaving. Thus the two papers were seen as making an £8 million profit in 1982 and double that in 1983.

Potential buyers had little time to ponder these dazzling predictions, for bids had to be in by the end of December. Bids were invited for both the whole company and the papers separately, on the understanding that a good bid for the company as a whole would take precedence over the others. By adhering rigidly to the December 23rd deadline, Brunton ensured that nobody seriously interested could afford to wait and see what the others were doing – the way Murdoch for one preferred to do business. It minimised the chance of a buyer coming in at the end and picking up the papers for almost nothing as a bidder of last resort, as Murdoch had done with the *Sun*. In effect, only people who had made a serious bid for the whole company by December 31st had a chance of being chosen as the purchaser.

Brunton's announcement that the papers would close in mid-March if the deal was not completed by then, left ten weeks for negotiation after the closing of bids. The most important result of this was virtually to rule out any reference to the Monopolies Commission – which usually takes about three months – unless there were to be a break in publication. This was important because neither Murdoch nor Rothermere, with their important Fleet Street holdings, could expect an easy time from the Commission. In all, the procedure for the sale amounted to an expert piece of stage management. It was like those London conferences in the 1950s and 1960s that took Britain's African and other colonies to independence: the constitution was cleverly drawn up to ensure victory for the party Britain wanted to see win the elections – although, as it turned out, once that party was in full control there was no effective check on whatever excesses it had in mind to carry out.

Though Brunton had made up his mind to sell the papers as a unit, both Rees-Mogg and Harold Evans thought they would be better off separated, for the marriage had never been an especially happy one. Brunton once had sympathy for that view. In conversation with Louis Heren a few months earlier he had spoken of the desirability of pushing the papers apart somewhat, and the reorganisation of the boards in June had been a move in that direction. The reason he now gave for wanting to sell them together was that, without the potential profits of the *Sunday Times*, *The Times* would be hopelessly unviable and might not survive.

Sudden shocks often make people act out of character, sparking responses that surprise even themselves. Allowing for that, though, Rees-Mogg's reaction to Brunton's announcement was altogether remarkable. During the last few months his colleagues had noted that the suspension of the paper and the troubled year since had left the editor with an ineffable weariness, persuading some that he was losing interest in his job and in the paper. But its impending closure concentrated his mind wonderfully, almost miraculously. By philosophy and emotion, Rees-Mogg had always been opposed to the collective ethic, thundering against it in the leader columns of *The Times*. Yet what he proposed, when he called the staff together on the afternoon of the Thomson statement, was a new form of ownership for *The Times*, a modified co-operative of journalists and managers, financed by outside capital. The paper would operate with a reduced staff and lower overheads, probably printing under contract outside London, making full use of advanced technology.

During the 1979 suspension a group called Journalists of *The Times* (JOTT) had been established to be in a position to rescue the paper should its owners abandon it. The brainchild of Hugh Stephenson, editor of the Business

News section, this ill-organised outfit had formed itself into a limited company, with one share issued to each journalist who chose to join. Now Rees-Mogg was proposing that he should ally himself with this group, his name bolstering its credibility to those who would have to put up the money and had never heard of Stephenson.

When he told this to his stunned staff – their second shock following the announcement of the sale – Rees-Mogg adopted a revivalist tone. "I do not myself think we should wait for the arrival of a new proprietor on a white horse," he cried. "If we are to secure the future of the paper we must do it ourselves . . . I have already begun working on trying to put these ideas together . . . We now have two choices: we can leave it to other people to save us or we can work to save ourselves." He added that he was going to Canada and America at the weekend to fulfil a long-standing engagement and would take the opportunity to speak to Lord Thomson about his plan and sound out prospects for American investment in the consortium. Before he left he met the journalists again, and in the two days since the previous meeting he had become more than ever gripped by the power of the idea. "I think what we are trying to do will very possibly emerge as the best future organisation for Fleet Street," he enthused. "People still think in terms of a Don Quixote on a white horse claiming to be proprietor and I find this extremely annoying . . . Any ultimate decision will be taken in a collective spirit." And he took the opportunity to dismiss the only Don Quixote who had declared himself, Robert Maxwell. "I certainly do not consider him suitable . . . Not only is he unsatisfactory but he has not got a great deal of money either." He rubbed in the objection by repeating it to Maxwell's face during a television discussion.

Armed with his new alliance, Rees-Mogg headed for America to shake the dollar tree, but found it for the most part unshakable. It was not surprising, when you thought about it, for in his editorials about the suspension and the sale of the paper, he had given vent to his most dire musings about the appalling state of Fleet Street's industrial relations: hardly an effective lure for a prospective backer. And most Americans thought the idea of a workers' co-operative, however hard Rees-Mogg tried to avoid using the word, was . . . well, a bit flaky. He saw Katharine Graham at the *Washington Post* and the senior executives at *Time* magazine. He also went down to the office of the *New York Post* to talk to Rupert Murdoch.

Although it was only a few days since Murdoch had seemed to declare his lack of interest, Rees-Mogg received the impression that he would bid for the *Sunday Times* if it could be separated from *The Times*. For that reason, the Australian seemed supportive of Rees-Mogg's consortium plan, even suggesting that if the newly-constituted *Times* were to come into being, he might be able to print it at Worcester, where News International owned the local Berrow's newspaper chain. It was conceivable, Murdoch calculated, that if a viable plan could be devised for *The Times*, headed by so reputable a figure as Rees-Mogg, Thomson's might after all be persuaded to sell the papers separately.

There was no doubt about Murdoch's interest in the *Sunday Times*, for he spent some time praising Harold Evans in the most effusive manner, describing him – as he was to do publicly a few months later – as the greatest editor in the world. If this appeared an impolite observation to make to a man who might think *he* was in the running for that accolade, Rees-Mogg did not seem to notice. Indeed, like many of his class after their first meeting with the mature Murdoch, he went away with a much more favourable impression than he had anticipated. Basing his expectation on what he had read in his own and other newspapers, he had been prepared to meet an un-couth ogre with a rough accent, but was instead surprised at the tycoon's smoothness and refined manners. What gave Rees-Mogg more pleasure than anything was to be served a thoroughly English cup of tea (not normally encountered in Manhattan offices). It came on traditional blue and white china, in gracious and comfortable surroundings. As he sipped and clinked cup on saucer, Rees-Mogg reflected that it is the *detail* that is so important on occasions of this kind, and Murdoch had the detail just right. Could he, surrepti-tiously, be a gentleman after all?

In Toronto the itinerant editor found Thomson fairly

receptive to the idea of a *Times* consortium, but cautious, stressing that Brunton was the man who would decide. Brunton, hearing reports from Thomson's aide John Tory on Rees-Mogg's adventure, was furious. How dare he patch together some harebrained scheme for a journalists' co-operative and then dash off to America trying to get backing for it, without so much as a by-your-leave? Why, the papers were not his to sell. They were Thomson's, and through him Brunton's, and Brunton was going to dispose of them as *he* wanted. Certainly he was not going to hand over the prerogative to an effete intellectual with utopian plans for a consortium.

Arriving back in London, Rees-Mogg was summoned to see Brunton for a dressing-down. "William, for God's sake, don't pursue this," Brunton pleaded, stressing his view that the only chance for the survival of *The Times* was in harness with the more viable Sunday paper, and that he was jeopardising it by pursuing his idea. Rees-Mogg, surprised by the ferocity of Brunton's reaction, quickly agreed to tread water for the time being, reserving the right to resume his efforts in earnest if Brunton could not find a buyer for the group as a whole. The consortium was now a fall-back position solely, and Brunton for one was going to do his utmost to see that he never had to fall back on it.

So when Rees-Mogg saw the staff again on his return, he began with a long preamble explaining how Thomson was looking for a single buyer for the whole company. He had his doubts about whether one would be found, and if it did not happen, then the consortium idea would come into play. Planning went ahead but, after his meeting with Brunton, the editor's crusading spirit waned. The ringing confidence of the previous week was no more. "We are not in a position to make a bid for the whole company and we are therefore not in the first stage, in considering the future of *The Times*," he told his new partners, the journalists. "But I believe we are in a position to say that we shall be able to carry on *The Times* if *The Times* is to be carried on on its own . . . rather than being dependent on some stray millionaire walking in off the street." This was already rather distant from his heady vision of co-operative ideals taking over not just at *The Times* but in all of Fleet Street.

Rees-Mogg telephoned Harold Evans to tell him about his meeting with Murdoch and to report that the Australian seemed interested in the *Sunday Times*, especially in its editor. "Why don't you phone him?" Rees-Mogg suggested, but Evans did not do so. He had long been under the impression that Murdoch did not much like him – a belief based on previous brief encounters and on reports from colleagues. For his own part, while he could admire Murdoch's energy and skills in tabloid journalism, he had no reason to think they could work profitably together. Rees-Mogg's report of how Murdoch had sung his praises only made Evans wary, for he was now engaged in consortium-building himself. At his right hand was Bernard Donoughue, an economist who had been an adviser to Harold Wilson at Downing Street and a close friend of Evans since then. Donoughue had long been appalled at the condition of Fleet Street, seeing it as an extreme example of the ills that beset much of the rest of British industry. He had become convinced that the only future for national newspapers lay in their workers having a real stake in their success, discouraging the strikes and go-slows that constantly hampered production. With Evans, he devised a formula under which journalists would have the chance of buying £1,000 worth of shares each and the production unions could also invest in the company. The main capital would have to come from outside and, given that the paper had made a profit in seventeen of the last twenty years, it was not too hard to raise. American investors *were* interested in the *Sunday Times*. Charter Oil of Pennsylvania, owners of the Philadelphia *Bulletin*, pledged support and in Britain there was backing from the Scottish Widows Insurance Company. Evans also made approaches to *The Guardian* and Granada Television, both of which expressed initial interest but were unable finally to agree to take part in a consortium. Addressing a meeting of his staff, he stressed that his scheme would be a lot preferable to being owned by any of the "seven dwarfs" who tended to sniff around whenever papers were for sale. (He was referring to Rupert Murdoch, Robert Maxwell, Lord Rothermere, Sir James Goldsmith, Tiny Rowland, Lord Matthews of the

Express group and Lord Barnetson of United Newspapers.) Most of his listeners agreed.

As December wore on, Brunton waited in some trepidation for expressions of interest to come in and, rather to his surprise, several did, quickly mounting to double figures and as high as fifty before the deadline was reached. When Brunton and Thomson thought of Times Newspapers the only figures dancing in their heads were in red ink, or were images of obstructive printers and undelivered newspapers. Yet to many people the idea of owning one or two such famous titles was inordinately seductive. To own *The Times*: wouldn't that be a passport to the top tables, the most influential circles in the land? And wouldn't that be something worth having? For fifty hopefuls, it would.

Most of them, though, failed to fit the criteria the Thomson board had established. Some were financed, directly or otherwise, by Arab oil money, and Brunton was determined that the ability of the two papers to express themselves freely in Middle East disputes should not be compromised in this way. The Aga Khan, who owns a newspaper in Kenya, was among the more unlikely bidders, and another surprising name among them was James Sherwood of Sea Containers, perhaps trying to emulate fellow shipping magnate Victor Matthews of Cunard by adding a newspaper to his interests. Edward Du Cann, a Conservative MP and director of Lonrho, made powerful approaches to Brunton on behalf of Tiny Rowland, despite his disclaimer, but Brunton thought Lonrho's newspaper and other commitments in the developing world might, as with the Arabs, make *The Times* subject to unwelcome political pressure. Atlantic Richfield (Arco), the American oil company, made the running early on, but would surely merge the *Sunday Times* with the *Observer*, which they then owned, and Brunton did not relish that. (Soon after failing to acquire Times Newspapers, Arco sold the *Observer* to Lonrho.) Associated Newspapers showed interest, but more in the *Sunday Times* than the daily. Robert Holmes à Court bid for *The Times* alone.

Murdoch's instinct would have been to wait until after the December deadline on the assumption that there would by then have been no acceptable bid and he could have picked up the company – or the *Sunday Times* part of it at least – at a bargain basement price. But when he heard rumours of the other buyers in the field he decided he must make his move within the specified time if he was to stand a chance. He also realised that, because other bidders had expressed interest in the two papers and the supplements as a package, he must do the same if his bid was to be considered. Brunton's tactics had worked and had brought Murdoch to the point of decision. Did he really want to saddle himself with *The Times*? Was the undoubted prestige worth the equally undoubted strife? Well, yes, in the end it was. The shark, despite having declared himself a convert to vegetarianism, could not, when it came to it, resist the smell of blood. Addiction is never really cured.

In early December Murdoch telephoned Brunton from New York. "I want to put in a bid," he said. "Rupert, you'd better come over," Brunton replied. "We'll talk." Murdoch went to Warburg's to pick up the prospectus and quickly decided it was over-optimistic. All the same, he met Brunton at the London flat of Lord Catto, Murdoch's London banker, and the negotiations were under way.

What helped convince Brunton that Murdoch was the most serious and thus the most suitable potential purchaser was the fact that he oversaw the negotiations personally and was constantly on the phone to Brunton or one of his executives questioning this or that figure in the Warburg prospectus. No other bidder took such an interest. Moreover, from what Brunton knew of Murdoch – mainly from contacts in the Newspaper Publishers' Association – he was a straight-dealing man who would stick to a bargain and knew how to skirt Fleet Street's industrial booby-traps. Maybe his existing British papers would make curious bedfellows for *The Times* and the *Sunday Times* but at least they were competently run, which more than anything was what Times Newspapers needed. Murdoch was not the ideal owner for *The Times*, but then neither was Lord Thomson fourteen years earlier. You had to settle for the best available.

Before bids closed in December, Brunton had decided that he wanted Murdoch to buy the papers. His resolve was strengthened the following month when he called in the leaders of the print unions and asked them which of a list of potential purchasers they preferred. They strongly favoured Murdoch, on the grounds that they knew him, found him a tough but fair bargainer and because he had rescued the *Sun* – and with it many of their members' jobs. (More surprisingly, when Harold Evans took a similar poll among some *Sunday Times* journalists, he found the same majority opinion.)

Brunton recognised that Murdoch's initial bid of a million pounds was a sighting shot, a declaration of interest that would be improved upon. The final price of twelve million pounds was not the highest offer Brunton received. Associated Newspapers put in two bids – twenty million pounds for the company as a whole or twenty-five million for the *Sunday Times* alone. Rothermere badly wanted a Sunday paper to maximise the use of his *Daily Mail* presses, but Brunton was not convinced that his intentions towards *The Times* were motivated by an equal fervour. Rothermere, who lives in Paris, took no personal part in the negotiations. The Associated team was led by Mike Shields, the group managing director, and he consistently refused to give any pledge that he could keep *The Times* going. He calculated, though, that even if £20 million was a lot to pay for a loss-making business, it had to be set against the high start-up costs of the proposed *Mail on Sunday*, launched the following year, and against the probability that the *Sunday Times* presses could have been adapted to print all the *Mail* titles, enabling them to vacate their valuable but outdated premises off Fleet Street.

Rothermere was gloomy about the prospects of a successful bid, confiding to associates his conviction that Brunton had already decided to sell to Murdoch and that Associated were being used as a cloak of respectability to convince people it was a real contest. In the *Sunday Times* on February 15th, "one observer" (believed to be Brunton) was quoted as saying: "Rothermere's bid seemed rather fluffy; about as substantial as a snowfall in June." This provoked an angry letter next week from Shields, stressing that his firm's offer was serious, formal and properly made. "The 'observer' who told you differently may well have been motivated by something other than a desire to tell the truth," he wrote sinisterly.

Brunton's conviction that Murdoch was the right man was not in itself enough to ensure that he would be chosen, for to establish the purity of their intentions Thomson's had devised a "vetting" procedure under which the selected candidate had to submit himself to a committee comprising Hamilton, the two editors and the four national directors – now Lord Robens, the veteran politician, Lord Dacre, still better known as historian Hugh Trevor-Roper, former rail union leader Lord (Sid) Greene and the economist Lord Roll, chairman of Warburg's, whose dual role in the affair gave rise to suggestions in Parliament of conflict of interest.

The committee were to meet Murdoch on January 21st, the day final commercial terms of the sale were to be settled. The previous month they had already agreed a set of criteria roughly parallel with those of Brunton: the new owner would need financial credibility, stable management, no embarrassing political connections and would have to guarantee the independence of the editor. They had decided not to rule out American or Commonwealth purchasers but they believed British was best, if available. It was an interesting commentary on the altered status of *The Times* that the "national interest" was not mentioned this time round.

When they came to meet on January 21st at Thomson House – a solid Regency terraced house in Stratford Place, to the north of Oxford Street – the national directors discovered that they were not, as they hoped they might be, in a position to choose between rival candidates. The choice had effectively been made for them. As it was put to them, it was Murdoch or nothing. Their job was to approve Murdoch or reject him. If they exercised their undoubted right to turn him down, the search for a new owner (or owners) would have to be resumed less than two months before the deadline for closure. They were informed about the other contenders only in the context of why they had been ruled out. Associated Newspapers, they were told confidently, only wanted the company for asset-stripping purposes – they would keep the *Sunday Times* and sell off everything else. (Associated later denied this.)

Robens was abroad and unable to attend the meeting.
The other six, as they sat waiting for Murdoch to appear
before them, felt uncomfortable. They were, in effect, a
court of last resort, custodians of the public interest, the
final obstacle to a consummation which, only months earlier, most of them would have regarded as unthinkable.
Both editors had published articles condemning Murdoch
and the style of journalism he personified. He was one of
Harold Evans's "seven dwarfs". In September, at the
express insistence of Rees-Mogg, I had written an article
from New York about the poor repute in which Murdoch
was held in some circles there. I wrote of "the journalism of
the lowest common denominator" and "the breathless,
grubby vision of the world inherent in the Murdoch style".
The editor, pleased with my work, had given the article
unusual prominence, illustrated with a front page of the
New York Post bearing the headline: PREGNANT MOM
IN 911 TERROR.

Now Rees-Mogg was being asked to approve this man as
the proprietor of the paper he had nurtured during the last
fourteen years, and the others had equally painful adjust-
ments to make. Hamilton wryly recalled his leading part in
condemning Murdoch over the Keeler memoirs but, drawing as he often did on his wartime experience, he comforted
himself with the thought that the Australians had been the
best fighters on either side – the least disciplined but
tremendous in a scrap. In the current condition of Fleet
Street, this was a quality that would be needed above all.
When asked by Lord Dacre whether any undertakings
Murdoch gave could be relied upon, Hamilton had to admit
that what the Australian actually did was not always consistent with what he said he was going to do. But he recommended approval none the less, stressing that the new
owner should be made to put on paper specific pledges
which the Trade Minister, whose approval of the deal was
necessary, could give the force of legislation. Realistically,
despite their serious reservations, that was all the vetting
committee could do.

Upstairs, the negotiations between Murdoch and
Brunton were reaching their final stages. There was a
hiccup when Murdoch angrily accused the Thomson team,

in the person of Scottish accountant Ian Clubb, of misleading him over the valuation of the company's assets. Brunton leapt to his colleague's defence: "Rupert, you bloody well don't talk to my people like that," he shouted. "This deal is off as of now, but before you walk out of this room, bloody well apologise to him." That seemed to calm Murdoch. Clubb explained the disputed point again and Searby, who accompanied Murdoch throughout the discussions, said he now understood it. Both principals made much of that tiff in describing the deal later, with the aim of convincing people that they had negotiated toughly to the limit. Brunton used it as the basis for saying there had been "blood on the walls" at Thomson House and Murdoch told the *Sunday Times* that he had been shaking when he went up to meet the national directors. "These dignified gentlemen probably thought I was quaking with fear," he said. In fact, the dignified gentlemen noticed nothing untoward. In his book *Good Times, Bad Times*, Harold Evans describes how Murdoch entered 'like someone visiting a friend in hospital, walking quietly, speaking softly.'

Hamilton seemed almost apologetic at having to ask such intrusive questions about the bridegroom's intentions. He stressed the tradition of editorial independence on the two papers and Murdoch gave ringing assurances that he intended to respect it. And he accepted that editors could be appointed and dismissed only with the agreement of the national directors. At least one member of the committee thought he had given the pledges a little too readily. "One got the feeling that even if we'd asked for a different set of assurances he'd have given them equally easily," he said. "It wasn't too reassuring – very Australian." As well as promising to give the national directors the right to veto his choice of editor, Murdoch undertook to augment them by two. One would be Sir Denis Hamilton, though as a member of the Times Newspapers board he was not strictly independent at all. The other name proposed then was Lord McGregor of the Advertising Standards Authority, but he turned down the appointment because of the potential for conflict of interest. The national directors voted to approve Murdoch and, around midnight, Brunton opened the celebratory drinks.

Lord Dacre, for one, was sceptical about the amount of control that could be exercised over Murdoch once he had the titles, however many national directors there were. A few days afterwards he told Lord Longford: "We have put a paper hook through the nose of Leviathan." Nearly a year later, during one of the more serious crises that were to pepper the initial months of Murdoch's ownership, Longford asked him: "Where's your hook now?" "I did say," Dacre rejoined, "that it was just a *paper* hook."

The deal for Murdoch to buy Times Newspapers was conditional on his agreeing with staff unions about economies, but when it was announced the following day everyone assumed it would go ahead. "I have operated and launched newspapers all over the world," said a jubilant Murdoch at a press conference at the Portman Hotel in London. "This new undertaking I regard as the most exciting challenge of my life." The staffs at both papers were shattered by the development, although it had been rumoured for days. Many still entertained hopes for the Evans and Rees-Mogg consortiums, not recognising that they had effectively been non-starters almost since the beginning. Rees-Mogg had the sensitive task of explaining things to his journalists – some of whom thought that even now it might be possible for the JOTT consortium to make a bid to buy *The Times* from Murdoch. Rees-Mogg deflated that idea as gently as he could, then made a brave attempt to recommend the Murdoch deal as "the best that could have been achieved in the circumstances." He thought the guarantees of editorial independence would be effective, but pointed out it was not questions of editorial freedom that had taken the paper to its present pass. Bad management had done that, and Murdoch's existing Fleet Street papers had a better record there. "I think we have got with Rupert Murdoch a genuine chance of being very well managed." For the next morning's paper he wrote a leader making that point but giving the new owner a slightly tentative welcome.

The day after the announcement, Murdoch trotted excitedly round the Gray's Inn Road offices of his two new properties. "Who are you?" he would ask random people at desks. "Are you important?" He would not wait for a reply, but his patent enthusiasm for the most exciting challenge of his life was to lead him into an error that might easily have damaged his prospect of being confirmed as owner. He had two hurdles to clear yet – his negotiations with the unions and the possibility of a referral to the Monopolies Commission, which would have delayed matters beyond the Thomson deadline for closure. To encourage public opinion to oppose a referral, he had, in the early days, to be seen to be adhering strictly to his undertakings. Yet he could scarcely contain himself. On his first Saturday visit to the *Sunday Times* office, he noticed the paper was running an editorial headlined "Rupert Murdoch" and asked to see a proof. Written by Evans, it gave a more enthusiastic welcome to the new proprietor than Rees-Mogg's tepid leader of two days earlier. "He is certainly now preferred to any of the other would-be corporate purchasers," Evans wrote, "because of his energy, his directness, his publishing flair and, above all, the commitments he has given on editorial independence."

The argument of the editorial was that the Murdoch purchase ought not to be referred to the Monopolies Commission because the delay might jeopardise the papers' future. In support of his case, Evans listed the newspaper titles owned by other Fleet Street groups; but in his listing for Express Newspapers he omitted the *Daily Star*, a quite new and vigorous paper of which Murdoch was particularly aware because it competed directly with The *Sun*. Murdoch noticed the omission, made a mark on the proof and sent it to Evans suggesting it should be altered. In later editions, it was. Neither man saw it as an especially significant intervention – the simple correction of a fact. Yet when the left-wing weekly *New Statesman*, vociferously opposed to Murdoch and the acquisition, revealed the incident that week, it was able to present it as an alteration in Murdoch's favour of the balance of the argument in the leading article – the first instance of the new proprietor intervening to promote his self-interest. In a letter to the *New Statesman* the following week, Evans said Murdoch had promised not to do it again; but the slip did renew the fears of the many doubters that, however honourable his intentions, the "hands off" pledge would be one that, instinctively, he would find terribly hard to comply with.

While negotiations with the unions on manning cuts went ahead rapidly, the issue of the Monopolies Commission looked more menacing. The legal position was that any deal involving a change of ownership of a newspaper selling more than half a million copies had automatically to be referred to the commission unless the Government were satisfied that the papers were losing money and that the delay (generally about three months) might prove fatal. In the House of Commons Labour MPs urged John Biffen, the Trade Minister, to refer the deal to the commission but there was opposition from the print unions, who feared for their members' jobs. Murdoch, whose existing British newspapers were enthusiastic in their support of Margaret Thatcher, felt the Government owed him a favour and there was skilled and discreet lobbying in Westminster by Denis Hamilton. Persuaded, Biffen issued a White Paper declaring that, since both papers were in the red, the purchase would not be referred to the commission.

There was some suspicion that Brunton had set such a short deadline specifically to deter a reference to the commission, and Biffen hinted in the Commons that he shared this belief. The Thomson timetable, he said, had been "a disturbing aspect of this whole episode". Murdoch had made it clear from the beginning that if the deal was referred he might not go through with it, summing up his attitude in this snap answer when he appeared before the House of Commons Education Committee: "People seem to think they are doing me a favour in allowing me to take something that is losing thirteen million pounds a year."

A group of journalists on the *Sunday Times*, hoping that the favour might still be undone, decided to fight Biffen's ruling. While nobody could deny that *The Times* was losing money, the *Sunday Times*, according to the Warburg prospectus, was viable. The journalists suspected sharp practice with the figures and decided to institute legal action against Biffen to force him to refer the deal. They were motivated in part by their disappointment over the failure of their consortium. Their appetites had been whetted by the prospect of actually owning part of their newspaper, and they had entertained hopes for the consortium long after the disappearance of any real chance of its success. They became dismayed, though, to discover that the cost of taking legal action against Biffen could be hundreds of pounds for each of them, and most were thus quite relieved when Murdoch offered a compromise: if they dropped the action he would further strengthen the guarantees of editorial freedom and agree to the appointment of two journalists to the board of Times Newspapers – Louis Heren from *The Times* and Peter Roberts, managing editor of the *Sunday Times*.

Those journalists most fervently opposed to Murdoch were disappointed that they received no support from Harold Evans, who now seemed by his actions and his editorials to be committed firmly to Murdoch. (When his book was published in 1983, Evans sought to reopen the question of a Monopolies Commission reference, asserting that subsequent research proved that Biffen was working on falsified figures when he declared the *Sunday Times* unviable. Had he supported that proposition when made by his staff 2½ years earlier, he might have prevented Murdoch's acquisition of the papers.) Some suspected that Evans had been won over at a quite early stage by a promise that he could edit *The Times*, but both men have denied this. Evans's position was that, as a member of the vetting committee that had approved Murdoch, he could not in all conscience continue to work against him. He had suggested in January that he might quit the vetting committee to avoid such a clash but colleagues thought it important he should stay on it. His last formal act for the consortium was to make a last-minute bid for support to Associated Newspapers. He went to see the Associated directors accompanied by Donoughue, Peter Harland, an assistant editor, and Donald Cruickshank, finance director of Times Newspapers, who was helping organise the consortium. By that time they realised that to have any chance of success they would have to link in some way with *The Times* consortium to make a joint bid, since this was the only kind Brunton would consider. Mike Shields, Associated's managing director, said he wanted nothing to do with *The Times*, but Evans explained that after the joint purchase the papers could be split and go their own ways. Negotiations foundered on Shields' insistence that Associated should have a controlling interest of fifty-one per cent. (It was this meeting that led *Private Eye* to suggest he had been secretly plotting against Murdoch, but Evans stressed that it took place *before* Murdoch's approval by the vetting committee, and he threatened to sue the magazine.)

At a very late stage the two consortiums did place a joint bid. It arose from a meeting between Donoughue, Cruickshank, Stephenson and John Jackson, a businessman who was going to be chief executive of *The Times* if the bid was accepted. But it was by now clear that there was almost no chance that Brunton would consider selling to any kind of consortium even if the Murdoch deal did not go ahead.

On Monday, January 26th, five days after his positive vetting, Murdoch addressed the editorial staff of *The Times* in a crowded news room. He stressed the need to make *The Times* viable and recognised that this would take time – up to five years – and money. Asked to be specific about changes, he mentioned putting in a separate arts and entertainment section on Fridays – "an idea I have had" – and added: "We should really be lively in the sense of consumerism, I suppose: consumer service for our upper middle-class readers." That, and his suggestion that the circulation might rise to half a million, would have appalled the White Swan group and, even more, the opponents of the 1957 Cooper Report, with their scorn for the Reading Public.

Clifford Longley, the Religious Affairs Correspondent of *The Times*, is, as befits his subject, a man of rigid moral standards, wary of compromise, difficult to please. At the start of the shutdown in November 1978 he wrote a letter to the *Guardian* suggesting in the strongest terms that Rees-Mogg had failed his staff and should resign. A few days later, as penance, he wrote another letter saying he was wrong. Now, in the news room, he told Murdoch that not all the staff had been won over by the guarantees of editorial independence. "A lot of us are in two minds yet as to whether or not this is in fact the best thing or whether we should be satisfied," he agonised. "Could you say anything further?"

Murdoch's answer was modest to the point of bleakness. "I can sell myself to you as the least of the alternative evils," he said. "I do honestly believe, with respect to the efforts of many of you, that it is me or Lonrho or Atlantic Richfield. As regards the guarantees themselves. . . I think I have locked myself in, particularly with the power I have given (to the national directors) of absolute right of hiring and firing of editors and given them the right to be a self-perpetuating body. . . What if I found a way of tearing up all those guarantees and fired an editor? The answer is there would be a terrible public stink and it would destroy the paper . . . I get on with these people or I get out. Otherwise I would destroy what I am attempting to buy."

The respectful, concerned tone of his remarks about *The Times* contrasted with disparaging comments he was reported to have made about the paper and its staff in public and in private. Marcel Berlins, the legal correspondent, noticed the discrepancy and asked him about it. "Yes," Murdoch replied. "I had called *The Times* a dead duck. But perhaps I should have said a sick duck."

The journalists were sufficiently impressed for a group of them to draft a statement to the Press Association announcing that they now approved of the Murdoch purchase. An explanation for this new attitude had been made to foreign correspondents a few days earlier by Leslie Plommer, an astute young Canadian woman who worked on the foreign desk. In a circular to overseas bureaux, she wrote: "Most journalists seem in the throes of what we in the Pentagon siege-psychology section like to call Self Induced Mind Reversal, in which the subject seeks to persuade himself that the object of fear and loathing is not so bad, and even likely to be quite beneficial."

In Toronto Lord Thomson could scarcely contain his relief at having shed the dreadful burden, although he was able to muster a few decent words of regret. "It's a sadness to know that we are no longer associated with these wonderful newspapers," he said. "But we have committed the papers to the hands of someone who has the ability to make them work. Rupert Murdoch is a good newspaperman and businessman. I know that he has the desire to show the world that he can produce good newspapers as well as sensational ones."

A Thomson director said: "To my mind the best thing we did for *The Times* in all the years we owned it was the way we carried out the sale."

Chapter 9

THE TROUBLE WITH HARRY

Harold Evans . . . I regard as one of the world's great editors.
– *Rupert Murdoch, January 1981.*

Three weeks after the installation of a new administration is a busy and fruitful time for the hundreds of correspondents from all over the world whose job is to report and interpret the word from Washington. There are new government appointments to be reported and speculated about, straws to be plucked from the wind to see if they offer hints as to how sincerely campaign pledges will be fulfilled. New contacts are to be sought, phone numbers noted, dates made for lunch.

On February 12th, 1981, twenty-three days into the Reagan era, Patrick Brogan, the lean, grey Washington correspondent of *The Times*, would have expected to be engrossed in just such concerns. He had been nearly eight years in the capital, first as deputy chief correspondent and for the last four years in the top post. He had arrived as the Watergate drama was reaching its climax and this was his third presidential inauguration. He had seen Gerald Ford take the oath as the man who would heal the nation's wounds, then reported the single and in some respects singular term of Jimmy Carter. At the start of the new conservative era this talented correspondent, whose father, Denis Brogan, had been one of the most vivid of all British writers about America, was ideally equipped to interpret for his readers just what it all meant.

Yet on this wintry Washington Thursday he was in no mood to do any such thing and his readers would, for the most part, have taken only a passing interest if he had tried. He and they were preoccupied with a matter that affected them in a more personal way. Entering *The Times*'s spartan fifth-floor office in the National Press Building at his usual gentlemanly hour of 10 a.m., Brogan walked right over to the telex machine and perused a one-line message that had arrived a few moments earlier. It was not addressed to him but to Frank Vogl, his colleague, who wrote for the Business News section. It was terse and contained news that for weeks he had been dreading, though he had known there was no real chance of averting it:

IT'S THE DIGGER: OFFICIAL.

As Brogan stood and read in silence, the machine burst into life with a second cable, fuller than the first and unsigned. The indications were that it had been composed by one of the telex operators in the wire-room at Gray's Inn Road, keen to have his say and impart the news to the largely faceless folk across the Atlantic with whom he was in daily communication:

THE DIGGER NOW HAS OUR TITLES FIRMLY IN HIS POUCH.
SIGNING OF THE WALLABY DEAL 1500 GMT.
COVER YOUR PRIVATE PARTS.
NICE DAY IN LONDON AFTER OVERNIGHT FROST.
SUN SHINING OUTSIDE.
LONG LIVE THE TIMES.

Brogan smiled thinly at the line about private parts. It referred to a message he had sent to London four weeks earlier, when he had first, to his horror and amazement, heard that the negotiations with Murdoch were advanced and likely to succeed. Brogan, although only in his early forties, was an archetypal old *Times* man who had cared enough about the traditional standards of the paper to sign the White Swan letter in 1970. Murdoch, he was convinced, would destroy what little remained of those standards, not right away – even he was too subtle – but gradually, as he saw prospects for commercial success by the old route slip away. So a month ago, getting the first whiff of the change, Brogan had rattled out a feature about Murdoch's image in America, about how he had altered the *New York Post*, spicing his article with the hint of suspected scandal over the loan from the Export-Import Bank.

He had cabled the piece to London but, scarcely surprisingly in the circumstances, it had not been printed. Next day he sent off an uncharacteristically fierce enquiry, asking:

WHY WASN'T MY MURDOCH PIECE USED? OR
RATHER, WHOSE PUSILLANIMITY PREVAILED?
I AM TOLD THAT HE IS GOING AROUND
TELLING HIS COBBERS THAT HE IS
ABSOLUTELY DETERMINED TO BUY TNL.,
IGNORING COUNSELS OF CAUTION FROM SAID
COBBERS. THEN HE WILL CUT ALL YOUR
BALLS OFF, IF YOU HAVE ANY. REGARDS.

He had followed up that démarche with an exchange of telex messages with Rees-Mogg. "Mr Murdoch runs very many, very bad newspapers," he wrote, comparing him with Northcliffe. "I believe that Brunton, James Evans and the rest of them are betraying all the promises Roy Thomson made in 1966 and repeated frequently afterwards . . . When Thomson's intention to sell *The Times* was announced, you wrote that *The Times* would fight for her own survival and that you would join the fight. I hope you will continue to do so."

Rees-Mogg replied briefly, assuring Brogan that he took his message seriously but rejecting the comparison of Murdoch with Northcliffe. "I believe *The Times* will benefit from a stronger commercial drive, that he will not appoint an editor who is not worthy of the paper and that any editor who is worthy of the paper will, under the system of guarantees, be able to maintain his independence." He thought the Murdoch purchase was the only way of avoiding at least a temporary closure of the paper.

Brogan thought of that message, and of his career with *The Times*, as he walked to his desk with the two "digger" telexes. He considered, then rejected, the notion that perhaps Rees-Mogg saw all this as sweet revenge for his humiliation by the White Swan rebels. In the end, Brogan and those who thought like him had been able to ensure that the Thomsons kept the paper in something like the condition in which they had found it. He was not at all convinced that this was why they had failed to sustain it. Their management had, it was clear, been woefully inadequate. When they had screwed up their courage to get tough with the unions it had scarcely been a convincing performance. Murdoch would doubtless avoid those errors, indeed labour negotiations seemed to be among his strengths. Yet there was nothing in his record to suggest that he would want to nourish those qualities of rectitude, tolerance and moderation that had so impressed Brogan and others of his generation that they were proud to work for *The Times*. The Washington correspondent began composing in his mind a letter of resignation. He never wrote it but before the end of the year he had left.

There were the familiar last-minute alarums before Murdoch's purchase of Times Newspapers was finalised. He had not achieved the full cost savings he had hoped in his negotiations with the unions, and before the year was out he was to regret not having been tougher. He did reach agreement for the gradual introduction of new technology, but the unions claimed it was on the same terms Thomson's had been offered but rejected. The staff of over 4,000 would be reduced by some twenty per cent. Announcing the agreements, Murdoch warned that if there were further industrial trouble at Gray's Inn Road, "I will close the place down."

His other preoccupation in the days leading up to the agreement had been the appointment of a new editor for *The Times*. Rees-Mogg had made it known some time earlier that he would want to step down as soon as was decent after the new owner took command, and had he not done so voluntarily, it is likely that Murdoch would have found a way of persuading him to go, since he thought that, after fourteen years, a change was due. The identity of the new editor would be a crucial guide to the validity of his pledges about editorial freedom, for they would ring hollow if he were to bring in someone from his own stable. Among the Murdoch men rumoured to be in contention were the Australian Bruce Rothwell, the editorial page editor of the *New York Post*, and even Sir Larry Lamb of the *Sun*, who was after all the senior editor in the group. It always seemed more likely that Murdoch would consider it politic to appoint an editor from inside the paper, or at least from inside Times Newspapers. Of those, the front runners were Louis Heren, Charles Douglas-Home, Hugh Stephenson and Harold Evans. A switch of posts between Evans and Rees-Mogg had once or twice been rumoured during the Thomson ownership, but neither was keen then to make the move.

The forty-four-year-old Douglas-Home was the candidate favoured by the old Thomson regime of Rees-Mogg, Hussey and Hamilton. An Old Etonian, an officer in the Royal Scots Greys and briefly an aide-de-camp to one of the last colonial governors of Kenya, he is the nephew of Lord Home, the former Conservative Prime Minister. Somewhat ascetic – he does not smoke, drink or eat meat – he nevertheless enjoys traditional country pursuits such as hunting, though he is prone to falling off horses and hurting himself. He was Diplomatic Correspondent of the *Daily Express* until shortly before Lord Thomson bought *The Times*, when he was recruited as Defence Correspondent. This was on the initiative of Alun Gwynne-Jones, who had held the post until he was made Lord Chalfont and appointed to Harold Wilson's Labour Government. Douglas-Home had the confidence of Rees-Mogg and rose through a number of executive positions with a smoothness marred by only one setback, when it was discovered that he was keeping intimate personal dossiers on members of the reporting staff. Someone broke into his office and peeped at the documents. Douglas-Home was obliged to make a grovelling apology and undertook to discontinue the practice. In the six years or so since then, he had largely restored his reputation, and it was clear he saw himself as a potential editor, if not necessarily the next one.

Heren did not conceal that he would dearly like the job as the culmination of his life's work at *The Times*. He did not regard his age – sixty-two – as any handicap. To promote his cause he sent a long memorandum to Murdoch suggesting ways in which the paper might be improved: many were generalisations but some, like putting news on the back page instead of classified advertising and cutting back the Business News section, were put into effect.

Soon after Murdoch moved into Denis Hamilton's old office on the executive floor at Gray's Inn Road (Hamilton was shipped to the one formerly reserved for Thomson) he sent for Heren and they discussed senior journalists on the paper. Murdoch asked about Hugh Stephenson, the least likely of *The Times* contenders to win the editorship. Heren began to reply that he was a bright enough man although there were faults with the way he ran Business News, but Murdoch butted in: "No, he's no good; he's no good." He pointed to an article in that day's business section, illustrating his point that it was too much devoted to the discussion of economic affairs and there was too little hard City news. Then he moved on to discuss Margaret Allen, the features editor. Again, before Heren had the chance to frame a few kind words, Murdoch snapped: "No, she's no good." Heren believed these views were inspired by a talk Murdoch had about the staff with Rees-Mogg, but it would be consistent with his usual practice if they were a compilation of opinions gleaned on the telephone from his friends. People who have had similar discussions with Murdoch say he is never happier than when running down journalists and businessmen – equally those who work for him and those who do not – in outspoken and sometimes vulgar terms. Within a few months, both Stephenson and Allen had left the paper, although Stephenson had been offered and rejected the position of foreign editor.

On Monday, February 16th, Murdoch called in Heren, Douglas-Home and Stephenson for separate interviews. Stephenson was given a brief examination as though he were still a viable contender for the editorship, but he received a clear impression that he was not going to get the job. Heren was told bluntly he would not be chosen, chiefly because of his age. "I want an editor who will last at least ten years," said Murdoch, who has never been much of a prophet. Then, to drive the message home, he added: "By the way, I got a completely wrong impression. I always thought you were popular with the editorial staff. I've discovered that you're not." Heren composed himself after this surprise snipe. "Who can tell who one's popular with?" he asked philosophically. "My impression is that most people don't seem to mind me. I'm honest with them."

Murdoch pressed home the assault. "No, my impression is that Charlie (Douglas-Home) is more popular than you." He had gleaned that from Rees-Mogg, who had taken an informal poll among half a dozen assistant editors and reported to Murdoch that they favoured Douglas-Home by five to one. Before a deflated Heren left his office, Murdoch tried to cheer him up by breaking the news that he and Peter Roberts, of the *Sunday Times*, were to be the first journalist directors of Times Newspapers and that he could have a roving role on the paper, travelling and writing what he liked, though with no executive function.

The choice between Heren and Douglas-Home was anyway academic because the following day Murdoch revealed to the directors what had been rumoured for a while – that his nominee as editor was Harold Evans. The rumours had not been stilled by Evans's announcement only the previous week that he intended to stay with the *Sunday Times*. He had edited the Sunday paper for fourteen years and colleagues believed he was getting stale. In recent years *Private Eye* had reported that he would have liked to be Director-General of the BBC and he had been approached to edit the *Daily Mirror*, but turned the job down. *The Times* seemed a logical move for him, although he insists that Murdoch did not raise the question until their second meeting after Thomson's announcement that the Australian was the favoured purchaser. Evans spoke to Murdoch once during January before that announcement but declined to take any more of his calls because he was still hoping that his consortium might be successful. After the announcement, Evans and his fiancée Tina Brown, editor of the *Tatler*, went to dinner at Murdoch's Belgravia flat but the offer of *The Times* editorship was not made until a lunch the following week. He did not finally accept until after his approval by the board, when Murdoch took him to lunch at the Savoy Grill. On returning to the office to tell his *Sunday Times* colleagues he dissolved into tears.

For Murdoch, Evans seemed the ideal choice, a man within the organisation he had bought but not identified with the paper on which radical changes would have to be made. Not since the Stuart affair back in Adelaide had any of Murdoch's papers been involved in the kind of cam-

paigning journalism Evans was noted for at the *Sunday
Times*, but he still had a sneaking regard for it, illustrated
by the curious walking-on role he played in the most
famous of Evans's campaigns, the thalidomide affair. The
story is told in *Suffer the Children*, the book that Evans and
three members of his Insight team wrote about the scandal.
In 1972 a rash of savage posters were fly-posted all over the
country attacking the Distillers Group, who marketed
thalidomide. Most of them linked Distillers' main activity,
selling spirits, with the drug that had caused birth defects in
hundreds of children. In one of them, two men were
depicted in a bar with a bottle of whisky labelled thalidomide. "Have a thalidomide, old boy," said one. "Don't
mind if I do," was the reply. The posters amounted to
contempt of court, for litigation was still in progress over
compensation for thalidomide victims. For this reason they
were issued anonymously and only later did it emerge that
Murdoch was the man behind them. His idea had been that
the press, and his newspapers in particular, should report
the poster campaign as news, skirting legal bars to comment on the case. Graham King, an executive with the
News of the World, resigned from the paper to organise the
campaign and then was given an assignment in Australia as
soon as the posters began appearing. But lawyers advised
all papers, including Murdoch's, that to report the posters
would still amount to contempt, so not a word appeared in
print.

Not everyone agreed with Murdoch that the talents that
blossomed on the *Sunday Times* would stand Evans in good
stead on the daily paper. There are two basic techniques of
Sunday Times journalism, as created by Hamilton and
Evans. One is to make accessible the difficult but important
stories of the day – finance, industry, politics and foreign
affairs – by dramatising them and bringing out the personalities involved. The complementary skill is to use hard
reporting methods on essentially soft stories – probes by
the Insight team into antiques rings and phoney wine
labelling. By contrast *The Times* has traditionally treated
serious events seriously and trivial news trivially.

Murdoch took a more straightforward view. Evans was
reputed to be the best journalist in Britain, and that was

whom he wanted for *The Times*. First he had to convince
the board, especially the national directors, to whom he
had ceded the power of veto over the selection of editor.
They were one below strength, Lord McGregor having
rejected the invitation to be one of the two new ones
Murdoch promised to appoint. Casting round for a replace-
ment, Murdoch thought back to the man who had taught
him much of what he knew about popular journalism – Sir
Edward Pickering, his mentor at the *Daily Express* nearly
thirty years earlier. Though sixty-eight and in retirement,
Pickering was still active in the Commonwealth Press
Union and the Press Council. He had bumped into Murdoch now and again through the years, but he was surprised
to get a phone call one day in February, with Murdoch
asking a characteristic question: "Are you free to have a
bite to eat?" He was, and he accepted the directorship.

There had been no time to inform the other national
directors of this addition to their strength before the February 17th board meeting at which the editor was to be
chosen. The meeting was to begin in late morning and
continue through lunch into the afternoon. Lord Dacre had
warned Murdoch and the others that he would have to
leave at 3.30 p.m. sharp, when a car would be waiting to
drive him to Oxford to give a lecture. Dacre arrived a little
early and went to see Denis Hamilton. "Pickering's going
to be there," Hamilton told him. "He's the new national
director." Dacre was horrified. The high-handed action by
the new proprietor seemed to confirm all the fears he had
expressed at the Thomson House meeting in January. "We
can't have it," he said. "We are supposed to approve new
national directors." When Pickering arrived it was agreed
he should stand in the corridor until his appointment had
been confirmed. Murdoch was abjectly contrite, pleading a
new boy's ignorance of the rules. "I didn't know it was
wrong," he maintained. "I'll tell him to go away if you
like." The national directors approved Pickering's appointment, Dacre abstaining from the vote.

Murdoch was keen to get Pickering on to the board right
away because he anticipated difficulty in having Evans's
appointment as editor approved by the other national
directors and was sure Pickering would accept his choice.

The delay meant that they did not start talking about the editorship until after lunch. Heren said he thought the staff would accept Evans because of his reputation, but added that the paper might be embarrassed by his involvement in one of his periodic disputes with *Private Eye*, with litigation threatened.

Sterner criticism came from Hamilton and Dacre, who agreed with Rees-Mogg that Douglas-Home was a better choice. Dacre delivered some cautious personal criticism of Evans, and said the *Sunday Times* under his editorship was a tasteless paper. At first it seemed that the collective view of the national directors was in accord with Dacre's. Hamilton weighed in. He felt that his protégé Evans, while a tremendous editor of a Sunday paper, had the opposite qualities from those needed to edit *The Times*. He was emotional, inconsistent, brilliant in flashes. He did not have the required backbone, the gravitas, the solid worth. Douglas-Home's name was not mentioned in the discussion, for the arrangement is that only the management can nominate the editor: the national directors may simply approve or reject the choice. By the time Dacre had to leave for his drive to Oxford, he was sure that the mood of the meeting was for him, that Evans would be rejected and Murdoch be forced to nominate Douglas-Home. "I presume Lord Dacre is voting against," said Murdoch as he left the room. He was, but in the end his was the only negative vote, for Murdoch then made an eloquent plea for Evans, saying he desperately needed the services of the most able journalist in the land if he were to carry out his aim of reviving *The Times*.

The choice for the *Sunday Times* had been more difficult – though less publicly contentious – than *The Times*. The two main candidates from inside the paper were Ron Hall, editor of the colour magazine, and Hugo Young, the brainy political editor. Hall had been on the paper longer than Evans and the two were friends. Evans recommended him. Hamilton, though, plumped for Young, who would bring less technical expertise but greater political insight. Hall was notoriously uninterested in run-of-the-mill politics. Faced with these conflicting recommendations, Murdoch took a characteristic way out: he appointed Frank

Giles, the sleek deputy editor, who at sixty-two (the same age as Louis Heren) was regarded by most as too old to be considered. Murdoch's idea was that the two younger men should fight it out for the top job and he would then see who was the better at asserting himself. "He expected us to behave like Australians," one of them complained a few months later, when the ruse had clearly gone wrong.

The board also decided at that meeting that Sir Denis Hamilton should remain chairman of Times Newspaper Holdings, with Murdoch as vice-chairman. This was a surprise: most people had assumed Hamilton would bow out. Later that afternoon Sir Denis called Heren to his office and handed him a long statement about the board meeting for publication in that night's paper, announcing all the new appointments except the editor's. He said it should appear unaltered, including a statement from Sir Denis on the subject of himself. "Until a few days ago I had intended to make a clean break with Gray's Inn Road," the statement declared, "but I have been persuaded that I could be of help to old and new colleagues to bridge a transitional period."

Heren returned to his office where a bit later Murdoch dropped in. He asked Heren what he thought of the announcement, then chuckled. He said he had actually been expecting Hamilton to leave, but let him stay on because he was keen to do so. "He's a great survivor," he said, adding: "And so's William Rees-Mogg." "What do you mean?" Heren asked. "He wants to keep an office here and write a political column in the *Sunday Times*." "Are you going to let him?" "It's up to the new editor."

The idea for the column had been concocted by Rees-Mogg and Evans at a lunch in January, before Evans knew he was going to move to *The Times*. Murdoch had told Rees-Mogg he favoured the idea but Frank Giles, who had never got on specially well with Rees-Mogg, was less keen. In any case, Rees-Mogg, knighted in 1981, was now making other arrangements for his future. He would soon assume senior posts on the BBC and the Arts Council, and he bought Pickering & Chatto, an antiquarian bookshop.

Apart from masterminding the choice of editor, Murdoch was prevented from imposing changes in editorial personnel by the conditions of his purchase. He had agreed with the NUJ that no journalist would be dismissed, though he sought thirty voluntary redundancies. One hand thus tied, he decided to make a virtual clean sweep on the commercial side of the paper, where no such restraint applied. He made his intention plain from the beginning. On the day of his first visit to the paper's offices he went to see Bryan Todd, the bluff, portly advertisement and marketing director for *The Times*. On his office wall were photographs of recent promotional campaigns. There was the "Open Your Mind and Say 'Ah'" series of advertisements and their successors: "Have You Ever Wished You Were Better Informed?", illustrated by a bridge whose two spans failed to join; the assassination of Julius Caesar; and the Trojan horses. Murdoch was patently unimpressed. "What circulation have we put on as a result of these campaigns?" he asked Todd, who thought it impolitic to tell his new proprietor that he thought the question simplistic, that with *The Times* it was not straight numbers that were significant but the quality of circulation, the proportion of high-income AB readers.

Todd could see changes were coming, but like many of his colleagues, he clung as long as possible to the belief that he would survive them, as in battle the soldier thinks, until the very moment the bullet strikes home, that he will be the one to dodge it. Soon he discovered that one of the bullets did have his name on it. A day or two after Murdoch's takeover was formalised, Todd was summoned to see Gerald Long, the newly-appointed managing director of Times Newspapers. A former foreign correspondent, Long had run Reuters news agency for nearly two decades with a vision and efficiency that had impressed both Murdoch and Hamilton. He had a reputation for being difficult with subordinates, but that had never been regarded by Murdoch as a disability: nor did he mind his lack of experience in running newspapers. Long had shown at Reuters an aptitude for managing a business profitably, which recommended him not just to Murdoch but also to the commercial people at Times Newspapers. Todd felt well disposed towards him, despite what he had heard about some slight eccentricities, including an interest in Zen Buddhism.

Long, a gaunt man with a droopy moustache, had just moved into Nisbet-Smith's old office, furnished with a shaggy white carpet and little else. (Nisbet-Smith had resigned when the company changed hands.) In one corner were a card-table and two chairs and in the other, as Todd entered, knelt Long, his bottom pointing at the visitor. "My God," thought Todd, "I've caught him at his devotions," but Long soon stood up and held out to him a large glass ashtray bearing small white candles. "It's my eyes," Long explained. "I can't bear tobacco smoke. The man who had this room before must have smoked morning, noon and night." Nisbet-Smith had been an enthusiastic pipe-puffer and Long was applying camphor to drive away the fumes.

He put down the ashtray and perched on the card-table. "I know nothing about advertising," he began, and Todd guessed what was coming. When people say they know nothing about a subject they are about to deliver their opinion on it. "I can only tell you," Long went on, "that *The Times*'s promotional advertising is the worst in the world. Furthermore we pay huge sums of money for it. You've seen the note. We don't have marketing here any more. So perhaps you'd like to go and see Tudor Hopkins [personnel director] and arrange your redundancy."

The note Long referred to was one that had been sent round the previous day, announcing that the new regime had abolished marketing as a word and as a concept. Murdoch thought it effete and over-elaborate. He did not accept the argument of the Thomson marketing people that because *The Times* could not be sold to advertisers as value for money in terms of total readership it was a question of burnishing its image as the sort of paper that enhanced the goods and services advertised in it. "If we get the product right – and we will – then we don't need to sell on special situations, special editions, that sort of thing," Murdoch told Sheila Black in an interview for *Media World*. "Advertising is something you earn and, if you've got the product, you go out and do a hard sell on it."

Before Todd went off to see Hopkins, Long had a

thought. "Perhaps you might go and see Ruda and see if there's a job in sales for you." Mike Ruda was the newly-appointed advertising director brought in from the *Sun* and the *News of the World*. He had grown up in the shadow of Bert Hardy, a master of the foot-in-the-door selling technique and of gaining advertising by offering discounts on the rate-book price and cobbling last-minute deals to fill space in the paper. (Years earlier a senior advertising man from Times Newspapers was discussing with Hardy the training of representatives, saying how carefully his men and women were instructed in the skills of learning the client's requirements and talking him round. He asked Hardy how he trained his people. "I give them an order book and a pencil and if they haven't sold enough after a month I fire them," Hardy replied. Murdoch could scarcely have put it better.)

Hardy had pioneered the idea of group selling, persuading advertisers to buy space in all the group's publications. With the *Sun* and the *News of the World* that was not difficult, and Ruda had continued the technique. Only once, in the late 1960s, had Thomson's tried it but they found that, because the size and the quality of the readership varied so widely between the papers, they simply sold more space in the *Sunday Times*, the easy sell, and less in *The Times*, which needed a subtler form of persuasion. Subtlety is not a weapon in Ruda's armoury. When the advertising department were called to meet him on his first day, he instructed them to make the telephone "red hot with activity" as they contacted their clients with the glad news that Rupert was in charge and Times Newspapers in business with a vengeance. This they dutifully did, creating some astonishment among contacts used to a gentler approach, but winning few fresh orders. Ruda concluded his lecture by telling his staff they would not like all his ways, and he would soon find out which among them would fit into his scheme of things.

Try as he might, however, Ruda discovered hardly anyone on the existing staff who measured up to his exacting standard. Todd went to see him, as Long had suggested. "I'm sales director," said Ruda, "and we obviously don't need two sales directors, so you'd better go and see Hopkins." Todd reflected ruefully that he had in effect been fired twice. He was out of the office by the end of the week.

Others went just as quickly. Gary Thorne, advertising and marketing director for the whole group, had decided not to stay on but to form his own agency, which was awarded *The Times*'s meagre business for a year. Andrew Shanks, marketing manager of the *Sunday Times*, had already accepted another job and was told not to go back to his office except to clear his desk. Donald Barrett, Thorne's grey, precise deputy, had been asked by Ruda, early in his first week, to draw up some proposals for increasing advertising revenue. At nine o'clock the following Thursday morning Ruda asked to see him. Scarcely had Barrett begun to present his thoughts when Ruda cut him short. "Let's approach this from a different angle," he said. "Let's not muck about. There's not going to be room here for the two of us." Barrett trotted to see Hopkins to arrange severance terms and was told: "Don't come back on Monday." He took his son to the office on Saturday to clear away his things – a sudden end to twenty-six years with the Kemsley and Thomson groups. The following week friends told him that his desk was out in the corridor of the executive floor.

Panic and confusion gripped the advertising and marketing staff as Ruda began to scythe through them from the top downwards. Until the blow was actually dealt nearly all, like Todd, thought it could not possibly happen to them. For a few weeks, something close to hysteria reigned. By the middle of the year, scarcely any of the old people remained.

On Saturday, March 7th, Rees-Mogg printed his farewell address to his readers at the top of the main feature page. Headlined "My Assumption of Liberty", it was a sprightly and interesting piece but angered many of his former colleagues on *The Times*. The imagery, they felt, was unfortunate. "As the shades of the prison house close round Mr Harold Evans (and even cast a somewhat fainter shadow over Mr Rupert Murdoch) I feel like the prisoners at the end of *Fidelio*, bursting out of their jail-house with a song of joy on their lips." It was a bit much, *Times* men felt, to be likened to convicts. Worse, there were none of the conventional farewell remarks about how lovely it had all been and how grateful he was to his friends and colleagues. It was all about Rees-Mogg. "I have been too sensible for too long and now I need not be sensible again, at least for the time being."

The following Monday the staff had their first meeting with the man who would now have to be sensible in his stead, Harold Evans. His voice still weak after a bout of 'flu, he entered the news room to address the prisoners, who reflected wearily that in recent months they might have spent more time listening to harangues than working. At least this should be the last pep talk for a while. Evans put on a frisky performance in the circumstances, though his answers to specific questions about long-term aims were imprecise. He was firm on such uncontentious issues as the need to improve the quality of the newsprint, but when it came to circulation targets he hedged. "Obviously I don't think that as a marketing strategy we just want numbers, as in 1966," he said. "We all learned something of a lesson from that . . . We are not going hell-for-leather for sales but it is not a healthy situation at the moment. *The Times* is at 270,000 – 100,000 behind the *Guardian* . . . We are not looking for readers, we are not seizing them by the scruff of the neck, but we would be glad as more and more of them climb aboard in the next year or so." He added that he did not see his new *Times* as being modelled on the *Sunday Times* and rumours that he would go for a circulation of 750,000 were "absurd, can't be done."

Actually, the staff were rather more interested in how the new editor's methods would affect their working lives than in such generalisations. "How do you work with the sub-editors?" one of their number asked him. "Do you write headlines, captions?" "If you give me a decent count sheet (a book of type styles and sizes) I would be very happy to write headlines. I would like to be involved. I intend to be involved in all parts of the paper at all times. It's called the editing theory of maximum irritation." He thought Murdoch would be a good proprietor because he was active and interested – better than one who was never there – though he did deplore the sackings in the advertising department: "There has been some sadness on my part too at some of the departures over there . . . I think it would be safe to say that period is ended now . . . If I am accused of anything . . . it is of being a little too kindly." But he understood the anxieties his arrival had brought, on top of the agonies of the suspension and the change of ownership. "You have had an absolutely dreadful time and I hope we are now going to have a period of stability and a period of adventure together." Adventure, certainly . . .

One of the questions to the new editor was in the true *Times* tradition of pedantry. It was whether he would bar the use of new-fangled expressions such as "shoot-out" and "look-alike" on the grounds of "editorial excellence and quality". Everyone has his pet peeves in this area and Evans, in reply, gave vent to some of his own – "none were" and "finalised" – while adding: "I don't want to rob the English language of some of the idiom which enriches it." The exchange obviously set Evans's mind racing, for the first general memorandum he sent to the journalists, three days later, was on a question of style: "Please let us not confuse 'less' with 'fewer'. 'Less' is right for quantities – less coffee, less sugar. It means a less amount. 'Fewer' is the correct word for comparing numbers – fewer people, fewer houses. Nobody would think of writing 'fewer coffee' but every day someone writes 'less houses'." Like Rees-Mogg's first executive act fourteen years earlier, when he broadened the cricket coverage, this initiative from Evans was presumably designed to show the old *Times* people that in his heart of hearts he was one of them. But, unlike Rees-Mogg, he wasn't really.

In his memorandum to Murdoch about *The Times* and its future, Louis Heren conceded that, like all organisations, the paper had some dead wood. Murdoch and Evans went further: they thought the tree was rotten through and through and could be saved only by cutting off as many branches as possible and grafting on new shoots. So Evans took with him from the *Sunday Times* a layer of senior people that he would impose on the old structure, calculating correctly that those who could not bear the new order would take advantage of Murdoch's offer of voluntary redundancy, leaving him extra gaps that he could fill from his stable of favourites. Edwin Taylor and Oscar Turnill, experts in layout, were brought in to pep up the design. Anthony Holden, once editor of the Atticus gossip column and the young author of a successful biography of Prince Charles, became features editor, bringing with him as assistant the even younger Peter Stothard. Peter Watson, who used to edit the *Sunday Times* Spectrum pages, took over the Diary. Brian MacArthur, news editor of *The Times* before going to the *Evening Standard* and then the *Sunday Times*, moved back to take charge of the Daily at night. Bernard Donoughue, Evans's guru, became assistant editor for policy, a kind of one-man think tank. High-priced recruits from elsewhere included Frank Johnson, a writer of whimsical Parliamentary reports that Evans had admired in the *Daily Telegraph* and Sir James Goldsmith's short-lived weekly news magazine *Now!*, and Julian Haviland from Independent Television News, who became political editor. Adrian Hamilton, Sir Denis's son, was recruited from the *Observer* to edit the Business News section.

One appointment, essentially a by-product of the new influx, provides an illustration of Murdoch's wholesale and indiscriminate approach to the news business. MacArthur's new position made Michael Hamlyn, the previous night editor, effectively redundant and something had to be found for him to do. (Hamlyn had himself been recruited from the *Sunday Times* by Rees-Mogg just after the Thomson takeover.) Between them, Murdoch and Evans decided to make room for MacArthur by appointing Hamlyn as New York bureau chief for all Murdoch's British and Australian publications. The one bureau would serve the needs of *The Times* and the *Sun*, as well as the *Daily Mirror* and the *Australian* in Sydney, the women's magazines – everything. When it was put to him that the peculiar requirements of *The Times* might need rather more individual attention, Hamlyn would shrug and say, apparently quoting Murdoch, "a story is a story is a story". Unfamiliar Australian bylines began appearing in *The Times*. The move was, in addition, an example of Murdoch's theory of creative tension, of deliberately placing his senior people in positions where conflict with colleagues is inevitable. The Australian papers already had a head of bureau, Ross Waby, whose executive function Hamlyn was to take over – and it was left to Hamlyn himself to break the news to a distraught Waby when he visited New York to cast an eye over his new empire. The man in charge of the New York office of Times Newspapers was Old Etonian Robert Ducas, formerly president of the American subsidiary. While he had no journalistic function, some of his administrative tasks would be reassigned to Hamlyn. Ducas had been invaluable to Evans, an old friend, in organising American financing for his proposed *Sunday Times* consortium and did receive the courtesy of a telephone call from Evans warning him of Hamlyn's impending arrival and asking him not to make waves. "Don't worry," he said. "I've taken a lot of trouble to work this out with Rupert."

That day Ducas went to see Murdoch in his office at the *New York Post*. Was it, he ventured, realistic to expect the same New York reporter to be filing for the *Sunday Times* and the *News of the World*? "You know what journos are like," Murdoch replied, "particularly journos overseas. They're bone idle – live off their expenses. I'm not having three people from my group going to cover the landing of the space shuttle: it's absurd." A few weeks later, after raising the question of his reduced status, Ducas was dismissed. A telex message, with Murdoch's name at its foot, instructed him to vacate his office within forty-eight hours. Ducas phoned his friend Evans. "I've done all I can," said the new editor, in tones of anguish.

Ducas's departure was involuntary: but soon many decided to take the offered redundancy money – a month's pay for every year of service. The target of thirty was eventually reached, but the offer was kept open and over fifty members of the editorial staff left within the first year. They included important writers such as Bernard Levin, Hugh Stephenson, Peter Hennessy – who specialised in revelations about the Civil Service – legal correspondent Marcel Berlins and Roger Berthoud, chief feature writer. Their departure damaged the paper by alienating readers of long standing, while the new recruits, according to the disappointing circulation figures, were not proving as attractive as Evans had hoped. It was the opposite approach from that of Rees-Mogg in 1967. He had brought in only three people from the *Sunday Times* and few of the existing staff left because no voluntary redundancy terms were offered then.

Evans was conscious of the danger of a rift between the old and new people but did not truly see what he could do to prevent it if he was to change the paper as he wanted. Despite his soothing remarks at the staff meeting, his actions indicated a conviction that hardly any of the old *Times* people were any good at all at journalism as he understood it. Only those he had brought with him were admitted to his confidence. "It's all cronyism," one long-serving senior executive complained.

Evans equates good journalism with energy and bustle. He believes the quality and thoroughness of a piece of reporting are related directly to the amount of chivvying and prodding that has been carried out by him on its authors, and by them on their sources. The technique – the one he called maximum irritation – had worked spectacularly on the string of investigative reports he presided over at the *Sunday Times*. He believes the validity of the technique to be self-evident and is convinced that anyone who winces at it can be motivated only by idleness. But the many old *Times* people who *did* wince admitted to no such motive. They thought – as they had thought of the Thomson changes in the late 1960s – that it was all very silly, not at all what *The Times* ought to be doing, a great deal of energy expended for something that in the end they would prefer not to see in the paper. That dread word "authority" was being muttered darkly again. Often the irritation would get out of hand, as Evans tried to adapt to a paper that appeared daily a technique developed on one that came out once a week. "The trouble with Harry," said one disgruntled veteran, "is not that he won't come to a decision but that he comes to six different decisions on the same subject."

Like all zealots, the newcomers were amazed that the transparent rightness of their concept of journalism was not immediately recognised by the old-timers. They failed, as the Thomson people had, to realise that if you come into an organisation and tell those in it that what they have been doing for the last umpteen years is quite worthless, a product of a lazy, old-fashioned and pedantic approach, the view is likely to be resisted.

The leader writers had always been the most conservative group on the paper, least welcoming of change. Under the control of Owen Hickey, a man of stern and rigid views, they seemed to the newcomers to regard themselves as members of an Oxford college, with Hickey the tutor and the rest undergraduates who would write essays to be discussed and then put in the paper. Donoughue, now in charge of policy matters, wanted to see editorials about subjects closer to the concerns of readers than the political situation in Bolivia. He wanted firmer opinions expressed, less of the "on the one hand, but on the other . . ." posture that *The Times* would adopt on many issues. And he wanted to pre-empt events rather than react to them, occasionally to start a debate instead of just taking part in it. The leader-writers resented such criticisms and thought them unfair: many of the things he was proposing were what they had been doing – or at least believed they had been doing – for years. Donoughue was at root against the whole collegiate approach, believing it part of what was wrong with modern Britain: no firm leadership, everyone chiming in and expecting to be heard, resulting in drift and a lack of decision. He and Evans would try to be patient, but the atmosphere was one of mutual suspicion.

The split widened. At the depressingly frequent farewell parties for departing staff, the new recruits would huddle together, not mixing with the old timers. Evans scarcely discouraged the division. After he had been editor for a few weeks he arranged a boardroom lunch where Murdoch could meet key journalists, mainly his new people. It produced one telling moment. The conversation had turned to American politics and someone said that, following the defeat of President Carter, the country might be in for a series of one-term presidents. "Then that gives Harry four years," piped up Peter Watson, jocularly. When the chuckles had died down Murdoch allowed a second or two of silence before rasping: "At the outside!" The laughs this time were hollow and edgy.

At *The Times* such carnage was novel and quite alarming. It was altogether familiar at the *News of the World*. Concerned at the slide in his Sunday paper's circulation, Murdoch approached Barry Askew, the young editor of the *Lancashire Evening Post*, who was making a name for himself as a campaigning journalist. When Askew put it to Murdoch that to be one of his editors was not the most secure of positions, the proprietor smiled and disagreed. "Either they get another job in the organisation or they get the crock of gold," he observed.

Askew moved to Bouverie Street in April, 1981. His slide towards the crock of gold began, he believes, the following October, in a dispute over a proposed front-page exposé of John De Lorean, the American car magnate given many millions of British government money to build his dramatically-conceived sports car in Northern Ireland. Based on an interview with a former secretary in his office, the article cast doubt on how De Lorean was using the government funds. Murdoch, in London, expressed reservations about the piece on the grounds that it seemed unsafe legally. The paper's lawyers agreed with him, and at the last minute on Saturday afternoon the story was removed from the paper. Next day the *Daily Mirror* printed it and other papers picked it up, though De Lorean claimed it was a malicious fabrication. Within a year his car firm was bankrupt and he was arrested in California on a drugs charge. Askew is convinced that the seeds of mistrust between him and his proprietor were sown on that Saturday. At the year's end he was dismissed and moved back to Lancashire.

On March 11th, 1981, Murdoch was fifty. Anna organised a party at the Cavan ranch, mainly for members of the family. It was an overnight affair and motel rooms were booked for those who could not be put up in the house. It began on the Saturday evening with dancing to a group of country musicians to set the mood; then came an elaborate dinner, followed by twenty minutes of fireworks organised by two Vietnamese refugees Anna had discovered living in the vicinity. The evening ended with a film Anna had organised, made up of clips from newsreels and television profiles, illustrating highlights of Murdoch's life. Next day a small plane flew overhead pulling a streamer that read: HAPPY BIRTHDAY, RUPERT. Sky divers dropped from it and landed on the lawn, to the delight of the young family members. Anna announced her special surprise present – a commission for a portrait of Rupert to be done by his favourite Australian artist, Fred Williams. But for most guests the highlight of the weekend came on the Saturday night, after dinner and before the film, when the birthday cake was brought in for Rupert to cut. It was iced to resemble the front page of *The Times*. Everyone laughed and cheered. *Bon appétit*.

Evans made some cosmetic changes to the paper right away. He began using larger pictures and the layout became clearer and better thought out. The first big story the paper had to cover, the day after his arrival, was the Budget. Although he and his new people could hardly have had time to sharpen their pencils, at least one press critic purported to identify changes for the worse already. Paul Johnson, the conservative commentator of the *Spectator*, wrote an article suggesting that in a matter of days the paper's entire tradition of moderation and objectivity had been eroded. "Gimmickry and sensationalism, speculation and guesswork, have to be avoided," he wrote sternly, then went on to illustrate how, in his view, they had not been. The headline: "Harsh budget for workers but more for business" seemed to Johnson more appropriate to the Communist *Morning Star*. The accompanying story was "a curious muddle of budget snippets, lobby gossip and speculation". Later in the week came more sensationalism, in Johnson's view, notably the headline: "Chancellor under savage attack from all quarters." It was clear that the establishment, in so far as the maverick Johnson can be said to represent anything so specific, were going to keep a close watch on the new editor as he tinkered with their morning reading.

A story Evans could really get his teeth into occurred on March 30th: President Reagan was shot and wounded as he left a Washington hotel after lunch. Evans stayed in the office supervising the development of the story as edition followed edition. By the time of the last edition, the one sold on the streets in London, the front page had been given over entirely to Reagan in a layout of astounding impact. The headline went across all eight columns. Across six columns just below it were three pictures, one on top of the other, simulating newsreel clips of the actual shooting. The main report was set across two columns all down the left of the page with articles on other aspects of the shooting lower down on the right, continuing on an inside page. It was all in larger body type than is customary, for extra drama. By coincidence the issue of March 31st was also that in which Bernard Levin announced his impending departure: "My decision is in no way based on any disquiet on my part at the change of editors or proprietor, nor on any lack of confidence in the paper's future, and anyone saying or writing anything to the contrary is, and for all material purposes should be treated as, a liar." (Levin returned to the paper in 1982, as did Peter Hennessy.)

Over the next few months more changes were made. Classified advertising was removed from the back page, where Rees-Mogg had placed it fourteen years earlier to mitigate in part the loss of revenue the paper suffered when it was taken off the front. The back page was now split in two, the top half being used for stories that turned from the front and for lighter writing and pictures: later, Frank Johnson's parliamentary reports were to find a home there. On the bottom half came an innovation called The Times Information Service, a collation of facts about the weather, that day's events, road conditions, editorial comment from other newspapers – anything a *Times* reader might be thought to find useful and that lent itself to the capsule form. That was generally agreed to be a sensible use of space and was well received, although a hint of the confusion that now reigned in the organisation of the paper came a few weeks later when, for no good reason, the Information Service suddenly switched to listing the *following* day's events rather than those on the day of publication. This proved so muddling that the decision was reversed after a few days. Another popular introduction was a Friday pull-out section, printed in tabloid format, called "Preview", providing a critical listing of arts and entertainments, mainly in London.

In an interview before taking over, Evans had said: "Changing a newspaper should be like good surgery. The reader shouldn't feel any pain at all." *Times* readers, though, do not anaesthetise easily. They scream unabashedly when things begin to hurt. They wrote prolifically, some in support of the changes but many opposing them with fervour.

A sardonic account of the goings-on at Gray's Inn Road appeared in the magazine *Harpers and Queen* in September, in a pseudonymous article headed: "O Tempora! O Mores!" The new *Times*, it declared, was "masterminded by a crack squad of the upwardly mobile", and it went on to give a hilarious, though partly inaccurate, account of the arrival of Evans and his team.

"Evans was never in the style of *The Times*," the author wrote. "Where others saw eccentricity, authority and charm, he saw public-school cliques, pomposity and fancy verbiage. He preferred the *Guardian*, with its dynamic layout, its lively, colloquial style, its feel for the modern world." And the article concluded: "There it is, a fallen lady whose heart has been plucked out by whizz-kids and replaced by a more up-to-date model."

Evans reacts sharply to criticism. Several facts, or half-facts, in the article were in error and he insisted on a full correction. A couple of months later the magazine apologised and listed fifteen mistakes. Peter Watson, it noted solemnly, had never had a football trial for Bristol Rovers. Anthony Holden's wife did not play the harpsichord, and so on. The retraction made the new *Times* team look even more ridiculous than the original article. The knowing deduced that it must have contained more than a trace of truth, to provoke such an exaggerated response; and the knowing were to be proved right.

The most puzzling and disappointing aspect of the first few months for Evans and Murdoch was that, despite their radical surgery, circulation was scarcely improving. After three months it was still well under 300,000, up only by 13,000 from the figure when they took over. Murdoch gave increasingly gloomy reports to the board at their meetings during the spring and summer. In April he said that losses so far were around two million pounds for Times Newspapers as a whole, but by June the rate of loss was twelve million a year. Advertising was poor, partly because of the reorganisation of the department and partly because advertisers had been reluctant to book space ahead during the recent uncertain period. A five pence price rise for the *Sunday Times*, to thirty-five pence, had taken 30,000 off the weekly sale. He was still confident, though, that the money Evans was spending on editorial changes at *The Times* would eventually be translated into increased circulation and revenue. When, at the April board meeting, he let slip the figure of 500,000 as a target, he was taken to task by alarmed directors who foresaw a replay of the Thomson attempt to popularise the paper in the late 1960s. He hurriedly assured the doubters that half a million was "a distant objective" and there was no intention of moving down market to achieve it.

In September came the first serious industrial dispute under the new ownership and the first threat by Murdoch to close the business if labour relations did not improve. The particular dispute, like many in the industry, was over differentials. The Murdoch management had inherited a promise by Thomson's to increase the pay of NATSOPA members in the *Sunday Times* press room. The machine managers, who belong to the NGA, said this eroded a traditional differential. They asked for compensation in the form of extra shifts and payments. When this was refused the NGA men said they would not guarantee normal production of the edition of Sunday, September 27th, so the management decided the paper would not appear at all. The next day the dispute halted production of *The Times* and Harold Evans declared: "This is the most serious situation I have ever seen in Fleet Street." Murdoch threatened to close the papers if agreement had not been reached by Wednesday but he backed off a bit when he met the staff in the news room on Tuesday. He said he was "not entirely pessimistic". He spoke of issuing a general call to work on Thursday to see who would turn up but if that failed the paper would close on Monday. The strength of that threat never had to be tested because *The Times* resumed publication on the Thursday and the *Sunday Times* the next Sunday. The NGA men won no extra money and agreed to negotiate a comprehensive press room agreement with the management and NATSOPA.

During this crisis the new owner had his first skirmish with *The Times* journalists. Alarmed by the threats of closure, the NUJ chapel asked Paul Routledge, their leader, to seek assurances from Murdoch that in that event he would keep to the house agreement, that "journalists' notice and redundancy entitlements will be honoured by News International" and that editorial guarantees would be observed. Murdoch replied quickly and testily that the house agreement would be observed, that "News International Ltd. does not employ anybody in any of its subsidiaries [a legalistic point] and certainly has no such obligation" and that "there has never been any question about the editorial guarantees, and I find your raising the matter at this time offensive." No messing.

Although he had weathered his first crisis and chalked up a small victory, Murdoch was still gloomy at that week's board meeting. "There have been few bright moments since the purchase by News International," he told directors. All over Fleet Street advertising volume was down. Circulation of both papers was improving only slowly while the three supplements were dipping. The most alarming figure was the circulation of *The Times*, which in July 1981 was less than 4,000 higher than in July, 1980, despite the greatly increased editorial expenditure.

Yet if part of his motive for buying the paper was prestige, it had already begun to pay dividends. Three months after his purchase of *The Times*, Murdoch tried to take over William Collins, one of Britain's most important book publishers. He has two profitable publishing houses in Australia – Bay Books and Angus & Robertson. Jan Collins, the chairman, sold his shares to Murdoch and was blunt about the reason. "Following News International's recent acquisition of Times Newspapers," he said, "it was clear to me that we could not hope for a better purchaser." In the event Murdoch managed to acquire only forty-two per cent of the company, and Jan Collins was dismissed as chairman by colleagues who opposed the takeover. Murdoch and his nominee, Sir Edward Pickering, were invited to join the board.

The day President Sadat of Egypt was assassinated by members of his army was pivotal not just in the history of the Middle East but also in the history of *The Times*. It happened on October 6th, 1981, the week after the paper's September crisis. Evans took charge in the news room, determined that this should be an even more impressive *tour de force* than the Reagan shooting coverage. Now he had been running the paper for seven months: this time he would show Fleet Street exactly how such big occasions should be handled.

Rushing, shouting, frenzied telephone calls, wild ideas put up and shot down – such signs of incipient panic intensified throughout the late afternoon. Evans and his chief advisers gathered in groups by the foreign desk, the back bench, the features department, all trying to talk at once. Then Evans would march away, leaving a half-formed idea in his wake, and a clutch of people would follow him, waving pieces of paper. As the time for the first edition approached, nobody was at all clear how the front page was to look. The first edition, by general consent, was a disaster – and a late disaster at that. High on the front page was a pointless little story about some relatives of Sadat's in Britain, but it lacked any kind of coherent account of the shooting itself. Peter Hopkirk, one of the paper's most experienced reporters, had been deputed to write the main story, wrapping up all the elements. Nicholas Ashford in Washington wrote a piece about the international implications that was tagged on to the end of Hopkirk's story. By the final edition it looked a bit more orderly, with the main story running up and down five columns, a couple of unexciting pictures and a diagram showing the position of Sadat relative to his assassins at the moment of the attack. The whole of pages two and three were given to related stories, with a strip of pictures illustrating Sadat's life across the top of both. That worked well, as did the five-column obituary on the court page. There were two articles about Sadat on the feature page and a long editorial.

In terms of quantity the event had been done justice, but the vital front page contained all the signs of the confusion that had reigned at its creation. In the rush to print the first edition Murdoch took himself down to the stone. "How's it going?" he asked, and was told the news page would be late. "No good producing the best paper in Fleet Street if you can't get it printed on time," Murdoch grumbled. Disillusion with his brilliant but disorganised editor was starting to grow.

For one veteran *Times* man it was not the beginning of disillusion but the culmination of months of it. Louis Heren had been having an unhappy time in his role as a writing associate editor with no executive responsibilities. He had, as promised, been able to give himself his own assignments and travel wherever he wanted. But the final part of his bargain with Evans was that his work would always be given a good display and this was not kept. A few of his pieces did not appear at all. Came the Sadat killing, and Evans sought the advice of his own men and a few of the old *Times* people as well. But not Heren. Here he was, the most experienced correspondent of them all, a former foreign editor, who had been reporting from the Middle East when most of these people were still at school: but nobody wanted to know what he thought, nobody felt he could be useful. A few days later he applied for redundancy. After more than forty years with the paper he deserved – and received – a generous settlement.

Until that night Murdoch's doubts about Evans had been concerned not with his competence but his over-spending. By the end of 1981, fifty-three people had left under the voluntary redundancy scheme. This was a burden on the bank balance but a one-time burden only. The trouble was that Evans had hired fifty-six new people in their place, nearly all at higher salaries. Murdoch had initially agreed with Evans that it was essential to clear away the dead wood among the staff and introduce new blood. But the essential weakness in all voluntary redundancy schemes is that the very deadest wood, the people with scant hope of finding employment elsewhere, cling on stubbornly. Those with marketable abilities pick up their tax-free redundancy cheques and move on. Thus Murdoch was committed to higher salaries and fat payoffs, with no commensurate increase in the quality of his staff. Evans tried to raise his proprietor's morale by describing the departing journalists in the kind of denigratory terms he knew Murdoch enjoyed using himself. Thus when the *Spectator*, in February 1982, published an article listing some of the senior people who had left to the detriment of the paper, a stung Evans responded with a note to Murdoch describing at least one of the departing as "bone idle" – a characteristic Murdoch phrase, a vice he detests. Transparently, Evans was trying to show Murdoch that he could be as ruthless and spiteful as any Australian. Many of his dealings with the proprietor can be explained in this way. They must have derived from the old suspicion that Murdoch did not really think much of him. He seemed always to be justifying himself. Far from resisting proprietorial influence, Evans would make a point of consulting Murdoch to a degree that seemed to irritate even a man who likes to keep his finger firmly in the pie.

When the *Spectator* criticism appeared, Evans and his acolytes derisively dubbed the named journalists "The *Spectator* Hall of Fame": but Murdoch did not join in the joke. He wrote a note to Evans deploring the departure of Hennessy, Berlins and Berthoud. For him it was the latest in a growing number of disconcerting factors. Losses for the second half of 1981 would be ten million pounds – a higher rate even than Thomson achieved in 1980 – and for his money he was getting an editor accused in the same *Spectator* article of treating his readers as half-wits and alienating many of the old staff. While Murdoch decries idleness, he is yet more averse to wilful extravagance. If the fifty-three departing journalists were bone idle, why were fifty-six needed to take their places?

Yet while he made it plain to Evans that he was overspending, Murdoch would never say by how much. One of the editor's constant complaints throughout this period was that he was not given a budget. He did not know how much he could spend on redundancies, new staff or anything. It was no use being told you had independence within your budget if nobody told you how much that was. For a while Murdoch worked through Gerald Long to try to curb editorial spending, and Long, recognising that Evans was hard to control, put pressure instead on John Grant, the managing editor, a solid and blunt northerner who had been with *The Times* since 1955. Grant had no power to restrain Evans but he did once or twice rebuke him sharply for having no concept of economy. Evans in turn was trying to persuade Grant to apply for redundancy. He wanted the managing editor's job for Brian Horton, a prickly New Zealander formerly with Reuters, whom Evans had appointed foreign editor at Long's suggestion, but whose effectiveness was hampered by his inability to forge cordial relations with most overseas correspondents.

Much of the chaos on the paper during Evans's editorship can be put down to two of his outstanding qualities: his good nature and his impulsiveness. Combined, they result in a failure to resist offering jobs to anyone whose talent he admires, whether or not there is a vacancy to be filled. The saga of Bevis Hillier makes an engrossing case study. Hillier's first job was on *The Times*. He joined as a trainee in 1963, aged twenty-three, and left in 1970 for the British Museum. Since then he had developed a reputation as a freelance writer specialising in art, antiques and leisure pursuits. At the suggestion of Denis Hamilton, Evans engaged him to write regular book reviews for the *Sunday Times* and then to edit the "Good Museum Guide" in the colour magazine.

A few days after Evans was made editor of *The Times*, Hillier bumped into him at the Garrick Club and asked: "When are you going to offer me a job?" It was like asking a drug addict whether he would like a fix, for in no time at all Evans had invited him to his office and dangled before him three jobs: editing the Diary, editing the Saturday Review – a weekly leisure section – or arts editor. *The Times* already had an arts editor, John Higgins, but, underestimating his tenacity, Evans and Holden believed that by whittling away his responsibilities they could persuade him to leave. They took the Saturday Review out of his empire and even appointed John Heilpern as American arts editor without telling Higgins. In the event, Higgins clung on longer than they did.

Hillier, in any case, did not want to be arts editor: he

plumped for the Saturday Review. Without making any firm commitment, Evans left him with little doubt that he would be offered one of the three jobs, and could expect a letter in two days. Nothing arrived for more than a week and when the letter came it said: "If you have other offers, it would be wrong of me to restrain you from accepting them." In other words it was a rejection. Six months later, when Hillier was considering accepting a position as curator of Gainsborough's birthplace in Suffolk, Evans wrote to him again, with a firm offer of "one of the positions we discussed". Hillier accepted, but when he arrived on November 3rd Evans told him: "You can have a desk but we haven't got a job for you yet."

His plan had been to move Peter Watson, not a great success as Diary editor, to New York as a feature writer, but Murdoch had balked at the extra expense and Watson was still in the job that had been earmarked for Hillier. After a while Hillier became an informal assistant to Philip Howard, the literary editor, helping him sub-edit articles and write headlines, only slightly embarrassed by the realisation that his salary of £17,000 a year for this agreeable pastime was higher than Howard's.

In January Evans and Murdoch agreed on Watson's New York posting and Hillier assumed he would automatically get the Diary job. But by now Evans was under pressure to promote more of the old *Times* people and the job went to Robin Young, consumer affairs correspondent and deputy editor of the Diary for several years before that. Finally, at the end of January, Hillier was made editor of the Saturday Review, with a promise of autonomy and a free hand. When he found those promises imprecisely fulfilled, he left on February 24th, taking with him six months' money in lieu of notice and a consoling letter from Douglas-Home noting cryptically that circumstances had changed dramatically from the moment he had been signed up for the paper. Hillier had been on the staff for less than four months, done very little work (through no fault of his own) and had been paid some £14,000 for his trouble, though it took him a while to get all his money. Long, furious at the incompetence surrounding the affair, at first refused to authorise his six months' leaving payment; but it had been committed to paper and Long accepted in the end that it was a cast-iron obligation.

During the last months of 1981 relations between the old guard and the new grew worse. Evans worked longer and longer hours and became less and less accessible to those old *Times* people who remained. His health was patently deteriorating. In the summer he had married Tina Brown in a well-publicised private ceremony at the Long Island holiday home of his friend Ben Bradlee, editor of the *Washington Post*. But for a newly married couple they saw precious little of each other. He was under pressure from his proprietor above and an increasingly discontented staff below. The stress was barely tolerable.

Evans's distraction during this period is a possible explanation of his acquiescence in two curious and perhaps related manoeuvres by Murdoch in December. At a board meeting on December 8th, Sir Denis Hamilton announced that he was going to resign as chairman. This came as a surprise to his associates, who had gained the impression that his intention was to stay with the company for two or three years. His own explanation was that he had never intended to stay more than a year, but even that does not account for his quitting in December rather than waiting until the February anniversary of the change of ownership. Many believe that Murdoch found him a hindrance, an unnecessary barrier to things he wanted to do. In particular, he may have wanted Hamilton out of the way before his extraordinary attempt the following week to change the ownership of the newspapers' titles.

At a board meeting on December 16th, attended by both Harold Evans and Frank Giles, Murdoch announced that he proposed to remove the titles of their two papers from the ownership of Times Newspapers and vest them in the parent company, News International. The two editors failed to see the possible significance of this move and they raised no objection. The national directors did not attend the meeting and were not informed of the change, finalised five days later at a meeting of only four directors, including Long and Murdoch.

The switch meant that if Murdoch were to put Times

Newspapers into liquidation, the titles would not be among the assets available to the receiver. This would prevent a rival publisher from buying them and starting the papers up again. It also appeared to violate the pledges Murdoch had given to Biffen – undertakings that had the force of law – in return for being exempted from examination by the Monopolies Commission. One of the pledges stated that there would be no change in the ownership of the newspapers or any interest in them without consulting the national directors.

On January 13th, 1982, the national directors met Murdoch to discuss a successor to Hamilton as one of their number. There was in fact no reason why Hamilton should have had to resign from the position, for now that he was no longer chairman he was more genuinely independent than before. But Murdoch gave Hamilton a strong hint of what was expected, when he wrote asking him to suggest a new national director to succeed him. At the January 13th meeting Murdoch did not mention that the ownership of the titles had been changed.

Indeed, the switch did not emerge until Times Newspapers was well into its next labour crisis. On February 8th Murdoch wrote to all the staff saying that unless the unions would agree to six hundred redundancies "within days rather than weeks", the papers would close. The letter was similar in tone to the ones employees had become accustomed to receiving from the Thomson management, but blunter. The alternative to the redundancies, wrote Murdoch, "is no work for anyone and only the statutory minimum payoff". The group stood to lose fifteen million pounds in 1982. "The most dramatic contribution to our loss comes from the fact that we are employing far more people than our competitors." Before leaving for New York on Concorde, Murdoch said he would want negotiations on the redundancies completed within ten days or a fortnight.

The unions at first resisted the measures but within a couple of days attention was temporarily diverted from the industrial difficulties when rumours of the switch of the newspaper titles began to circulate. They started when Murdoch was briefing senior executives about his impending showdown with the unions, and Charles Douglas-Home asked him whether the titles would be available to a liquidator. When he replied opaquely that they "might not be," a check by *Sunday Times* journalists at Companies House confirmed that the titles were no longer listed as assets of the company. On February 10th Long was asked separately by journalists at *The Times* and *Sunday Times* who owned the titles and he said he would have to check – despite having been at the meeting where they were shifted to News International.

It was clear that an announcement would have to be made, and on February 11th Long telephoned the national directors to tell them, so that they would not read it first in the newspapers. "Why was it done?" one asked him. "To protect the rights of the national directors," Long said. When it was put to him that the national directors should legally have been informed, Long replied: "You have a point there. Raise it at the next meeting."

It was hard to see how the move could do anything but weaken the influence of the national directors, for it meant that decisions about the future of the titles would be taken by a board of which they were not members. Even before that, some of them felt that the management were not taking them into their confidence, were pushing them on to the sidelines. On February 2nd, in the wake of Hamilton's departure, Lord Dacre had written to Lord Roll suggesting that the national directors should arrange private meetings outside the aegis of the board, to formulate common positions. When on February 8th Murdoch made a rare phone call to Dacre to tell him of the proposed ultimatum to the unions, Dacre phoned Roll to inform him of this uncharacteristic gesture of consultation by the proprietor. "Perhaps he's learning how to behave," Roll conjectured, though they agreed that was unlikely.

It was Sir William Rees-Mogg who initiated the public outcry over the titles. He had no formal status in the matter, but as one of the vetting committee who had cleared the way for Murdoch's proprietorship he felt some residual responsibility and was unwilling to let the manoeuvre slip past as a *fait accompli*, as Murdoch may have hoped. On February 13th he wrote to John Biffen, the

Trade Secretary, declaring the transfer of the titles to be unlawful because the national directors had not been consulted. In an interview with the *Observer*, Rees-Mogg said: "What Rupert wants is to liquidate the present company and keep the titles to himself. That is clearly his intention." If it was, he was thwarted, for in the face of criticism Murdoch retreated swiftly. He accepted that the matter was a legitimate one for the national directors and when they did not agree to the move it was reversed.

In other matters, though, he was getting his own way. His decision to brazen it out with the unions coincided with his conviction that editorial changes were needed on both papers. The *Sunday Times* had predictably lost much of its bounce since Evans's departure. Ron Hall and Hugo Young were not, as he had hoped, vying with each other to displace Frank Giles. Young had none of the practical expertise to replace Evans's flair for layout and presentation, and he did not try. Murdoch, in any case, did not warm to him: too cerebral, the kind of person, he suspected, who was saying clever, superior things about him behind his back, to politicans and the like. As for Hall, although skilled in those technical areas where Giles and Young were weakest, he was disinclined to get involved in running the paper. He had accepted the joint deputy editorship, and the useful salary increase that went with it, but kept largely to editing the magazine and resisted suggestions that he should appear in the office every Saturday. Murdoch was egging him on to "use your elbows" against Giles. "How are those elbows going, Ron?" he would ask when they met, with a wink and the hint of a leer. The truth was that Hall was keeping them closely tucked to his sides. Convinced Giles's editorship would fail, he wanted to distance himself from it rather than try to redeem it. Murdoch became impatient.

While nobody expected Giles to be as forceful an editor as Evans, it was a surprise that *The Times*, too, should be suffering from lack of leadership. Evans was away from the office for a period after Christmas, recovering from an injury sustained when putting up decorations at his house. Douglas-Home was taking a month-long sabbatical, leaving Brian MacArthur in charge. When Murdoch phoned from Australia or New York he would be connected to MacArthur and was impressed with his competence. Perhaps here was a man with elbows sharp enough to nudge Giles into producing a better paper. Using the pretext of a dispute over a new women's section in the magazine, Murdoch had Giles dismiss Hall and appoint MacArthur as deputy editor, leapfrogging Young, who was relegated to number three in the hierarchy to the dismay of his colleagues, who tried to get Biffen to intervene here, too. Young scowled and bore it.

There was one further distraction from the main event of the showdown with the unions. On February 6th, the Saturday before the ultimatum, a curious article by Gerald Long appeared on the feature page of *The Times*. It was an account of a portentous correspondence in which he had engaged with Albert Roux, proprietor of Le Gavroche restaurant in London, on the subject of French farmhouse cheeses. In the course of a debate about whether the cheeses served at Le Gavroche were indeed all farmhouse cheeses, as was claimed on the menu, Long paraded his great knowledge of the subject; but he could not avoid the appearance of being a pedantic and over-fussy customer.

Long is proud of his accomplishments as a gourmet and also of his elegant prose style. He would employ the latter on disgruntled readers of *The Times* who wrote to complain about some of Evans's changes to the paper. His replies were models of correct English and he used to show them to Evans, who was impressed. When Long showed him his correspondence with Roux, Evans kept it and talked Long into letting him publish it. Neither man appeared to appreciate how ridiculous it made Long appear. "How do I come out of it?" he asked Anthony Holden, the features editor. "In the great tradition of British eccentrics," Holden replied carefully. "Eccentric?" snapped Long. "What's eccentric about it?"

Murdoch was furious when he saw the article in print. Not only was it an example of the high-minded pretentiousness he despised, but it also – and Long knew this – came only a few days before he was about to issue his ultimatum about the 600 redundancies. Evidence of the costly sensual passions of the company's managing director could not

have been produced at a less suitable time. When in
London Murdoch tries to visit the *Sunday Times* every
Saturday, and on this day he made no attempt to hide his
anger. Usually Long strode alongside him as he made his
tour of the production areas, but today he was a few paces
behind, confessing to bystanders that he was for the time
being out of favour.

The article was supposed to have been an appetiser for a
series of critical reviews of British food by a French and
German arch-gourmet. This project, which cost more than
£10,000, was close to Long's heart and he had written
profiles of the two fastidious men, due to appear in the
following week's paper. At Murdoch's insistence, Long
had his name removed from the profiles. A few weeks later
he was transferred from managing director to a post as
special adviser to Murdoch on unspecific matters, perhaps
reflecting ruefully that he should have taken the advice of
one of the didactic memorandums he had recently sent to
staff: "All executives of the company are reminded that
written authorisation is required for any proposed action of
whatever nature. There is no exception to this rule."

Murdoch's demand to the unions for manning cuts was
made in the most dramatic way possible. He sent his
hectoring letter to each staff member and to union leaders
and, as he climbed aboard Concorde, announced: "*The
Times* is not for sale. We will just close it if we don't have
agreement." Owen O'Brien, the general secretary of
NATSOPA, pointed to the difference, as he saw it, between
this warning and those periodically issued by Thomson's.
"The trouble is that Mr Murdoch is not someone who usually
cries wolf. Our experience is that when he says something
he usually seems to mean it." Barry Fitzpatrick, head of the
clerical chapel on the *Sunday Times*, was blunter. He said
Murdoch's plans amounted to a "straightforward mug-
ging". John Mitchell, secretary of the London machine
branch of NATSOPA, said: "We can conclude that Mr
Murdoch is trying to put a façade over his real desires,
which seem to be to let *The Times* and the *Sunday Times*
go."

The talks continued in Murdoch's absence and little
progress was made. On February 18th the company

announced that the number of applications for voluntary redundancy had fallen short of the 600 needed. Two days later Murdoch, now back in London, said: "The state of negotiations remains bleak. If the deadlock is not broken we shall have to close the two papers. There are no plans to reopen them." And Peter Wilby, head of the journalists' chapel on the *Sunday Times*, said: "There is a feeling that this edition may be the last – at least for the time being."

On Monday, February 22nd, Murdoch announced that, because no agreement on voluntary redundancies had been reached, 210 workers in the clerical departments would be dismissed. After an anguished reaction from Fitzpatrick, Murdoch relented slightly the following day, saying the dismissals would be rescinded if enough volunteers came forward: but the union was discouraging that by threatening to take away the membership cards of people who did apply.

Negotiations continued during the weekend and, despite Wilby's fears, the next issue of the *Sunday Times* duly made its appearance. Deadlines were made and extended. Murdoch was now playing a more personal role in the talks and figured in one incident that immediately became part of trade union lore, enhancing his reputation among workers. The leader of the machine-room chapel at the *Sunday Times* is Roy (Ginger) Wilson, a strapping Cockney, more than six feet tall, noted for his colourful use of language. After working the Saturday night shift at the *Sunday Times*, he was asked to go back to the office at 10 a.m. on Sunday for talks with Murdoch. He did so, but the day wore on and he was not summoned. His patience snapped and he stormed into Murdoch's office, with Owen O'Brien trailing behind. Murdoch, who had been sitting pensively behind his large desk, put out a hand and said: "Good to see you."

"Good to see me?" stormed Wilson, using an abusive oath. "Good to see me? I've been working all night making your [expletive] profits and you [expletive] keep me hanging about here. Good to see me?"

Murdoch grinned broadly. "Sit down," he said. "You're just the kind of man I can do business with."

It was mid-March before the business was completed and Murdoch was able to announce that the future of the papers was secure, with seventy per cent of his proposed reductions agreed. This meant 430 redundancies and more than 400 shifts abolished, for a cut of some eight million pounds in the annual wage bill.

By this time a new drama was under way, more gripping than the battle with the unions because it was a personal struggle between Murdoch and his star editor, Harold Evans. In *The Times* of March 12th the report of the successful outcome of the redundancy negotiations carried this cryptic paragraph at its foot: "Mr Harold Evans, the editor of *The Times*, said he had no comment to make on reports circulating about his future as editor. He was on duty last night as usual."

The reports referred to had been circulating for a month. They began in February with hints in the William Hickey column in the *Daily Express* and in *Private Eye*. The Hickey item pointed out that Evans was away from the office during the paper's time of crisis. "I've got 'flu," he explained plaintively to Hickey. The *Private Eye* story said Murdoch had already informed the board that he was thinking of removing Evans. Murdoch was persuaded to respond swiftly and unambiguously, calling the rumours "malicious, self-serving and wrong", and adding: "Mr Evans's outstanding qualities and journalistic skills are recognised throughout the world, as are his improvements to *The Times* over the past twelve months."

Indeed they were, in particular by the Granada Television programme *What The Papers Say*. In Granada's annual awards, announced the following week, Evans was named Editor of the Year. No such award can ever have been less opportune. In his acceptance speech Evans felt obliged to refer both to the rumours about his departure and Murdoch's threat to close the papers. Returning to the office, he addressed a mass meeting of the staff, stressing that the award was really for them rather than him, and handing his medal round for the journalists to touch. They were less than impressed, preferring to quiz Evans on his role in the attempted transfer of the titles. The mood was sullen, not festive.

The breach between Evans and the majority of his staff had now become more open and more personal than that between Rees-Mogg and the White Swan group twelve years earlier. The issue was the same, but the White Swan people had not aimed their anger directly at the editor, whom they saw was not himself wholly committed to the Thomson strategy. Evans, though, *was* the new strategy, the man whose idea, shared with the proprietor, was to make *The Times* attractive to readers of the *Daily Telegraph* and the Sunday colour supplements by introducing features that could have served equally well in the *Telegraph* or the supplements themselves.

Since Christmas, Holden and Donoughue, Evans's closest allies, had become convinced of a plot to have Evans dismissed and they suspected that Douglas-Home, his deputy, was part of it. They thought they detected a more abrasive, less co-operative attitude from him when he returned from his sabbatical in mid-January. Donoughue summoned Douglas-Home and put to him directly the suggestion that he was working to undermine Evans. Douglas-Home became angry. He not only denied the allegation but avowed in strong terms that he would never edit a paper for Murdoch, whom he believed to be a 'monster' and the cause of most of the disruption at *The Times* and the *Sunday Times*. Murdoch's technique, as he saw it, was to break up useful combinations and alliances in his companies, in case they should ever become a threat to him. Douglas-Home repeated his assurance to Evans and, at a second meeting with Donoughue, said he was finding things so difficult that he was thinking of resigning.

Evans would have had nothing to fear from Douglas-Home or anyone had he been able to rely on the loyalty of his patron. That he could not depend on Murdoch's backing was the crucial weakness in his position. Evans's allies were right to detect a move against him, but the instigator was his proprietor rather than his deputy. By the end of the year, Murdoch had become convinced that Evans was not the man to produce the low-cost, higher-circulation paper he wanted. He would return fewer and fewer of his editor's calls forcing him to compose long memoranda on trivial topics. In January Murdoch began taking soundings among senior staff to see how they would react if Evans were replaced. Owen Hickey was among those called to see him. Then one evening he wandered into the Business News section for a long talk with Adrian Hamilton, its editor. He said he was growing convinced that Evans did not have the support of the senior staff. What did Hamilton think? Hamilton said that was not his impression and the conversation turned to more general matters, including a ritual denunciation by Murdoch of the quality of the old *Times* journalists. He said he would be asking for more staff cuts, and stressed the urgency by browbeating everyone who came to use the copying machine near where they were talking. "Do you know how much each copy costs?" he asked them combatively.

It was evident that Murdoch, frustrated by Evans's failure to deliver as large a readership as had been hoped, was looking for a pretext to pounce. He found it when John Grant, demoralised by his rows with Evans and Long over money, decided to apply for redundancy. Grant confided his intention to Douglas-Home, who found this further nibbling away at the core of the old guard more than he could bear. He told Grant that he too would leave if Grant went through with his plan, but first he decided to go and see Murdoch, who saw this as the opening he needed. Told that both the deputy editor and managing editor wanted to quit, he advised Douglas-Home to defer a final decision, for there might be a change in the offing.

Before moving against Evans, Murdoch sought the view of Fred Emery, effectively number three in the paper's hierarchy, in charge of home and foreign news reporting. Emery was about to go on a skiing holiday but drove to the office on the eve of his departure on Murdoch's summons. When Murdoch asked him if he could work with Douglas-Home as editor, Emery said he could.

His lines thus cleared, Murdoch asked for Evans's resignation on Budget Day, March 9th, 1982. "Why?" Evans asked. "The place is in chaos. You can't see the wood for the trees and the senior staff are in turmoil," Murdoch replied. Evans declined to go quietly and pointed out that if he was dismissed he would expect a large redundancy payment. Murdoch's initial offer was £25,000, half his annual salary. Evans wanted nearly ten times that; but as news of the attempt to dislodge him spread, he and his allies insisted that the dispute was not over money but over

Murdoch's right to dismiss him so summarily. Should the national directors not be brought into it?

Murdoch had taken the precaution of giving the directors advance warning of his intention. "I have to admit that Lord Dacre was right and I was wrong," he told them. "Mea culpa, mea culpa." The directors agreed that a resignation was a matter between the editor and the proprietor. If the editor felt improper pressure had been exerted on him, it was up to him to complain to the national directors and they would take it from there. Evans did raise the issue informally with Lord Robens who advised him there was no point in staying on if he was constantly going to be at loggerheads with the proprietor. Spurred by Donoughue, he ensured his departure was played out publicly. "It's all over," Donoghue told him, "but what we're discussing is the *style* in which you'll go. There are important principles here and the longer you hold on the more it may be possible to focus attention on the principles." Anthony Holden, emerging as Evans's spokesman, said there had been political pressure. He claimed that Murdoch had expressed his dismay at Evans's and Donoughue's apparent support for the new Social Democratic Party, and at the liberal tone of editorials on racial matters and foreign affairs, specifically Poland and El Salvador. Donoughue claimed to have heard on his shadowy "network" of contacts that Margaret Thatcher, the Prime Minister, had expressed displeasure at this centrist drift, and that Murdoch had promised her that *The Times* would be firmly in her camp by Easter. In his book, Evans maintains that she had been thinking of offering him the chairmanship of the Sports Council to get him away from Gray's Inn Road.

On Friday, March 12th, the day Murdoch announced that the future of the paper was secure, the first leader of *The Times* bore the headline "The Deeper Issues". In that heated atmosphere almost anything could be read as having a double meaning, but in this case it was deliberate. Evans and Donoughue had composed the editorial as a swan-song to the Evans editorship. Superficially about the issues behind that week's Budget, it was supposed to read as a comment on the implications of Evans's dismissal and his policy differences with Murdoch.

"There is a whole number of areas where so far Government has done nothing to ameliorate life and in some cases has damaged its tone and quality," Evans wrote. "Unemployment is a social scandal," he continued, going on to speak of the "erosion of hope and a collapse of vision in the role of Britain as a leading member of the international community." These were broad points, but the editorial then concentrated on the role of the newspaper. "Underlying the view of *The Times* on these matters is a conviction of the value of the individual free spirit and of free debate. We favour a more competitive society as against one which is subject to the monopoly powers of capital or the trade unions, or too great a concentration of power in any one institution: the national press itself, to be fair, is worryingly over-concentrated."

Having taken an explicit jab at their proprietor, Evans and Donoughue broadened the theme to disclaim any political commitment. "No single British party has a programme which matches the needs of this great but troubled nation . . . What is necessary at this time is leadership and vision that will lift the British people beyond the current dogmas and disputes. A society is judged not only by what it achieves but by what it aspires to achieve."

Evans's terminal negotiations with Murdoch were being conducted on a less lofty plane than that. When Holden dropped into the editor's office he found Richard Searby, Murdoch's urbane, long-time friend and lawyer, ordering Evans in unambiguous and abusive terms to vacate his chair for Douglas-Home. The outspoken Searby has a special place in the demonology of the Evans camp, based partly on his once having told Tina Brown that the paper her husband edited was a "smelly rag". (Searby denied making the remark in a letter to *The Times* in 1983, but Evans repeats the assertion in *Good Times, Bad Times*.)

The drama was gaining increasing public attention. Radio and television teams and reporters from rival papers were constant visitors to Gray's Inn Road, and cameras were placed almost permanently outside. On that same Friday, Evans was intercepted on his way to the office by a radio reporter and managed to sustain a chirpy mood. "I am editing *The Times* and I'm going to do that now," he said. "And as Mark Twain said, rumours of my death have been greatly exaggerated."

Next day the right-hand column of the front page was headed "*The Times* and its editorship." It began: "A day of speculation about the editorship of *The Times* ended inconclusively last night." Murdoch was reported as saying that terms had been agreed for Evans's departure, but the editor continued to deny it, saying: "It is and has been an argument about principle and the constitution of *The Times* as agreed in the articles of association laid before Parliament." Anthony Holden said there had been a series of policy disagreements between Evans and Murdoch but Murdoch denied this: "At no point has there been any difference, stated or otherwise, between Mr Evans and myself about the policy of the paper," he said.

Next day the Sunday papers carried articles based on the assumption that Evans was about to go. The lunchtime radio programme, "The World This Weekend", contained a long segment on the dispute. Among those interviewed was Lord Robens, who gave the first public explanation of the position of the national directors. If Evans felt he was being unfairly pressed to resign, he asserted, he could approach them, but he had not done so and "it is not possible for the national directors, on rumours that he may have resigned, to take any action at all . . . The initiative, if Harold Evans thinks he is being pressurised or persecuted, is certainly with Harold Evans . . . He is the most protected editor in the world. He can't be forced to resign if he thinks it's improper pressure. If he has resigned you can be sure he has got good reason for resigning." It was not true that Evans had made no approach to the national directors. By now he had discussed the matter with all of them except Pickering. But despite his fury he could see the wisdom of the advice Lord Robens and others were giving him: he really had no choice but to quit.

The next person interviewed in the programme was Geoffrey Smith, a leader writer, a pillar of the Old Guard and a committee member of JOTT, the organisation of *Times* journalists that on Saturday had taken the unusual step of issuing a statement urging their editor to resign and make way for Douglas-Home. "Our concern is that the gradual erosion of editorial standards from within might leave us with no paper worth saving," they wrote. "The way the paper is laid out and run has changed so frequently that stability has been destroyed."

Smith, quivering with self-righteousness, had something more gripping than that to read to Sunday radio listeners. "I have here," he began, echoing Neville Chamberlain, "a copy of a memo sent by Harold Evans to the chairman Mr Rupert Murdoch on February 24th this year. It concerns the coverage of the Budget in *The Times* this year." The contents of the memo were a bit of a let-down. Evans was asking Murdoch his views on how the Budget should be reported in *The Times*. It was soon clear that Smith's motive was to combat Holden's claim that Murdoch's reason for wanting to be rid of Evans was political.

"Here is the editor," Smith raged, "going to the proprietor for his guidance on what are matters of editorial decision. I do not believe it is possible to say that the man who wrote that letter is the man who must remain as editor if the editorial independence of the paper is to continue." The next extract was even tamer. Evans was asking Murdoch's opinion on an idea for a series of articles and concluded: "If you like the idea, I'll take it further." Said Smith: "That does not sound to me like an editor eager to preserve the independence of his office . . . It doesn't sound to me like an editor behaving like an independent person in the way that is traditional with the holding of that office." The explanation for the memos was not as sinister as that; indeed it was a bit pathetic. Because Evans was finding it harder and harder to get Murdoch to talk to him on the telephone, he was forced to consult him by memorandum – a form of communication Murdoch dislikes and seldom uses. All the same, the introduction of secret documents gave the affair a conspiratorial flavour, recalling Watergate. Smith would not say how he came by them, but since Douglas-Home had access to Evans's correspondence many saw his hand in it, recalling the scandal of the dossiers years before. Douglas-Home is a genial enough man but some detect in him a submerged shiftiness that encourages conspiracy theories.

Holden was next to be interviewed on the programme.

"I'm surprised and saddened by the depths to which Mr Evans's opponents are sinking in their hour of apparent victory," he began. "I would only point out that the deputy editor and putative next editor is copied in and sees all the editor's correspondence with the chairman and was privy to these at the time, whatever he may or may not be doing with them now." He defended Evans's consultation with Murdoch on budget coverage and the feature series on the argument that it was a question of cost and thus a legitimate area for discussion with the management. He said he knew for a fact that Murdoch had tried to interfere politically and spoke of "dirty tricks which don't augur well for the new editorship of *The Times*". Illustrating that, he revealed wryly: "Last night I was asked by three different people if I was on a percentage of the editor's payoff money. I had, alas, emphatically to deny that."

By the following day Evans had still not confirmed his resignation, though Douglas-Home was effectively editing the paper. Smith's reading of the editor's memoranda on the radio had heightened the atmosphere of suspicion and unreality. (In his book, Evans maintains that his private secretary was suborned by Douglas-Home and was giving detailed reports about the people who had been to see him and his telephone callers.)

Evans arrived late in the office and closeted himself there with Donoughue. At lunchtime John Higgins, the arts editor, who had a few days earlier privately declared his support for Douglas-Home, asked Philip Howard, the literary editor, to lunch at the Garrick. On the stairs, as they walked down from the bar to the dining-room, they encountered Evans and Donoughue walking up. "How are you bearing up in these terrible times?" Evans asked Higgins. "That question should be addressed to you," Higgins replied. Without saying more, Evans grasped Howard's shoulder melodramatically, then released it and proceeded to the bar, where friends buzzed round him for the latest word.

There were still several hours to wait for the final resolution. The first edition of *The Times* that night carried an announcement to the effect that Evans was still editor, but by the time the paper appeared that was no longer true. He

had alerted Independent Television News to be ready for a
statement at 9 p.m., in time for their News at Ten. The
cameras were in place outside his office when he left it.
"The differences between me and Mr Murdoch should not
be prolonged," he told the nation. "I am, therefore, resigning tonight as editor of *The Times*. I have enormously
enjoyed my fifteen years as editor of the *Sunday Times* and
The Times, and I look forward to a future as exciting and
interesting."

Back home in Pimlico Evans's wife Tina had organised a
party to keep everyone's spirits up. Apart from professional colleagues like Donoughue, Holden and Ron Hall, the
guests included Melvyn Bragg, the novelist, and John
Mortimer, the playwright and lawyer. A little after 9.30
p.m. Evans arrived clutching a piece of paper and everyone
went quiet. "I have just made this statement to ITN," he
announced gravely, and then read it out again. Someone
turned on the television and after a few minutes the guests
saw the scene re-enacted. They noticed that the cameras
had lighted on one of Evans's secretaries, sobbing quietly.

Murdoch might have been weeping as well: he had to pay
Evans a six-figure sum in compensation. But the proprietor
said nothing in public. Certainly, it was a while since he had
last described Evans as the greatest editor in Fleet Street.
Murdoch had proved that an editor can only be as great as
his proprietor allows him to be. It was an expensive way to
make a point.

Within weeks the most important of the men Evans
brought with him had left. Holden resigned in sympathy,
with no payoff, while Donoughue was asked to leave
because he had not informed the paper in time for the first
edition that Evans planned to quit. Peter Watson, who had
been in New York only a few weeks, was told his job no
longer existed, as was John Heilpern. Adrian Hamilton
gave up the editorship of Business News because he could
not accept Douglas-Home's plan to reduce its size and
scope even more drastically than Evans had done, turning it
into a strictly City section resembling the *Daily Telegraph*'s.

In the week of Evans's resignation, Holden and Murdoch
confronted each other at a cocktail party where the Queen
and Prince Philip were the chief guests. Holden

approached Murdoch pugnaciously and said he was "a deeply misguided man" for having ditched Evans. "You will never work for me again," Murdoch fumed, and stalked away.

As for *The Times*, it had fended off one more attempt to compromise its character. An old *Times* man, an aristocrat to boot, was now in charge, and his supporters claimed their rewards. John Higgins was made executive editor in charge of features and John Grant spent his last nine months on the paper as deputy editor, with the promise that after he retired he could edit the crossword. The counter-revolution was complete. If *The Times* does not survive the Murdoch proprietorship it will at least succumb with quiet dignity, its self-image intact.

The Times reminds me of that appealing literary character, Mehitabel the alley cat, whose unpunctuated adventures with Archy* the cockroach were chronicled in several American publications between the wars. Despite degrading encounters with a variety of lusty tom-cats, Mehitabel emerged with claws at the ready and, in her own catch-phrase, always the lady. "Class is the thing that counts, archy," she would confide, "you can't get away from class." And in a memorable verse she penned at the end of a sordid affair with a coyote:

> "i have had my ups i have had my downs
> i have been through the mill
> but i said when i clawed that coyotes face
> thank god i am a lady still."

*Don Marquis, *Archy's Life of Mehitabel*, Faber & Faber, 1956.

Chapter 10

CHICAGO . . . AND BEYOND

It's very wrong to say I'm the most powerful man in Australia.
I'm not even there.
        – *Rupert Murdoch interviewed in 'Town and Country'*
        magazine, New York, November 1982.

Scarcely had Murdoch wiped away the blood from the
Evans skirmish than he was in the thick of another battle in
New York. The circulation struggle between the *Post* and
the *News* had intensified in the second half of 1980 and been
at a high pitch since. It was, on the face of it, an unbalanced
and an unlikely contest. On one side was the powerful
News, long established as a monopoly in the morning
tabloid field, owned by the mighty *Chicago Tribune* and
boasting the largest daily circulation in the country except-
ing the *Wall Street Journal*. Against it, the *Post* had scarcely
half its sales and, proportionately, even less advertising.
Yet the *News* management were worried by the *Post*,
almost to the point of obsession.

Part of this was due to what they saw as Murdoch's
blatant treachery over the 1978 strike, but mostly it was a
product of his fearsome reputation, embellished by tall
tales told in journalists' bars and by his own boasting. "We
will bleed them to death in five years," he said of the *Daily
News* in 1981, an echo of the claim his father made of an
upstart rival – and fulfilled – in Melbourne some fifty years
earlier.

The *News* people could not blame Murdoch entirely, or
even chiefly, for their horrific plunge in circulation in the
1970s. The paper began the decade selling more than two

million copies a day and three million on Sundays. By 1981 the daily circulation had gone down by 600,000 and on Sunday by a full million. Not all the lost readers had switched to the *Post*. What was really hurting the *News* was the changing population pattern of New York. Working-class readers were leaving the declining outer boroughs as fast as they could afford to. They moved to Long Island, Westchester and New Jersey, where they switched to thriving papers like Long Island's *Newsday*. As the old readers died their college-educated children subscribed to the *New York Times* or the *Wall Street Journal*, papers that served their interests better.

But Murdoch is a great tease. Colleagues recall how he used to chivvy Lord Ryder of the *Mirror* at meetings of the Newspaper Publishers' Association in London. Now he lost no opportunity of sniping at the *News* in public, mocking it for going over the head of its audience, boasting of his aim to drive his rival out of business, or even buy it himself.

Since Murdoch's abortive attempt to start a morning paper during the strike, executives at the *News* had convinced themselves he would try again or that he intended, by progressively advancing the printing time of his first edition, to turn the *Post* into a twenty-four hour newspaper. In the summer of 1980 they decided to make a pre-emptive assault. They announced that the *Daily News* would start an evening edition, called *Tonight*. It would seek to be everything they felt the *Post* was not – lively yet intelligent, aimed at Bloomingdale's shoppers rather than shoplifters, including the closing market prices, an authoritative business section and up-market consumer features, to attract *New York Times* readers on their way home. Some twenty million dollars was budgeted for the launch and the initial circulation target set at a modest 200,000. With a nice sense of retribution, the *News* people hired Clay Felker as editor.

The concept of *Tonight* had been devised by marketing strategists, but to those unversed in their mysteries there were some peculiar things about it. For one, it was going to be sold at news-stands only in Manhattan south of Harlem. The traditional *News* readership in the outer boroughs was to be ignored. Part of the reason for this decision lay in another dubious strategy. *Tonight* was not to be an entirely separate paper but an afternoon edition of the *News*, carrying many of the same feature articles as the next day's morning paper. That is why there was no real attempt to sell it where the *News* already had a strong hold on the morning market.

Murdoch is energised by such blatant declarations of hostility. As soon as he had wind of the *News*'s plan he summoned meeting after meeting of his executives to devise a counter-strategy. When preoccupied with something he will discuss it with anyone who comes to talk about any subject. When David Schneiderman went for one of his infrequent meetings about the *Village Voice*, he found Murdoch bubbling with enthusiasm for the impending battle with the *News*, asking advice on what moves he should make. "He was like a general in a war," said Schneiderman, and it was only with difficulty that he was able to steer the conversation round to the *Voice* at all.

The main decision was to meet the challenge by printing the *Post* earlier in the morning, to compete with the *News* on the news-stands and on railway stations while people were on their way to work. The time of the first edition was advanced to 7 a.m. There was a debate on whether to reduce the price from thirty cents to twenty-five. Most people advised him not to, but Murdoch, always a low-price enthusiast, did it anyway. As a result of these moves the *Post* won about 100,000 new readers, roughly the sales figure *Tonight* settled at after the curiosity impact had worn off. The *Post*'s price cut meant it would be out of the question for the *News* and *Tonight* to go up to thirty cents. With their large combined circulation, this cost them much more than the *Post* forfeited by its reduction.

Felker did not prove a judicious choice as editor. His recent experience and his greatest success had been with magazines. Many felt he might not be strong in news gathering and presentation – areas that are paramount in all newspapers but especially tabloids that appear in the afternoon. Most of his major hirings were of columnists and feature writers, such as Richard Reeves and Gary Wills, skilled at turning out exquisitely crafted and thoughtful articles of several thousand words – splendid stuff, but not the kind needed in an afternoon paper, which must first of all be a fast read. Of the handful of writers he lured from the *Post*, the most notable was Claudia Cohen, the successful young editor of the page six gossip column that had been one of Murdoch's earliest innovations. The circumstances of her departure illustrate the fervour with which Murdoch was conducting the war.

Roger Wood, the editor, was away on the day she announced she was leaving, so she handed her notice to John Van Doorn, deputising for him. When Wood phoned to ask how things were going, Van Doorn told him about Cohen. "You'd better call Rupert," said Wood, although Van Doorn had not thought it necessary to inform the publisher of anything so trivial. Murdoch was in the South of France, but Van Doorn took the advice and phoned him. "Good," said Murdoch when he was told. "Have her out of the office by tomorrow." Van Doorn protested that she had given the required two weeks' notice and he saw no need to rush things. "Get her out, get her out," Murdoch insisted, apparently fearing she would use her final two weeks to damage the paper, to hit back at her enemies or steal secrets to take across to the *News*. Murdoch reinforced the instruction with a call to Wood, who phoned Van Doorn again. Cohen left within a couple of days.

Van Doorn sees that as evidence that Murdoch has an essential dislike of journalists. Soon after his arrival as managing editor he had a small problem with reporters who left for home after work without checking with him or another senior editor. He wrote a wry memorandum reminding the offenders of the news-room tradition of getting a "goodnight" from the news editor. Murdoch found this cordial approach to staff infuriating. "You treat them like that and they'll come after you," he said. "No sense in being funny, they'll get after you." This is consistent with his observation to Robert Ducas, when head of the *Times* office in New York, that journalists are chronically idle.

It was soon clear that *Tonight* had been badly misconceived. It was not simply the long features; it just did not look newsy. The front page was too sedate, lacking the compelling urgency of the *Post*'s screaming headlines. And there was a confusion of identity with the morning paper.

Readers could not remember whether the features and special sections duplicated those in that morning's *News* or the next morning's. Part of its circulation was taken from the old late-night edition of the *News*, on sale as people left theatres, cinemas and restaurants. They bought that because it was the next morning's paper. They were getting a jump on the news. That edition was stopped when *Tonight* was launched, but fewer night-owls were attracted to an afternoon paper, several hours stale.

By the spring of 1981 it was apparent that *Tonight* was a failure. Its circulation had struggled to barely over 100,000 copies a day and had then dropped below 80,000. They were having trouble giving it away: commuters to Westchester and Long Island were being handed coupons entitling them to take it free for a week, but even that did not convert many of them. When the sales figures for the six months ending on March 31st were available, the *Post* was able to trumpet that its circulation was up to 732,158 from 654,314 a year earlier. Over the same period, despite the launch of *Tonight*, figures for the *News* were lower, at 1,491,556, as against 1,554,604 for the six months ending March 31st, 1980. Felker was replaced as editor of *Tonight* by Dick Oliver, a man with a background in hard news, and the paper became thinner as the controlling company in Chicago decided to cut losses. On August 15th, 1981, Michael O'Neill, the executive editor of the *News*, and Robert Hunt, the publisher, called the staff together in the news room and announced emotionally that *Tonight* would cease publication at the end of the month. Hunt had other rigorous measures to reveal – a wage freeze for all and a cut of ten per cent in the salaries of the company's eleven senior executives.

This substantial victory for Murdoch was sweetened by another success he was enjoying that summer. A few years earlier he had teamed up with the Australian film producer Robert Stigwood in a company called Associated R. & R. Films. (The initials are for Rupert and Robert. Had they used their surnames it would have come out as S. & M., indicative of films of a less proper kind than they planned.) Their first production was Peter Weir's *Gallipoli*, and Murdoch admitted that he had been drawn to it because of his father's role in that campaign. The film was released in New York in 1981 and was a deserved success. Queues formed outside the cinema on Third Avenue and 59th Street, where it had its first run, and Murdoch was not to know that at the end of some performances a faint hissing could be heard from the audience when his name came up on the credits. That image problem again.

Although the *Post* had trounced *Tonight*, it was still losing more money than his other American enterprises were making. He was certain by now that the only way he could significantly increase his share of city advertising, short of driving the *News* off the market altogether, was to force his circulation up still further. There were already some phenomenal days when the *Post* was selling all it was physically capable of printing: on the day President Sadat was assassinated they sold 1,050,000 copies, but that was an isolated event. To try for a longer-lasting increase Murdoch turned to a device that had proved effective, though horribly expensive, in London and Australia: bingo.

This is a perfect gambling game for newspapers because it obliges players to buy the paper every day to see whether they have won. Long popular in Britain, where a non-newspaper version is played in hundreds of converted cinemas all over the country, it involves each player checking numbers against a personal card. The first to check a complete line, or the whole card, wins the prize. Since in the newspaper version the numbers are available only in the paper, it is a cast-iron circulation builder.

The 1981 bingo craze began in Britain. It started on the *Daily Star*, a tabloid launched by Trafalgar House, the new owners of Express Newspapers. The *Star* was aimed at the bottom end of the market, competing directly with Murdoch's *Sun*, even to the extent of publishing daily pictures of nude women. But its circulation stuck at around a million – less than a third that of the *Sun* and the *Daily Mirror* – until the introduction of bingo. The *Daily Star* management mailed a million cards to householders, pointing out that the only way to find out whether they were winners was to buy the paper. Circulation rose by 75,000 within a week, and continued to climb.

Murdoch, characteristically, decided to fight back on a

more ambitious scale. The *Sun* was to have a bingo game that every person in Britain would have the chance to play. Cards were mailed to every household in the country. Prizes would total a million pounds in the first few weeks. The impact on circulation was so sensational that the *Daily Mirror* had no alternative but to join in as well. The game, or versions of it, spread to London's two more sober tabloids, the *Mail* and the *Express*. Now everyone had to have bingo, just to keep up with the others. Once started, it was hard to see how the games could be abandoned without a mutual self-denying agreement among the proprietors – a device foreign to Murdoch's nature. He prefers to continue the games, and the drain of funds they involve, believing that his opponents will weaken before he does, and he will reap the reward. If bingo expenditure were to force the *Daily Star* to close, the *Sun* would be the beneficiary.

Delighted with the initial success of the London bingo promotion, Murdoch decided to do the same in Sydney, where it would, he saw, be an ideal way for his *Daily Mirror* to steal a march on its afternoon rival, the *Sun*. It worked there too and, like his London competitors, the *Sun* in Sydney had to improvise its own bingo game to stay in the race.

From there, New York was a natural progression. With the *Daily News* demoralised by the closure of *Tonight*, it was time to press home the advantage. At the beginning of September 1981 the *Post* began mailing a sheet of weekly cards to every household in New York city and some of the inner suburbs – more than six million altogether. The name bingo was unavailable for copyright reasons, so it was called Wingo. At the *News*, something close to panic set in when they first caught wind of what Murdoch was planning. They cobbled together a rival game, calling it Zingo. If they were to compete they had no time to plan their own mailing, so the cards were printed in the paper itself and promoted by intensive television advertising. This is less effective than direct mailing, where the potential player has the card in hand, uncertain whether it is a winner of thousands of dollars but having to spend only twenty-five cents a day to find out. In the early stages the *Post*'s circulation vaulted by some 200,000 to nearly a million a day. The *News* put on readers, too – but fewer. As the circulation gap between the two papers narrowed, the *News* continued to be afflicted by a debilitating haemorrhage of confidence until in December 1981 the Chicago Tribune Company announced that it was for sale. It was still the largest-selling city newspaper in America but now it was limping and bruised, its spirit damaged, apparently mortally, but its brush with the formidable Australian. It had lost eleven million dollars in 1981 and the projections were for losses of thirty million in 1982 and fifty million in 1983. Not surprisingly, there was no immediate rush of buyers, but in the first weeks of 1982 a number of corporations were said to have made discreet inquiries.

On March 31st it was announced that Joseph Allbritton, a tough, fifty-seven-year-old Texas millionaire, would buy the *News* provided he could negotiate cost savings with the printing unions. Allbritton had bought the *Washington Star* in 1974, before selling it at a loss four years later to *Time* magazine, who have since closed it. In 1981 he bought the *Trenton Times* in New Jersey and made Draconian cuts in staffing. On April 5th he said he wanted to shed 1,600 of the 3,800 unionised full-time workers on the *News*, saving eighty-five million dollars from the $200m annual payroll. Stanton Cook, President of the Chicago Tribune Company, commented: "If these negotiations fail we see no alternative but to cease publication of the *News*."

The Allied Printing Trades Council had since the 1978 strike engaged the inevitable Theodore Kheel as their permanent adviser. Kheel could see that Cook's naming of Allbritton as the buyer of last resort made the unions' negotiating position dangerously weak. To offset that, he persuaded the Allied to investigate purchasing the *News* themselves under an Employee Stock Ownership Plan (ESOP) – a scheme offering tax advantages to companies selling stock to trusts for the benefit of the employees. The union leaders, though, were nervous about such a departure from tradition and doubted whether they were capable of running the paper without a proper proprietor.

At about this time Kheel was at a dinner party in

Manhattan and sat next to Donald Kummerfeld, president of News America, Murdoch's American operation. "It occurs to me that if the *News* survives, the *Post* will be in trouble," Kheel told Kummerfeld, to whom the thought had certainly occurred also. Kheel went on to say that the unions he represented were almost as concerned for the future of the *Post* as for the *News*, although it provided substantially fewer jobs for their members. "Why not call Rupert?" Kummerfeld suggested.

Relations between Kheel and Murdoch, having reached their nadir during the 1978 strike, had improved since the settlement of Kheel's libel action against *New York* magazine – a settlement that some felt was made at the expense of the article's author, Richard Karp. The possibility of bringing Murdoch in as a second bidder, to outflank the *News*'s strategy of dealing only with Allbritton, had been dawning on Kheel for some time. The thought crystallised when Kheel and the unions were allowed to see the letter of intent Allbritton had signed to buy the paper. As Kheel saw it, the terms offered meant that the Tribune Company were in effect paying the Texan to take the paper off their hands. In return for shouldering the potential burden of some thirty-seven million dollars in severance pay and around fifty million dollars of unfunded pension liability, Allbritton would receive assets worth about seventy-five million dollars. He was risking very little and, if he succeeded in negotiating the staff cuts he planned, he could make a profit of eighteen million dollars in his first year.

Kheel did not contact Murdoch direct but instead telephoned Martin Fischbein, his former employee, then a senior executive at the *Post*. (Fischbein died in a motor accident in 1983.) "Do you know the *News* is up for grabs for nothing?" Kheel inquired. A meeting was arranged between Kheel, Murdoch and George McDonald, the president of the Allied, at Murdoch's apartment. Further meetings took place at the University Club, the restaurant "21" and other fashionable midtown locations. It was agreed that Murdoch should express his interest in buying the papers, possibly in partnership with the proposed ESOP.

The union leaders preferred Murdoch to Allbritton

largely because he was the devil they knew. For sure, he was a tough negotiator but at the end the deal was always struck. Allbritton was an unknown quantity. What they would have preferred was for the Tribune Company to change its mind and continue publishing the *News*, but Murdoch would be a good second best. They recognised the risk that he would close one of the two papers once he had acquired both; but there was in any case always the danger that after they agreed to Allbritton's manning cuts one of the papers would close anyway, leaving the other with a much reduced staff.

On April 7th Murdoch gave a press conference to stress that, to defend his trading position, he would have to insist on manning concessions at the *Post* equal to any negotiated for the *News*. The *Post*, he said, had lost twenty million dollars in 1981 despite its increased circulation. Asked why he had not sought such cuts before, he replied that he had not then thought it possible to achieve them. He said: "I feel passionately that the *News* ought to survive and the *Post* ought to survive too." He left it to McDonald to make public the suggestion that he might bid for the *News*. Murdoch, although by now virtually committed to a bid, said for the record only that he would think about it. Allbritton was furious at McDonald's move. He suspended talks with the unions, although the Tribune Company reiterated that the paper would close if he did not buy it.

There was never any real doubt that Murdoch would go along with McDonald's and Kheel's suggestion. Here was the chance to end at a stroke the losses on the *Post*, which clearly could not continue indefinitely at their present rate. What is more, a monopoly of the New York tabloid press would put him in the pleasing position of being able to cock a snook at advertisers too proud to do business with him: now it would be him or nobody. It was an unmissable opportunity.

On April 12th he announced formally that he was in the hunt for the *News*. The direct competition of the two tabloids, he declared, was a "dance of death" that would end with the disappearance of one or both of them. He would publish both papers, he promised, if the unions would agree to cuts to cover their current losses. He would spend $150 million on a new joint printing plant, with modern equipment that would bring costs down to the level of those on competing suburban newspapers. Employees would be allowed to buy stock up to half the value of the new company.

The Tribune Company, fearing they might be forced to negotiate with Murdoch if Allbritton withdrew from the contest, persuaded the Texan to resume talks with the unions, whose bargaining position had been strengthened by Murdoch's announcement. A Tribune statement called the bid "a transparent attempt to destroy and shut down the paper" and Stanton Cook made the point that Murdoch, having shown no interest when the paper was put up for sale in December, now declared himself through a press announcement. "This is really a curious approach, even for Mr Murdoch, if one is really seeking to acquire a property."

Though Cook declined to deal with him, Murdoch continued to pile on the pressure, trying to dissuade the unions from agreeing to Allbritton's terms. He hinted he might shut the *Post* if the unions gave so many concessions to the *News* that his paper could not compete effectively. The *New York Times*, too, said they would want to benefit from any new manning agreement. Five days later the talks between Allbritton and the unions broke down on his insistence on a wage freeze and a five-year contract, but Allbritton agreed to resume them after an appeal from Mayor Koch.

Then on April 28th the board of the Tribune Company met in Chicago, to discuss some disturbing advice they had received from their labour relations lawyers about possible liabilities if Allbritton's negotiations with the unions failed and they closed the paper. They were told that Murdoch's intervention might have changed matters radically. As well as severance pay and unfunded pensions, they might now be liable to pay off the job guarantees of a significant group of printers until their contracts expired in 1984, making a total liability of between $200 million and $300 million. The lawyers explained that the question would go to arbitration and that the ruling might go against the company if they closed the paper while another buyer – Murdoch – was willing to buy it. The chances were that the decision would be in favour of the company, they advised, but the snag was that if the arbitrator decided differently there was no appeal against his ruling. Payments on that scale would be quite insupportable, the board decided. The softer option – given their continued aversion to dealing with Murdoch – was to reverse their December position and continue publishing the *News*, after trying to secure concessions from the unions on something like the scale Allbritton had suggested. They announced this decision and fixed a meeting with union leaders for April 30th.

But Murdoch was still not finished. The day after the Tribune announcement he tried to contact Cook by telephone to formalise his offer and, on failing to do so, hurriedly dictated a letter to Cook's secretary. "Since there are apparently no other qualified buyers for the *News*," he wrote, "I am advised there should be no legal barrier to purchase by News America Publishing, Inc. Under these circumstances I hereby offer to sign a letter of intent with Tribune Co. containing the same terms as those set forth in your letter of intent with Allbritton Communications Co. . . . Despite public speculation to the contrary, I do not wish to see the *News* closed. I believe it is in everyone's interest to seek a solution that assures continued publication of both the *News* and the *Post* under sound economic conditions."

This provoked a furious reply from Cook, which he published, along with Murdoch's letter, in the *News* under the headline: TRIB TO RUPERT: DROP DEAD. It began: "I acknowledge receipt of your message to me dictated by you to my secretary when you called my office yesterday after business hours. Although a public announcement of the availability of the New York *News* for purchase was made on December 18th, 1981, no representative of yours made any attempt to contact us until after a contract was signed by our company with the Allbritton interests on March 31st, 1982. Even then, your initial apparent communication to us was casual, vague and lacking in any substance or meaning. You now, on the eve of our meeting with the unions, present an 'offer' that is so contingent that it is patently illusory on its face . . . You have no right to intrude upon or attempt to 'spoil' our negotiations with the unions and your only motive for doing so is anticompetitive. We view your claim that you are presently a qualified buyer of the *News* as an anticompetitive and predatory act and you should govern yourself accordingly."

It took six months for the *News* to complete its negotiations with the unions. They resulted in a potential saving of some fifty million dollars a year, while a five-cent price increase would generate additional revenue of fifteen million dollars. The contract with the unions was extended from 1984 to 1987, making it unlikely that the Tribune Company would think about closing the paper until then. By 1984 it was making a useful profit. Murdoch, meanwhile, was losing a million dollars a month on the *Post* and it was hard to see any prospect of its being profitable.

Just after Allbritton began his ill-fated negotiations, he met Kheel and McDonald in his suite in New York's exclusive Carlyle Hotel, at Madison Avenue and 76th Street. Kheel raised the question of the impact any concessions to the *News* would have on the viability of the *Post*. Allbritton replied that there was no need for worry on that score. "Rupert's ego is so big that under no circumstances would he shut the *Post*." When Kheel reported that conversation to Murdoch, he responded: "Let me tell you something. We are now a public company and regardless of my ego I have to be concerned about continuing losses."

All the same, Allbritton was expressing a view widely held in New York. When McDonald was negotiating new contracts with *Post* executives in 1981 and they pleaded poverty, the union leader told them: "You make a profit in Australia and you've just bought the London *Times*. Here in New York you've elected a mayor and a governor and a president and you've got a loan of $380 million from the Export-Import Bank. The *Post* is worth a fortune to you. We have to look at the whole picture when you say you can't afford a pay increase."

It is hard, as McDonald implies, to separate Murdoch's political from his commercial interests. Although the *Post* had by now lost all traces of the liberalism that had characterised it under Dorothy Schiff, there remained one policy area where it stayed constant – support of Israel. No doubt this sprang partly from Murdoch's own conviction, but it was also true that the business people who had to take decisions on whether to advertise in the *Post* were overwhelmingly Jewish. In recognition of his stance the American Jewish Congress in New York named Murdoch Communications Man of the Year in April 1982. "My whole life has been with newspapers and so has my father's," he said when he received the award at the New York Hilton. "You could say my destiny is to be in love with newspapers." The president of the Congress is Howard Squadron, his New York lawyer.

Soon afterwards Murdoch suffered an unexpected political setback. Mayor Koch had decided to seek the Democratic nomination for governor of New York State, largely at Murdoch's behest. The *Post* had organised a ballot among its readers, who overwhelmingly urged the mayor to run for governor. after his landslide victory in the previous year's mayoral election, everyone assumed Koch would easily win the primary: but despite the wholehearted support of the *Post*, he was beaten by his old rival Mario Cuomo. In the election itself, in November, the *Post* came out for the Republican Lew Lehrman but again their man was narrowly defeated and Cuomo won the office. Murdoch had temporarily lost the knack of supporting winners.

Undaunted by his continuing losses on the *Post*, he continued to bid for new properties. His next pass was at the *Buffalo Courier-Express*, the morning paper in the declining industrial city on the Canadian border. In August 1982 Cowles Media, the Minneapolis-based chain that had bought the paper in 1979, decided to close or sell it, because they saw no way of stemming losses running at $8.5m a year. They approached Donald Kummerfeld. After getting Murdoch's go-ahead, he began an investigation into the paper's viability. He and his team visited Buffalo and concluded that the paper could not make money without staff cuts so deep that the unions would not accept them, and they told Cowles they would not go ahead. On September 7th Cowles announced that the *Courier-Express* would close in twelve days' time.

The unions, keen to preserve at least some of their jobs, urged Murdoch to reconsider. Their leaders flew to New

York to meet him and his senior executives, who laid down stern conditions for a takeover. Chief among these was a six-month grace period during which Murdoch's people would evaluate journalists on the staff and have the right to dismiss those they thought unsuitable. The object was to reduce the editorial staff of 157 to ninety, of which twenty would be brought in from Murdoch's existing publications. This meant that fewer than half the existing journalists would keep their jobs.

"We look at a newspaper somewhat differently than many other publishers," explained Bob Page, vice-president of News America. "We want control of the newsroom. We want to determine the quality of the staff. We want to put out the type of newspaper we want."

All this was too much for the Guild, the union representing the journalists and other non-printing staff. They concluded that they would sooner see the *Courier-Express* fold than be converted into an ersatz *New York Post* and decided overwhelmingly to reject Murdoch's conditions. "We voted to die with dignity," a reporter told the trade magazine *Editor & Publisher*: and die they did.

By now Murdoch had become one of the people newspaper proprietors automatically thought of when they wanted to unload their titles. And it was not only proprietors. His next acquisition came about partly at the instigation of an editor – who quickly qualified to join the long honour roll of Murdoch victims.

Bob Forst had been editor of the *Boston Herald American* since 1979. Some twenty years earlier the *Boston Herald-Traveler* had been the city's leading serious paper, outselling its rival the *Globe*, which was then so folksy that its editorials were signed "Uncle Dudley". In the 1960s the *Herald-Traveler* declined, partly because of a debilitating law suit over a television station it owned. In 1972 it was bought by the Hearst Corporation who merged it with their vigorous tabloid *Record American* to form a new broadsheet, the *Herald American*. The hybrid paper never did well. Editors came and went. Forst was hired from Hearst's *Los Angeles Herald-Examiner* to halt its declining circulation.

He had been there only a few months when he was

surprised to get a call from Murdoch, asking whether he would like to be considered for editor of *New York* magazine. It was a highly desirable offer but Forst did not see how in conscience he could accept it. He was only just beginning to get to grips with the *Herald American*. He had hired some good new people and it would be wrong to abandon them.

In 1981 the paper became a tabloid and achieved a small reputation for its snappy headlines: REDS' BREZH DEAD and GAUCHOS BLITZ BRITS were two of the more notable. But circulation remained stagnant. Forst detected dwindling interest from his proprietors in the unprofitable paper and in 1983 he thought it time to move on. So he telephoned Bob Page in New York and inquired whether Murdoch was still interested in him. The answer came back that there were no vacancies at present. Half in jest, Forst then asked Page: "Why don't you get Rupert to buy this thing?"

Not long afterwards Forst was summoned from an editorial conference to take a call from Page. "Rupert's coming to town," Page told him. "He wants to talk to you." Elated, Forst returned to his conference. "Do you hear that bugle?" he asked his executives. "It may be the cavalry."

At lunch in St Botolph's, a discreet Boston restaurant, Murdoch quizzed Forst about the paper's commercial and editorial prospects, then invited him to spend a day at his recently-acquired country place at Old Chatham, in upstate New York. It was not a good day for Forst. He began by spilling coffee on the floor: the frugal Anna took the blame for having glued the handle inadequately on to a broken cup. Later, while walking in the nearby woods with his children, Murdoch sprung his surprise: yes, he was going to bid for the *Herald American* but no, he was not going to ask Forst to edit it.

To soften the blow, he invited Forst to stay on as assistant publisher during the first three months of the new ownership. Then he discussed other roles the deposed editor might play in his organisation. Perhaps he would like to go to England for six months to work on one of his papers there? Or join the *Village Voice* as editor or publisher? Or maybe start a new financial weekly that Murdoch had been pondering for some time?

"It was like he was a waiter bringing the dessert menu over," Forst was to say later. "I didn't know whether I wanted the éclair, the chocolate mousse or the strawberry tart. I wanted it all." The offer, when it came, was a stale rock bun. He was asked to be third managing editor at the *New York Post*, which had never had more than two managing editors and probably needed only one. Forst declined and left.

"I found him very charming," Forst was able to say when the passions of the moment had passed. "He charmed me right out of my underwear."

Forst's *Herald American* was selling only 228,000 copies a day – less than half the circulation of the *Globe*. Murdoch offered the Hearst Corporation one million dollars for it, plus another seven million dollars out of any future profits. He hoped to save seven million dollars by cutting staff. The deal was concluded in his favourite combative style. It had been hard to get the unions to accept his proposed cuts and Murdoch accused the *Globe* of trying to sabotage the negotiations, much as he had himself been charged with spoiling by the *Daily News* in New York. The *Globe* had indicated they would want the same manning concessions the unions were giving to the rival paper. (They did not get them.) The last deal with the last union was struck only minutes before the deadline on December 3rd, 1982. The *Herald American* was his.

He quickly changed the name to the snappier *Boston Herald* and imported two of his best men from New York to change it into an authentic Murdoch tabloid – Joe Robino-witz from the *Post* and Leslie Hinton, an Englishman, from the *Star*. Bob Page was appointed publisher. The layout of four columns to a page, which Murdoch finds dreary and pretentious in a tabloid, was changed to seven narrow columns, designed for faster reading. The reporting and editing were made sharper, less leisurely. Murdoch and his disciples dislike the American habit of writing tricky intro-ductions to news stories, which seem clever to the writer but often baffle the reader. (For example, a story in the pre-Murdoch *Herald American*, about a teenager breaking the windows of a taxi, began: "In the end, they shook hands and went their separate ways.")

As everyone expected, Murdoch introduced a Wingo game which produced the anticipated circulation boost. But not all the changes were in a down market direction. Some months earlier Forst had removed the daily list of stock prices, to save money. Murdoch had them reinstated.

Initially, the rival *Globe* showed distinct signs of panic at the prospect of the fierce new competition and began to act out of character. Surprisingly, they outbid the *Herald* for the serial rights in a revelatory book by the ex-wife of Mike Torrez, a former pitcher for the Boston Red Sox baseball team, full of the kind of steamy secrets with which the sober *Globe* would not normally be expected to concern itself. The *Herald* retaliated with a ruse straight from the streets of Sydney – they interviewed Mrs Torrez, who revealed nearly all the secrets from her book, which the *Herald* proceeded to print before the *Globe* began its serialization.

It soon became apparent, however, that the *Globe* had little to worry about. For although the *Herald* put on readers quickly – 100,000 in the first year of Murdoch's ownership – it was not taking them from the *Globe*, whose sales remained stable at just over half a million. More significantly, the *Herald* was suffering from the same disability as the *New York Post*, in that the greater circulation was scarcely being reflected in terms of advertising share. By the end of 1983 only 16.3 per cent of the city's daily newspaper advertising was going to the *Herald* – a bare one per cent increase over the previous year. The *Globe* held the rest. The 100,000 new readers, attracted largely by Wingo, were presumably people who had not formerly read any newspaper, and they were not a group of much interest to advertisers. So the *Herald*'s cheeky boast that "we've got the *Globe* on a string", made in advertisements and on T-shirts, proved empty.

Murdoch's next acquisition came in another historic American city with a formidable newspaper history. The 1930s play *The Front Page* had immortalised the highly competitive and sensational approach to journalism for which Chicago had been noted and which Murdoch has always thought of as the right way to produce popular newspapers. But in the last dozen years or so Chicago journalism – like that in other American cities – had changed. Reporters now came not from the blue-collar housing projects but from schools of journalism where paramount among the qualities instilled into them was an onerous sense of responsibility, the idea that newspapers were important as a tool of democracy. As a consequence the press now took itself far more seriously. Both surviving Chicago papers – the *Sun-Times* and the *Tribune* – prided themselves on the sobriety of their reporting, the wisdom of their editorials and the high quality of their writing, even though the *Sun-Times* was a tabloid.

Murdoch decried the graduates of journalism schools, believing they had lost touch with what the ordinary people of America really wanted to read. His papers in New York and Boston embodied that philosophy. He had been keeping his eye on the *Chicago Sun-Times* since soon after he arrived in America in the early 1970s. He went for lunch at the paper's office with Marshall Field, grandson of the department store magnate who founded the *Chicago Sun* in 1941. Field, then the publisher of the *Sun–Times* and its joint proprietor with his younger brother Frederick, invited a group of senior journalists to meet Murdoch, including Jim Hoge, later to become publisher. The Australian visitor asked some shrewd questions about the paper's commercial condition, made some mental notes and went away for nearly ten years.

In the spring of 1983 Marshall and Frederick Field, after disagreements between themselves, put the paper up for sale. It was making an unspectacular profit – some six million dollars in the previous financial year – and Frederick, who lives in California, had other uses for the money. Hoge guessed that Murdoch would be among those interested in the paper and, worried by the tales he had heard of Murdoch's methods elsewhere, he persuaded Marshall Field to rule out the Australian as a qualified bidder. Field agreed. Hoge announced publicly that Murdoch would not be considered as a potential purchaser.

Murdoch had other ideas. He flew to California to see Frederick Field and put it to him that, in fairness, the paper should be sold to the highest bidder. Frederick made that point to Marshall who summoned Hoge and told him that Murdoch would be allowed to make a bid, but only for the purpose of pushing up the price. He still did not anticipate selling to him.

Hoge was meanwhile forming a consortium of local businessmen, as Evans (an old friend) had done for the *Sunday Times* in London. He raised sixty-three million dollars. This was scarcely enough to secure the paper and the Field Syndication Service that was being sold with it, so a bid was made for the paper alone, leaving the syndication service, valued at twenty million dollars, to be sold separately. This out-stripped the *Washington Post*'s bid of fifty million dollars but was seven millions less than Murdoch's ninety million dollar tender – the most he had ever offered for a newspaper. Marshall Field said that, left to himself, he would not have sold to Murdoch. "My sentiments were that we should try to have a local owner if possible; and I was willing to give up something to do that," he stated. "To be perfectly frank, my brother felt that he wanted to maximize what he got for the paper. Our agreement is such that he has a perfect right to do that. So it took control out of my hands." On November 1st, 1983, it was announced that agreement had been reached in principle to sell to Murdoch.

It was a desirable property, one of the few papers he had ever bought that was making a profit at the time of his purchase. And what made the deal especially poignant was that it opened up a second front between him and the Chicago Tribune Company, owners of the *Daily News* in New York. He had failed to wrest the *News* from them the previous year and his *New York Post* was still proving a substantial drain on his American profits as a result. Now he had the chance to challenge them on their home ground. It was irresistible.

Murdoch offered a public pledge to maintain the high standards and reputation of the *Sun-Times*. He said he planned no radical changes. At lunch with Hoge and other senior journalists, though, he indicated the kind of changes that might be required. He spoke of switching from a four-column to a seven-column layout, as he had done in

Boston. He said he wanted more competitions and more human interest stories. When he was taxed about the Son of Sam excesses in New York, and other instances of what some saw as irresponsible reporting, he replied: "Journalists take the news too seriously. You guys ought to have more fun."

Hoge, for one, doubted whether there would be much fun for him in working for Murdoch and that hunch was confirmed a few weeks later when he read Evans's book, a cautionary tale for all those foolhardy enough to believe that, with their exceptional talents, they might be able to succeed where others had failed in taming the beast. On the day the sale was announced, Hoge declined to discuss his future in detail with Murdoch, promising only to do what he could to smooth the transition between owners.

In December they talked more fully. Murdoch said he wanted to feel free to intervene on the paper editorially. He had not spent ninety million dollars or more to let someone else have the fun. Hoge said he knew that was how Murdoch liked to operate but he had his own ideas about the prerogatives of a publisher, which did not seem to square with Murdoch's. It was probably better if they parted company from the start, rather than implement Murdoch's suggestion of a three-month trial period to see whether they could work together.

Murdoch had a similar discussion with Ralph Otwell, the *Sun-Times*'s veteran editor. He grabbed a copy of that day's issue of the paper and, quickly flicking the pages, told Otwell just what, in his view, was wrong with it. After that chastening experience, Otwell was a little surprised to receive the same ninety-day offer, and thought it prudent to decline.

Another of the paper's stalwarts was unhappy about the sale to Murdoch. Mike Royko, who wrote a daily column, is without much doubt Chicago's most celebrated and popular journalist. In the issue of December 15th 1983 he devoted his column to a report of the annual satirical revue staged by the Chicago Bar Association, and in particular a skit about the sale of the *Sun-Times*. In it, a group of reporters complained to the Field brothers about letting Murdoch have the paper. A man supposed to be the Fields' lawyer sang a song in their defence, to the tune of "The Gambler". It related how Murdoch came in quest of the paper but the Fields would not at first sell it to him because of his reputation.

Then:

> He said: "I can understand that.
> I appreciate your spirit,
> I admire your dedication
> And respect the way you feel.
> Would it help salve your conscience
> If I paid you ninety million?"
> They said: "Murdoch, you're a scoundrel,
> But you've got yourself a deal."

After writing that column – and complaining that the word "sleazy" had been omitted from his description of some Murdoch papers – Royko took himself off on leave pending the transfer of ownership. Interviewed on television, he gave his opinion that no self-respecting fish would want to be wrapped in a Murdoch-owned paper and advised the tycoon to "go kick a kangaroo some place."

At this point there was a hiccup in negotiations for completion of the purchase. Murdoch found he would have to assume responsibility for the pension arrangements and that this would cost nearly ten million dollars. He wanted the price reduced to take that into account. The Fields reopened the auction and received a new local bid of £100 million. Murdoch was obliged to match that and, despite the renewed protests of Hoge and those who thought like him, the deal was confirmed. Murdoch took control on Monday January 9th, 1984. The previous Friday Hoge, Otwell and two executive vice-presidents on the commercial side resigned from the paper. Bob Page came from Boston to replace Hoge as publisher. Several dozen members of the editorial staff applied for jobs at the *Tribune* or in other cities.

When Royko was on holiday the *Sun-Times* customarily published old columns he had written a year or two back. That had been happening since mid-December and Page continued the practice. It was generally assumed that the columnist would not want to work for the paper, given the uncomplimentary remarks he had already made about the new proprietor. On Tuesday, January 10th, the *Tribune* announced that Royko would in future be writing for them. Some thought he could take as many as 100,000 readers with him to his new paper (in fact, he took some 20,000). Page, claiming he was in breach of his contract with the *Sun-Times*, said he would initiate legal action to prevent him leaving. "The *Tribune*'s malicious interference into our business is intolerable," Page stormed.

He sought an injunction to prevent Royko from writing for the *Tribune*. The following day, before there had been time for the case to be heard, the columnist had the rare distinction of being published in both of Chicago's morning papers. The *Sun-Times* printed one of his old columns and the *Tribune* the first of his new ones – inevitably about Rupert Murdoch. Royko looked back on some of the jobs he had held before becoming a journalist more than twenty years earlier. He had worked in a bowling alley, a lamp factory, a department store and a bar. He had settled into journalism because he liked sitting down but Murdoch was now contesting his right to sit in his new employer's premises. "Can you imagine a guy coming all the way from Australia just to tell me where to sit?" Nobody had ever threatened legal action to prevent him from doing his earlier non-sedentary jobs. "Ah, Rupert, where the hell were you when I needed you?"

Page did not get his injunction and Royko continued to write for the *Tribune*. Murdoch would no doubt have loved to be able to supervise the fray in person but he was in Geneva trying to raise money to wage the larger battle he had initiated a few weeks earlier. He was trying to gain control of Warner Communications, the conglomerate based on the old Warner Brothers studio which over the years had built up powerful holdings in the film and entertainment industries. To buy the controlling interest he sought would cost around $1,000 million.

To understand the Warner bid it is necessary to go back a few months, to April 1983, when Murdoch bought a majority holding in the Inter-American Satellite Television Network, changing its name later to Skyband, Inc. Soon afterwards he acquired control of Satellite Television plc, a British company operating in Europe. Both companies are in the nascent business of beaming television programmes by satellite, an alternative to cable in rural areas where the houses are too far apart to make cable installation economic. There are estimated to be twenty-six million such homes in the United States. Each needs to be fitted with a dish to enable it to receive satellite signals. Modern technology has reduced the size of the dishes to a diameter of three or four feet and enables them to be sold at a price which makes individual ownership feasible.

Murdoch has always been fascinated by the potential of new forms of communication. As soon as he had bought the two TV companies he made arrangements to lease space on a commercial satellite. In his annual report, written in the summer of 1983, he wrote: "Within a few months, we expect to be operating the first nationwide satellite-to-home broadcast network in the United States . . . At first we will function essentially as a distribution system with programming purchased from outside sources. Eventually we will bring our own creative resources into play so that we can produce and broadcast our own entertainment and information services." In an interview, Murdoch told Michael Schrage of the *Washington Post* that he expected the American satellite network to gross some $325 million by 1986, but he confessed it was a risky enterprise. Other companies had been making satellite plans but he thought he would reap the advantage of being first in the field.

"What it's going to look like is either a bloody battlefield with a lot of red ink strewn around or a brilliant success," he declared. "The upside is enormous. It's well worth the risk, but I would be the first to say that it will take three or four years to pay off." He told Schrage that he hoped to use his tri-continental muscle to finance feature films and assure his satellite stations of a flow of programming.

Only weeks after that interview, though, Murdoch announced that his plans to start satellite broadcasting would have to be postponed. There appeared to be two problems. The first was that the technology was not as advanced as he had supposed and the small, cheap satellite dish not widely available. The second was a shortage of suitable programmes to transmit. It was then, presumably to solve that second difficulty, that he began buying shares in Warner Communications.

Warner's had endured a volatile recent history. In 1976 Steven Ross, the flamboyant chairman, seemed to have made an astute acquisition when he bought Atari, then the leading company in the new field of home video games and computers, for $28 million. Between 1979 and 1982 Atari made profits of more than $680 million for Warner but in 1983 the video game market collapsed and strong new competitors entered the home computer field, resulting in a damaging price war. In the first nine months of that year Atari lost $536 million and Warner Communications lost $425 million. The share price fell from a high of sixty-three dollars to twenty-three dollars.

In the summer of 1983 Murdoch, absorbed in his satellite venture, paid a call on Ross. He had heard that Warner were planning to merge their loss-making Movie Channel, a cable TV service, with a rival outfit called Showtime. Murdoch wondered whether he might be included in the deal and offer the service on his satellite channel. Ross turned him down. Soon afterwards, Murdoch began to buy Warner shares at their depressed price. By the time he had bought seven per cent of the stock, at a cost of around $100 million, he had become the largest shareholder. The financial press began to take notice of his purchases, and so did Ross.

On December 9th the two men met again, this time at Ross's request. He was anxious to know Murdoch's intentions. Did he seek control of the company? At that stage Murdoch was describing his share purchases simply as "an investment". That left open the possibility that he would wait for the price to increase and then sell at a profit, as he had done after his failed takeover bid for the *Melbourne Herald*. But most analysts assumed he would be after at least a seat on the board and a possible deal for the rights to Warner's extensive film library.

Ross explained that he would be against any move to share control for two reasons. First, because of Murdoch's controversial reputation as a newspaper proprietor, some of the best creative people in Warner's profitable film division might prefer not to work for him and take their talents elsewhere. Secondly, there were rules against owning television franchises in the same area as newspapers. Warner had eleven cable franchises within the circulation area of the *Boston Herald*. Murdoch appeared unimpressed with the arguments. A worried Ross looked to his defences. On December 29th he announced a deal with Chris-Craft Industries, owners of a number of television stations, under which Warner acquired 42.5 per cent of Chris-Craft and Chris-Craft would get nineteen per cent of Warner in exchange. Then Chris-Craft would make further purchases on the market to bring their holding to twenty-five per cent. This not only made it much harder for Murdoch to gain a majority shareholding but also raised the possibility of further clashes between newspaper and television interests, since among Chris-Craft's TV stations is one in San Antonio, Texas, where Murdoch owns two newspapers.

Murdoch was not deterred. At the beginning of January he filed a declaration with the Justice Department – as by law he was obliged to do – of his intention to acquire at least twenty-five per cent and up to 49.9 per cent of Warner stock. Two days later he said he might solicit proxies from shareholders. At the same time he initiated legal action in Delaware – where Warner is registered – to halt the Chris-Craft deal on the grounds that its chief purpose was to entrench Warner management. He made no attempt to hide his rage at Ross's manoeuvre.

"I'm very angry about it," he told the American magazine *Business Week*. "We told them when we bought the stock. We are clients of theirs overseas. Then we woke up to find that paranoia had overtaken them. There is a question about whether those people can run TV stations. I'm not even sure they could get a casino licence . . . I think we could easily win a proxy fight . . . I don't think it is well run. Look at the results . . . It is run by dealmakers rather than managers."

And he offered a revealing insight into his personal motive for entering into a fight with Warner: "Someone can beat you up or run over you, but if you don't give them a few bruises in return, they can do it to the next person who comes along. It is also important for News Corp. to show that it won't be pushed around. It would be very bad for News Corp. for people to think we were a patsy that can be run over and disenfranchised in this way."

This kind of legal action is customarily conducted without restraint on either side. Allegations of shiftiness and dishonesty flew from both directions. Murdoch's reference to the question whether Warner could get a casino licence related to one of the grounds of his law suit, the past record of some senior officials. In February 1981 a Warner director pleaded guilty to transporting stolen money across state borders and resigned from the company. The following year the assistant treasurer was convicted of financial offences and a sales and marketing executive pleaded guilty to tax evasion. Murdoch implied in his court papers that these offences cast doubt on the probity of senior management. Warner vigorously denied this in their response and initiated a counter-suit, seeking to prevent Murdoch from purchasing more shares in the company.

One of the grounds of the Warner action was Murdoch's record. They quoted a passage from Harold Evans's book, seeking to show that Murdoch's word could not be relied upon. Their complaint continued: "Murdoch is now well known in the United States and England for purchasing reputable newspapers and converting them into a sensationalist format, emphasising violence, scandal and sex. Murdoch has already destroyed the journalistic reputation of the (New York) *Post* and the (Boston) *Herald* and there is widespread fear that he will do the same to the (Chicago) *Sun-Times* . . . Except in publications controlled by him, Murdoch has frequently been described as deceitful and untrustworthy by persons who have worked for him . . . Murdoch has also been accused of slanting and distorting his newspapers and television stations in order to gain an unfair advantage for his interests."

Murdoch's attempt to win an injunction preventing the Chris-Craft deal failed and the share swap went ahead. But the legal cases continued, too. Both sides undertook investigations of the other's record, hoping to find something murky. Warner did this in the conventional way by hiring a firm of lawyers noted for that kind of work, but Murdoch used his own resources. Steve Dunleavy, metropolitan editor of the *New York Post*, hero of the "Son of Sam" investigations some years earlier, was assigned with another reporter to finding out all they could about Ross. The two men told Ross's associates that they were working on an article for the *Post* but Howard Squadron, Murdoch's lawyer, confirmed to the *Wall Street Journal* that they had been asked by counsel to get the information. They went about it thoroughly, even contacting Ross's old schools for his educational record. Murdoch was fulfilling his boast to *Business Week*: nobody was going to push him around. When he did pull out it was on his own terms – and, characteristically, with a profit of $41.5 m. on the sale of his shares back to Warner. Then he caused a flutter in another film company, Disney, by buying some of their shares.

His aggressive and apparently indiscriminate approach to acquisitions was viewed with awe in America. Reporting the 1982 Boston negotiations, *Newsweek* quoted a source close to him as saying: "He keeps a stable of acquisition people in his office. I used to think they did things according to a grand design, but really they're just a bunch of guys with suitcases and airplane tickets." That he is prepared to continue making ambitious bids, borrowing against his turnover and global assets, is a tribute to Murdoch's tenacity and optimism. While his satellite operation remains grounded the viability of his American interests still depends primarily on whether he can stem his losses on the *New York Post*. With the *News* now in profit, it is hard to see how the *Post* can get into the black in the near future, despite a steady increase in circulation.

The expansion into Boston and Chicago suggests that George McDonald's view of Murdoch's motivation is right – that he is concerned as much about political power as making profits. There is a strong feeling in America that he is seeking to buy the *Los Angeles Herald-Examiner* and the *Baltimore News American*, which he would distribute in nearby Washington. If politics is a prime concern, he is likely to continue funding the *New York Post*'s losses for as long as he is able, as he will those of *The Times* in London and the *Australian* in Sydney. Rumours that he is about to shut the *Australian* surface from time to time, as its editors come and go. One of them, Colin Chapman, set an unenviable record in 1982 when he sat in the editor's chair for less than forty-eight hours. Then Sir Larry Lamb, who left the group in 1981, returned briefly to take charge at the *Australian*. In September 1982, after a five-day strike, the management reduced the staff by thirty-nine and made fresh menacing sounds: but Murdoch has kept the paper going tenaciously for twenty years and it does not lose anything like as much money as the *New York Post* or *The Times*.

At *The Times*, despite intermittent strikes and the now almost routine threats of closure, things were looking up by the beginning of 1984. Circulation was growing steadily as a result of changes designed to make the paper accessible to a broader readership: more features on consumer affairs and more lightweight articles, plus the introduction of an easier crossword for those who could not master the traditional one (which was retained as well). The aim was to make inroads into the circulation of the *Daily Telegraph*. The hiring strategy was significant: two men, a sports columnist and a new financial editor, came from the tabloid *Daily Express*. Douglas-Home was a more reclusive editor than Evans and seemed more skilful at keeping Murdoch at arm's length. But he was not universally popular with the staff, many of whom disapproved of the down-market direction the paper was taking. And both he and his paper – as well as the *Sunday Times* – were made to look foolish by trumpeting a "scoop" in the shape of Hitler's wartime diaries, quickly shown to be fakes.

Evans's book, *Good Times, Bad Times*, published in October 1983, provoked no formal response from Murdoch, despite the monstrous picture Evans painted of his former proprietor. He was, however, persuaded to comment by Terry McCrann in an interview in the Melbourne *Age*. Murdoch asserted that Evans would go into his office, gesticulate and rattle off a series of half-finished and meaningless sentences: "You've done all this and what can we do . . . you don't know . . . what are we . . ." Then Evans would say: "You must come here more often. It's wonderful to have you here." Murdoch imitated Evans returning to his own office, holding his head in his hands and saying: "My God, the *pressure* I'm under. You don't know."

This was the same interview in which Murdoch made a remarkable attack on Mrs Thatcher – whom Evans had accused of complicity in his dismissal. Murdoch was bewildered by her failure to support President Reagan over the American landing on the Caribbean island of Grenada. "She's gone out of her mind," Murdoch said. "I don't know what she's about. I just think she's very overtired. I know it sounds silly but I think it is a very human thing . . . She's run out of puff. She's not listening to any of her friends."

His other concerns about Britain were related more directly to his business. The *Sunday Times* had been losing circulation since Frank Giles became editor, and Murdoch persuaded him to take early retirement in the summer of 1983. Most of the staff had assumed that Brian MacArthur was being groomed to succeed him but instead Murdoch went outside the paper's ranks and appointed Andrew Neil from the *Economist*. He had met Neil – at thirty-one younger than all the senior staff at the *Sunday Times* – at an occasion connected with cable and satellite television, for which the two men share an enthusiasm. Neil is fascinated by modern technology and most of his early changes to the paper reflected that. His arrival naturally ruffled the feathers of senior people who felt passed over. MacArthur, only two years earlier an apparently rising star in the organisation, soon resigned and went to edit a paper in the west of England. Many other senior men left in Neil's first year, including the respected Washington correspondent Stephen Fay and the already demoted Hugo Young, who had just won an award as Columnist of the Year. Neil's was a characteristic appointment.

There was also something distinctively Murdochian about a circular sent in June 1983 to holders of Special Dividend shares in News International. These are the only vehicles for investment in his enterprises that are traded on the London Stock Exchange and they carry no voting rights. For some time they had been quoted at around one pound until at the beginning of 1983 they began to increase in value quite sharply, along with other shares in newspaper publishers.

The reason for this general increase in newspaper share prices was a strong rumour that Reuters, the international news agency, was about to be publicly floated. The agency, owned jointly by major news organisations, had become highly profitable because of the successful development of its financial information division. Murdoch owned eleven per cent of the shares and would be able to realise about £120 million from marketing them. By June, News International non-voting shares stood at more than two pounds.

It was then that shareholders received an offer from Morgan Grenfell, Murdoch's merchant bankers. The offer document disclosed that Newscorp Investments, a subsidiary of News Corporation, had been buying the Special Dividend shares in the market and owned 78.5 per cent of them. Anxious now to acquire them all, they were offering £2.25 a share, the highest price at which they had recently traded. The document said that because so many shares were now owned by News Corporation, it may be hard to market them afterwards and "it is possible that when the offer closes the price may fall significantly below the offer value". A similar warning was repeated in a follow-up letter in July, which noted that, after the initial response, News Corporation owned 87.6 per cent of the issued shares.

Those who declined to accept the lure were rewarded for their stubbornness. By April 1984, with the Reuters rumour now hardened into a clear statement of intent to float the company, News International shares had more than doubled in value to £4.85. If any of the lucky shareholders were readers of *The Times*, though, they were punished for their temerity by having the News International share price withdrawn from that paper's daily stock list when the offer closed. They would have to read a rival sheet to discover how much richer their defiance had made them.

Murdoch's remorseless expansion would be slowed only if he were to encounter difficulty in raising money. So far there is no sign of that. Bankers find him a good risk. His assets are considerable and he has always been willing to dispose of them if need be. He sold his shares in London Weekend to help pay for his Sydney TV station and in 1983 he disposed of Ansett's 25-per-cent holding in Santos, an Australian minerals concern. His half share in Ansett could be sold to raise cash for his Warner bid or for other acquisitions in America. The *Sun* and *News of the World* continue to thrive and to make his British operation profitable. (In 1984 Murdoch was reported to have instructed the *Sun*'s editor, Kelvin MacKenzie, to curb a virulent campaign against the French on the question of farm prices, because he feared it might provoke French car manufacturers into withdrawing advertising. And yet another *News of the World* editor, Derek Jameson, was replaced prior to turning the paper into a tabloid to halt the decline in sales.)

"What makes Rupert run?" was a question asked by many reviewers of the original edition of this book. There seems no mystery in the answer. With Murdoch, what you see is what you get. He plainly wants to be the biggest and most powerful tycoon around, because he believes he does it better than anyone. So he will continue to live dangerously, bidding for almost anything that is going and buying some of it; hiring, firing, cajoling, telephoning, browbeating employees and politicians alike, living out of a suitcase and flying by the seat of his pants. There are critics who predict that one day he will crash on his head: so far he remains airborne.

Appendix

In the News Corporation Ltd. annual report for 1983, the company's interests were listed as follows:

Newspapers	Where published	Circulation
The Times	London	336,189
The Sunday Times	London	1,288,448
The Sun	London	4,170,909
News of the World	London	4,074,424
Times Literary Supplement	London	30,904
Times Educational Supplement	London	105,043
Times Higher Ed. Supplement	London	15,450
The Star	New York	3,824,792
New York Post	New York	961,044
The Boston Herald	Boston	309,697
Sunday Boston Herald	Boston	241,837
San Antonio Express	San Antonio, Texas	88,774
The News	San Antonio, Texas	75,614
Sunday Express-News	San Antonio, Texas	196,267
Village Voice	New York	160,929
Houston community papers	Houston, Texas	253,988
The Australian	Australia	110,843
Daily Mirror	Sydney	324,168
Daily Telegraph	Sydney	290,831
Sunday Telegraph	Sydney	640,718
The News	Adelaide	174,950
Sunday Mail	Adelaide	252,381
Daily Sun	Brisbane	105,281
Sunday Sun	Brisbane	364,890
Sunday Times	Perth	254,771
Cumberland Newspapers	Parramatta, NSW	579,682
Northern Territory News	Darwin	15,498
Northern Daily Leader	Tamworth	12,575
Wimmera Mail Times	Horsham, Victoria	10,109
Other provincial papers	Australia	17,411
Independent Newspapers (22 per-cent holding)	New Zealand	

Magazines

New Idea	Australia	772,000
TV Week (50 per-cent holding)	Australia	770,000
New York	New York	422,819

Book publishing

Bay Books	Sydney
Angus & Robertson	Sydney
Wm. Collins & Sons (41.7 per-cent holding)	Glasgow
Times Books	London

Television

Channel Ten-10	Sydney
Channel ATV-10	Melbourne
News Group Productions	New York
Skyband	New York
Satellite Television plc	London

Other enterprises

Associated R & R Films (50 per-cent holding)	Sydney
Festival Records	Sydney
Progress Press	Melbourne
Eric Bemrose (printers)	Liverpool, England
C. Townsend Hook & Co. (newsprint)	Kent
Convoys Group (transport)	London
Ansett Transport Industries (50 per-cent holding)	Melbourne
Shell Consortium (offshore oil and gas – 20 per-cent holding)	Bass Strait, Australia
News-Eagle partnership (offshore oil and gas – 80 per-cent holding)	Western Australia
F.S. Falkiner & Sons (ranching)	Australia

Bibliography

The first list is of books, containing information on Rupert Murdoch, the second list on *The Times*

ON RUPERT MURDOCH

Brendon, Piers, *The Life and Death of the Press Barons,* Secker and Warburg, 1983.

Calwell, Arthur, *Be Just and Fear Not.* Seal Books, Sydney, 1978.

Carydon, Les, *Paper Chase.* Herald and Weekly Times, Melbourne, 1982.

Cudlipp, Hugh, *Walking on the Water.* Bodley Head, London, 1976.

Edgar, Patricia, *The Politics of the Press.* Sun Books, Melbourne, 1979.

Evans, Harold, *Good Times, Bad Times.* Weidenfeld & Nicolson, London, 1983.

Freudenberg, Graham, *A Certain Grandeur.* Macmillan, Melbourne, 1977.

Inglis, K. S., *The Stuart Case.* Melbourne University Press, 1961.

Jenkins, Simon, *Newspapers – the Power and the Money.* Faber & Faber, London, 1979.

Regan, Simon, *Rupert Murdoch, a Business Biography.* Angus & Robertson, London and Sydney, 1976.

Somerfield, Stafford, *Banner Headlines.* Scan Books, Shoreham, Sussex, 1979.

Souter, Gavin, *Company of Heralds.* Melbourne University Press, 1981.

Sunday Times Insight Team, *Suffer the Children.* André Deutsch, London, 1979.

Walsh, Maximilian, *Poor Little Rich Country.* Penguin Books, Melbourne, 1979.

Whitlam, Gough, *The Truth of the Matter.* Penguin Books, Melbourne, 1979.

Windschuttle, Keith and Elizabeth, eds, *Fixing the News.* Cassell, Melbourne, 1981.

Zwar, Desmond, *In Search of Keith Murdoch.* Macmillan, Melbourne, 1980.

ARTICLES

Brogan, Patrick, "Citizen Murdoch". *New Republic,* New York, October 11th, 1982.

Chubb, Philip, "The Murdoch Machine". A series of five articles in *The Age,* Melbourne, September–October, 1980.

Cockburn, Alexander, "Rupert Murdoch Tells All". Interview in *Village Voice,* New York, November 29th, 1976.

Deamer, Adrian, "Being Both Australian and National". *The Review*, Sydney, November 13–19th, 1971.

O'Brien, Greg, "Rupert Buys Hub Rag". *Boston Magazine*, Boston, May, 1983.

Raskin, A. H., "A Reporter at Large: The Negotiation". The *New Yorker*, New York, January 22nd and 29th, 1979.

Sheehy, Gail, "A Fistful of Dollars". *Rolling Stone*, Los Angeles, July 14th, 1977.

Welles, Chris, "The Americanization of Rupert Murdoch". *Esquire*, New York, May 22nd, 1979.

ON *THE TIMES*

Drogheda, Lord, *Double Harness*. Weidenfeld & Nicolson, London, 1978.

The History of The Times, 4 vols. The Times, London, 1935–52.

Jacobs, Eric, *Stop Press*. André Deutsch, London, 1980.

Koss, Stephen, *The Rise and Fall of the Political Press in Britain*. 2 vols. Hamish Hamilton, London, 1981 and 1984.

Thomson, Roy, *After I Was Sixty*. Hamish Hamilton, London, 1975.

The Times, Past, Present and Future. The Times, London, 1932.

ARTICLES

Hodgson, Godfrey, "Private Power and the Public Interest: The Case of Times Newspapers". *Political Quarterly*, London, October–December, 1981.

MacBeath, Innis, "How They Put the Paper to Bed". *New Statesman*, London, December 19–26th, 1980.

Zeitlinger, James, "O Tempora! O Mores!" *Harpers & Queen*, London, September, 1981.

Index